The intricacies of Lutheran education in the twenty-first century exceed basic pedagogy and a clear confession of Lutheran doctrine. This volume delivers a multilayered treatment, which encompasses the wide spectrum of these educational, cultural, and theological complexities. The individual articles are crafted by a comprehensive cadre of subject-matter experts in a manner that is of benefit for every Lutheran educator, from the novice student of education to the master teacher. *The Pedagogy of Faith* is an indispensable resource for everyone involved in Lutheran education whether in the classroom, the home, or the parish.

—The Rev. Dr. Paul A. Philp
Director of Institutional Research and Integrity
Concordia University System

As I read the essays, they resonated with my own personal ministry journey through the years. They connected with the teaching that I have done, but more importantly now for me, with the mentoring and teaching of young people on their journey in preparing to become teachers and directors of Christian education in our schools and churches today. I was continually asking myself, "How can I use this wealth of knowledge and perspective as I lead young people in preparation for their chosen vocation?" The essays provide an opportunity to get into the lives of veteran teachers and leaders in the church and then reflect on their journeys and how that can impact your journey. I look forward to the opportunity of using this resource as I work with young people preparing to serve our church and our world.

—Dr. Ron Bork
Associate Dean and Head of Teacher Education
Concordia University, Nebraska

Dr. Bernard Bull, known throughout the LCMS as a faithful, creative, and innovative educator, has struck gold with this new collection of essays. *The Pedagogy of Faith* will push, pull, and challenge even the best Lutheran educators. Here is something for everyone. Anchored in the faith once delivered and our desire to raise children in the Gospel, the authors challenge us to deliver the best quality education in an ever-changing world. The task demands our constant attention and continued learning. This little gem should find itself on the desk of every teacher and administrator in the LCMS. It should be read, digested, and discussed by every teacher who desires to remain engaged in the hard work of educating the next generation.

—Rev. Bart Day
Executive Director
The LCMS Office of National Mission

The
Pedagogy
of Faith

ESSAYS ON LUTHERAN EDUCATION

Edited by Bernard Bull

CONCORDIA PUBLISHING HOUSE • SAINT LOUIS

Concordia
Publishing House

Copyright © 2016 Concordia Publishing House
3558 S. Jefferson Ave., St. Louis, MO 63118–3968
1-800-325-3040 · www.cph.org

Photographs on cover and pages 11, 91, and 173 © iStockphoto.com

Unless otherwise indicated, Scripture quotations are from the ESV® Bible (The Holy Bible, English Standard Version®), copyright © 2001 by Crossway, a publishing ministry of Good News Publishers. Used by permission. All rights reserved.

The quotations from the Lutheran Confessions in this publication are from *Concordia: The Lutheran Confessions,* second edition; edited by Paul McCain et al., copyright © 2006 Concordia Publishing House. All rights reserved.

Hymn texts with the abbreviation *LSB* are from *Lutheran Service Book,* copyright © 2006 Concordia Publishing House. All rights reserved.

Quotations from the Small Catechism are taken from *Luther's Small Catechism with Explanation,* copyright © 1986, 1991 Concordia Publishing House. All rights reserved.

Quotations marked LW are from Luther's Works, American Edition: volumes 1–30 © 1955–76 and volumes 58–60, 67–69, 75–78 © 2009–15 Concordia Publishing House; volumes 31–54 © 1957–86 Augsburg Fortress.

Scripture quotations marked NIV are taken from the Holy Bible, New International Version®. NIV®. Copyright © 1973, 1978, 1984 by Biblica, Inc.™ Used by permission of Zondervan. All rights reserved.

Manufactured in the United States of America

Library of Congress Cataloging-in-Publication Data

Names: Bull, Bernard Dean, editor.

Title: The pedagogy of faith : essays on Lutheran education / Edited by
  Bernard Bull.

Description: St. Louis, MO : Concordia Pub. House, 2016.

Identifiers: LCCN 2016008223 (print) | LCCN 2016009124 (ebook) | ISBN
  9780758654496 | ISBN 9780758654502 ()

Subjects: LCSH: Lutheran Church--Doctrines. | Lutheran Church--Missouri
  Synod--Education.

Classification: LCC BX8065.3 .P43 2016 (print) | LCC BX8065.3 (ebook) | DDC
  268/.841--dc23

LC record available at http://lccn.loc.gov/2016008223

2 3 4 5 6 7 8 9 10   25 24 23 22 21 20 19 18 17 16

Contents

Introduction

Bernard Bull

Look at the cover of this book and you see a simple bridge, representing your journey as a Lutheran educator. As one preparing for or serving in Lutheran education, you are standing on the edge of that bridge, which extends into an unknown destination. While our theological convictions remain firm and unchanging, we find ourselves (as did past generations) living in a world of constant change, with new challenges and opportunities in Lutheran education becoming evident to us daily. What Lutheran education will look like in the upcoming years and decades is neither certain nor clear, although we praise God that the final destination in each of our journeys is indeed clear and secure in Jesus Christ. "I go to prepare a place for you," our Lord reminds us (John 14:2).

This book was written as a guide and resource on your journey. In it, you will find words of wisdom from fellow sojourners, many with decades of experience in Lutheran education. Their journeys represent countless prayers, the study of God's Word, Christian fellowship, laughter, tears, failures, successes, frustrations, and moments of uncertainty, along with moments of great joy and humble gratitude for the honor of serving God and His children (young and old) amid the teaching ministry. This book is a travel guide for you on that journey, one written by dozens of veteran travelers. As such, may this guide serve you well. The authors of this text and I will not deceive you by claiming that it is an easy journey, but it is an important one. You are part of something that matters, a centuries-old tradition in Lutheran education that has touched the lives of countless people for eternity. As Gandalf shared with Frodo amid his perilous journey, we cannot choose the times or places in which we are born, but we can choose how we will respond to the times in which we find ourselves.

That bridge on the cover also represents our collective journey in Lutheran education. We have the past behind us, but that past has contributed to where we find ourselves in the present. We are on this journey, as were countless others who came before us, from those Old Testament prophets to the many who contributed to ministry in the Early Christian Church, from the apostles through the Reformation leaders and up to today. As the author of Hebrews reminds us more broadly, we are indeed "surrounded by so great a cloud of witnesses" (12:1).

The Pedagogy of Faith is the first of its kind in Lutheran education. Never before has there been a more diverse collection of authors and topics distilled into a single text on Lutheran education. Authors include theologians, university professors, classroom teachers, directors of Christian education, school leaders, missionaries, parents, and pastors. Essays explore topics ranging from theological foundations to the implications of brain research, the role of music in teaching the faith to addressing grading and assessment concerns, literacy research to inquiry-based learning, the impact of technology to fielding difficult questions, service learning to personalized learning, international perspectives on Lutheran education to teaching the faith in a post-Christian context, teaching young children to intergenerational education. The authors collectively represent hundreds of years of Lutheran education experience in diverse contexts ranging from the rural Midwest to other parts of the world. Even amid such a diverse collection, every author shares an understanding of the Scriptures as the inspired and inerrant Word of God, a recognition of the Lutheran Confessions as a "true and binding exposition of Holy Scripture," a commitment to excellence in Lutheran education, and a desire for it to flourish long into the future.

As such, it is with great hope and humility that I offer this text to those serving and preparing to serve in Lutheran education around the world, as one text added to countless others that have taught and blessed us over the decades. In the past, Lutheran educators learned from texts such as Painter's *Luther on Education* (originally published in 1889) and Edward W. A. Koehler's *A Christian Pedagogy* in 1930. Then, in 1960, Allan Hart Jahsmann gave us *What's Lutheran in Education?: Explorations into Principles and Practices*. In 1992, Jane Fryar wrote *Go and Make Disciples: The Goal of the Christian Teacher*, a text that continues to find use in some classrooms in Lutheran colleges and universities, along with William Rietschel's 2001 *An Introduction to the Foundations of Lutheran Education*.

Then, in 2011, Thomas Korcok provided us with *Lutheran Education: From Wittenberg to the Future*, a text that introduced many to and reminded others about our roots in Lutheran education, how our predecessors grappled with changing cultural challenges, and how we might learn from that past as we look to the future.

Each of these were created and shared with the help of Concordia Publishing House, The Lutheran Church—Missouri Synod's publishing house, one that has persistently demonstrated a commitment to placing good and important resources into the hands of future and current teachers of the faith. Of course, there are many other texts that have added to our individual and collective knowledge and practice of Lutheran education. This book is preceded by valuable texts from Moulds, Swope, Hansen and Mae, Bickel and Surburg, Stellhorn, Everist, Kretzmann, Menuge and Heck, Bartsch, Dovre, Keuer, Miller, Meyer and Rast, and many others. Even amid all these books, it is my heartfelt prayer that this addition serves as a useful guide as you explore the challenges, opportunities, theological foundations, and practical concerns associated with Lutheran education in the twenty-first century.

This is not intended to be an explicit blueprint as much as a starting point for your thought, prayer, and reflection about teaching the faith in Lutheran schools, churches, and other contexts. With that in mind, I offer three important pieces of advice: (1) read this text with the Scriptures open, (2) study it within a Christian learning community, and (3) join us by writing and sharing your own lessons learned in Lutheran education.

First, as with any text written by fallen human beings, this book is best studied alongside the Scriptures. Just as the Bereans studied the Scriptures daily to see if what Paul taught was true (Acts 17), so I urge you to be more than a passive recipient of what you read. Examine, analyze, and test it—not just with your prior knowledge and experience, but principally with Scripture, which we are reminded is useful for "teaching, for reproof, for correction, and for training in righteousness" (2 Timothy 3:16). Follow in the footsteps of Martin Luther and test it with plain reason and the Scriptures. After all, there are many matters explored in this text that are neither commanded nor forbidden in Scripture. They often represent praxis. This is not to say that Scripture does not serve as a lamp and a light for practice, but among some of the topics addressed in this text, there is room for reasonable, confessional Lutherans to disagree or have different perspectives. At the same time, we do not want to fall prey to completely subjective, personal whims and preferences on these matters. Scripture may not provide comprehensive prescriptions on confirmation, life in a contemporary technological world, intergenerational education programming, addressing questions about state and national standards, teaching methodologies, or even the concept of a school; but that does not mean that God is silent on these matters. The authors wrote these essays with a commitment to God's Word and the Lutheran Confessions and informed by their study and practice of Lutheran education; but at the end of the day, you must strive to learn from the wisdom of these authors (and others) while carefully and prayerfully testing their insights and advice with God's Word.

Second, while this text is useful for personal study, it was created with the hope that you will join others to study it, allowing "iron to sharpen iron." You might study it as part of a college class, as an orientation to a new position at a Lutheran school or other ministry setting, in a formal or informal study group with colleagues, or even in an online study group, connecting with others around the country or world. Regardless, there is something powerful about Christians gathering to study together, to learn with and from one another, to grapple with the text and its application to their current or future context, and to provide support and encouragement for one another. After all, at the heart of much great Lutheran education is a community that shares life together. As such, I invite and encourage you to enjoy this text, but also to find ways to talk about and study it in community.

Third, you will find that this book is not an exhaustive collection of essays. There are many topics that do not appear in this text. In fact, I confess that I had more than a few sleepless nights praying and considering what can and should be included in this text. Could or should we have included more essays about apologetics or theological foundations? Could there be more explicit direction for more traditional teaching methodologies? Could there be more guidance on teaching the faith across different disciplines and context? The answer to each of these questions and a dozen more is "yes," there could have been much more. Yet, this collection is broad and addresses many pressing questions and considerations. It is a good place to start, but that does not mean that we must end there. As such, I invite you not only to be a reader, but also to join the many in this text as an author and a teacher of teachers. As you notice topics that are missing and important to you, your context, or

Lutheran education as a whole, I urge you to act on such an observation and conviction. Write and share those important lessons. Do so with colleagues in your local context. Share them with others as you study this book together. Make use of the digital world to share your ideas with colleagues more broadly. In fact, we are exploring ways to actively engage you, the reader, with the community of other readers who use this book. For more information, I encourage you to visit cph.org/pedagogy. However you do it, share those lessons that you have learned. You have not been given those lessons to hide but to help.

In the end, this book is not nearly as important as your learning and growth as a Lutheran educator. From that perspective, this book is little more than fuel to start and grow the fire of your lifelong commitment to learning as a teacher of the faith. Each author provides yet another log for the fire. May the warmth and light fueled by each log better prepare you to embrace the joys, challenges, and opportunities as you serve in Lutheran education.

Foundations

The first of the three sections in this book is devoted to foundations in Lutheran education. This section includes three distinct approaches to foundations: (1) theological foundations; (2) foundational questions, such as the "why?" and "who?" of Lutheran education; and (3) foundations based on current and emerging research. Collectively, they give us several ways to look at and think about what is distinct regarding how we go about teaching the faith.

First and foremost, you will find essays that explore a theology of Lutheran education, how Lutheran doctrine can inform our thoughts and actions. As such, there is a series of essays that examine theological underpinnings for thinking about Lutheran education. How does Lutheran doctrine inform our thought and practice? What, if anything, is distinct about Lutheran education? You can think of this part as a sort of educational theology. Russ Moulds's essay on ten Reformation foundations provides the reader with a solid overview. In addition, both John Pless and John Oberdeck offer insights into how the doctrine of vocation can inform our thinking about the teaching ministry, helping young people think about future vocations, and how to think about the role of learner as a distinct vocation. Rodney Rathmann helps us ponder the ways in which the division of Law and Gospel leads to a distinct manner of thinking about education and classroom culture. In addition, John Pless brings us back to the foundation of our foundations, God's Word. Of course, all of the essays in this book are written in view of Lutheran theology and God's Word, but these first essays are a helpful primer that invites us to think theologically about the many other issues in the book.

A second part of this section looks at foundational questions, considering the "why" of Lutheran education. Terry Schmidt's and Rebecca Schmidt's essays invite us into the "why" by examining the role of Lutheran schools more broadly as well as the role and value of Lutheran early childhood centers. Jim Pingel further explores this by writing two essays that, at first glance, are written for school leaders, but upon more careful consideration are a challenge and invitation for all of us in Lutheran schools to "keep the main thing the main thing." After all, "if salt has lost its taste, how shall its saltiness be restored? It is no longer good for anything except to be thrown out and trampled under people's feet" (Matthew 5:13).

Finally, you will find essays in this section that draw upon more recent research about education and how that research might inform our fundamental thinking about teaching the faith. Becky Peters provides us with a primer on faith development, giving insight and cautions about such developmental theories, and Patti Hoffman devotes an essay to nurturing the faith of the young children whom God places in our care. John Oberdeck brings us into the growing field of brain research and its implications for education, but he does it in a way that recognizes the brain as "God's design." In essence, he helps us to consider how we might teach the faith in view of what we are learning about God's design of the brain, along with the important recognition that our brains have been tarnished by our sinful nature—like all other parts of us. Kim Marxhausen helps us think about how teaching the faith is not limited to a single curricular area, but is something that permeates the school day and our interaction with students. Finally, Amanda Geidel reminds us about the callings that we have to nurture the faith of children from diverse backgrounds and with a variety of gifts, talents, abilities, and callings. Just as God calls us by name, we in Lutheran education embrace an approach that sees every learner as a unique child of God.

While not exhaustive, these foundational essays are a useful starting point as we consider what is distinct, foundational, and critical to teaching the faith in a Lutheran context. From here we will go on to examine a variety of teaching and learning methods along with various important cultural and contextual factors.

1

KEY REFORMATION THEMES
FOR LUTHERAN TEACHING

Russ Moulds

As with many of our practices in the Church, Lutheran teaching is influenced by much in the broader Church—other Christian church bodies, books, church media, and well-known speakers. We are also influenced by much in the secular world around us, including the media and political, commercial, and cultural trends. Some of this influence is appropriate. For example, we no longer teach our subject areas in Greek, Latin, German, or Swedish, and that includes religion. Some of this influence is problematic. For example, this book will include discussions about marriage and divorce, worship styles, common core curriculum, and other controversies. We remain attentive to these influences and weigh the pros and cons. What's more, we assess them in terms of "a pedagogy of teaching the faith," for which this chapter serves as an orientation.

In this essay, we conduct a brief inventory of ten insights about the Gospel that help us sort out the influences on our teaching. These insights belong to the entire Church but have been particularly developed by the Reformation in Wittenberg and throughout the Lutheran tradition. To be sure, other traditions in the Church also have addressed some of these themes, often with their own contributions. But sometimes, those views differ from the Wittenberg Reformation with respect to their attention to the Gospel. We consider here what makes teaching within a Lutheran pedagogy distinct in terms of the Gospel for the benefit of the whole Church and for the world that God so loves (John 3:16).

1. The Spiritual Not Superior to the Material

In contrast to the common Christian notion that the spiritual and the material are absolutely separate from and even hostile to each other, Lutherans recognize God's divine work and blessing in "things visible and invisible" (Nicene Creed). God's work, while mysterious, is nevertheless plain to us in the physical world not only in creation but also through Jesus' incarnation and resurrection as well as in the Sacraments. When Paul writes in Colossians 1:16–17, "For by Him [Jesus] all things were created, in heaven and on earth, visible and invisible . . . all things were created through Him and for Him. And He is before all things, and in Him all things hold together," he is not endorsing pantheism but is saying all things have their being and reason in Christ. If a parable is an earthly story with a heavenly meaning, then all of life is a parable with a spiritual meaning connected to it. As Lutheran teachers, we are surrounded by spiritually loaded incidents and events every day. We can help students learn to see the spiritual intersecting with the secular in all sorts of ways.

> As Lutheran teachers, we are surrounded by spiritually loaded incidents and events every day.

2. A Biblical Anthropology and the Freedom and Bondage of the Will

Christians often speak imprecisely about "free will" as if we all have a will freed from sin and its damage. Lutherans are careful to recognize that the human will apart from the restoring work of the Holy Spirit is tainted by sin and that "the mind that is set on the flesh is hostile to God, for it does not submit to God's law; indeed it cannot. Those who are in the flesh cannot please God" (Romans 8:7–8). A freeing of the will comes only through a trusting relationship with God, empowered by the Holy Spirit. This freeing comes with faith and is completed at our resurrection (2 Corinthians 3:17–18). Apart from this freedom, we have only a limited will. We can choose a brand of clothing, a marriage partner, or to make a charity donation, but we cannot choose to have the goodness and righteousness of God in our lives and actions. Students confuse this real freedom with the increasing independence they experience as they get older. Our expressions and practices can help them sort out this confusion.

3. *Two Chief Words: Law and Gospel*

Law and Gospel, of course, apply to everything about the Christian life and about sharing our Christian faith and life with others. One important application of the distinction between Law and Gospel is the difference between legalism and antinomianism. Legalism is the belief and use of God's Law as though laws, rules, regulations, and consequences can solve sin, motivate good behavior, and create Christian community. This amounts to an idolatry of the Law. Antinomianism (Latin, meaning "against rules") is the belief that because God has forgiven us and freed us from the curse of the Law's punishment, we no longer need the Law. This amounts to cheap grace. Young Christians, whatever their age, often seek refuge in these two errors. We can help them avoid these errors by how we devise policy and practice, express and apply community structure and consequences, and sustain our relationships with them.

4. **Simul Iustus et Peccator**

Simul iustus et peccator is more Latin that means "at the same time justified and sinful." This is one of the great biblical paradoxes that characterizes the entire Christian life. The catechism applies it in the ideas of "old Adam" and "new you." We continue to live with our sinful nature and experience its influence until we die. But we simultaneously live as new creations of God despite this continued sinful condition. So Paul declares that "if anyone is in Christ, he is a new creation. The old has passed away; behold, the new has come" (2 Corinthians 5:17), and that, despite our sin, "you also must consider yourselves dead to sin and alive to God in Christ Jesus" (Romans 6:11). Young people are used to thinking in one extreme or another, one category or another. We help them recognize both by responding to their inquiries about our life together with that practical theological question: "Why do you want to know?" In other words, who wants to know about this issue—the old Adam or the new you? We need to create and practice community so that young people learn *simul iustus et peccator* as the certainty that enable sinners to live together as the saints of God.

5. *Two Kinds of Righteousness*

All Christians possess two kinds of righteousness: one that is their own and one that is not their own. All young Christians need help in sorting these two out, yet sustaining both of them. Lutherans recognize a *right*eousness that makes our life and relationship with God right, good, and fulfilled. This rightness comes to us as a gift from God and not through any efforts or ideas of our own. Luther called it an alien righteousness coming down from God through Christ in a vertical relationship. We also recognize another *right*eousness that makes our relationship with other people right, good, and worth living. In this horizontal relationship with others, our rightness consists in loving our neighbors as ourselves through our works and actions, and pursuing justice, one of God's own attributes. This second righteousness is a kind of "borrowed" righteousness as we use the gift of alien righteousness and extend it to others in our words and deeds. Our practice and policy must always be careful to clearly acknowledge, distinguish, and foster both kinds of righteousness—the first through God's Word and promises, the second through stirring one another up to love and good works (Hebrews 10:23–25).

6. *The Hidden God and the Revealed God*

Through the centuries, many observers have noticed that people are incurably religious, having endless ideas about God and what He is like. All cultures and societies have devised forms for both worshiping and denying God or gods they vaguely sense exist or at least wonder about. Lutherans also have noticed that people constantly speculate about "the hidden God." Most of this speculation, based

> Our opportunities come in the spiritually loaded incidents of ordinary daily events when we begin to examine them for their spiritual implications.

on guesses and inferences from nature, imagines a God who is majestic, glorious—and threatening. The God revealed to us through Jesus' life, ministry, death, and resurrection unveils a different picture. In Jesus, we see God in weakness, humility, and mercy. While it is true that in Jesus we catch an occasional glimpse of kingdom, power, and glory, we mainly see "crib, cross, and crypt" in the Gospel accounts. This is "the revealed God" of the God-man, Jesus Christ: "Christ and Him crucified" (1 Corinthians 2:2). Our practice and policy in community are part of God's project to reveal His hiddenness to us not through our speculation and guesswork but through the kind of living community that reflects Jesus' own revelation of Himself to us characterized by humility, service, and compassion but also by altercation. Our opportunities come in the spiritually loaded incidents of ordinary daily events when we begin to examine them for their spiritual implications.

7. *Theology of the Cross and Theology of Glory*

Rather than seeing God hidden in suffering and crucifixion, many Christians seek God in the majesty of His creation (Romans 1:20), in the power of nature (Psalm 8:3), or the glory and terror of His second coming and judgment (Revelation 6:15). While these are certainly biblical themes, Luther regarded them as secondary to all God was doing through the humiliation and death of Jesus. As Hebrews puts it, "But we see Him who for a little while was made lower than the angels, namely Jesus, crowned with glory and honor because of the suffering of death, so that by the grace of God He might taste death for everyone" (2:9). Not nature and creation, not miraculous events in history or individual lives, not judgment and the close of the age, not any manifestation of power, but the cross—that's the emblem of our theology and our image of God now. We locate God and glory where for all human purposes there can be nothing divine. Our young people, like most people, tend to look for God "in all the wrong places." Lutheran education, then, needs a coarse, splintered, blood-stained cross in every quad and courtyard to which every policy can be nailed.

8. *Christian Liberty*

Early in the Reformation, Luther composed a pair of statements within which he sought to locate all Christian decisions. His couplet has kept thoughtful Christians busy for centuries working out its implications. He began his *Treatise on Christian Liberty* this way:

> *A Christian is a perfectly free lord of all, subject to none.*

> *A Christian is a perfectly dutiful servant of all, subject to all.*[1]

If the Gospel is true—that God's grace actually covers all our sin and that nothing can separate us from the love of God in Jesus Christ (Romans 8:39)—then the Christian has perfect liberty to choose and act in any way he or she believes is in keeping with God's coming kingdom. Abraham was prepared to slay his own son. Ezra ordered the divorce of Jews who had married non-Jews. John the Baptist engaged in reckless criticism of Herod. Luther quietly sanctioned the bigamy of one of Germany's princes. Bonhoeffer joined in the effort to assassinate Hitler. No action or choice, no matter how misguided or wrongheaded, can cancel the saving power of the Gospel. Paradoxically, that same Christian

---

1   LW 31:343.

is also the most humble servant, or *doulos* (Greek for slave), to every neighbor. That Christian must make choices and take actions that serve others both temporally and eternally. This Christian liberty, then, is the liberty both to take action and to serve. The Christian is empowered and emboldened to enact this servant liberty by the absolute promise of the Gospel that no work of ours can jeopardize what God has already done for us in Christ. Therefore, Luther declares, "Sin boldly, but believe and rejoice in Christ even more boldly."[2] This kind of Christian ethics is not for the faint of heart, the biblically illiterate, or the impulsive youth. We need practice and policy for a firm structure of community within which we can then equip young people with a sound understanding of servanthood, a personal knowledge of God's Word, and a bold trust in His promises.

> The Christian is empowered and emboldened to enact this servant liberty by the absolute promise of the Gospel that no work of ours can jeopardize what God has already done for us in Christ.

9. Vocation

"God gets up every morning and milks the cows." With this peculiar claim, Luther sets out a linchpin doctrine of the Reformation: the doctrine of vocation.[3] When the farmer milks his cows, he is doing God's work every bit as much as any monk or priest (or Lutheran teacher or pastor). By milking those cows, the farmer provides sustenance for people either to continue their own lives for another day as God's people in service to others or else to live another day and have the opportunity to hear the Gospel and come to faith. So Lutherans insist that every Christian has a vocation, or a calling to faith and Christian living; that "vocation" does not equal "job"; and that no vocation—including church work—is more pleasing to God than any other. Lutherans honor God by honoring all people in all stations of life that provide service, work, care, and respect for others. The smallest child learning her ABCs and the oldest retiree providing care for that child have vocations from God. Lutheran education devises policies that esteem all vocations and promote vocations for students in whatever ways within whatever means that school may have available.

---

2   LW 48:281.
3   See Luther's commentary on Psalm 147, as discussed in Gustaf Wingren, *Luther on Vocation*, trans. Carl C. Rasmussen (Minneapolis: Muhlenberg Press, 1957).

10. The Two Kingdoms

There are, in fact, two kingdoms of God, not just one. This also is a linchpin doctrine of the Reformation. The right-hand kingdom, as Luther called it, is God's kingdom of grace that is ruled by Christ in which the Holy Spirit by the power of the Gospel makes Christians and forms disciples. The left-hand kingdom is God's secular kingdom of the world that is ruled through law by people in various stations of temporal authority to preserve order in a fallen, sinful creation. God has established both kingdoms. Christians in their vocation are called to live simultaneously in both kingdoms, devising ways to interject the come-and-coming right-hand kingdom into the left-hand kingdom without confusing or merging the two. This is not easy to do. It calls not for maintaining balance but for sustaining imbalance. Lutheran education must exist and conduct its ministry in both kingdoms. This is not easy to do. We have the difficult task of conducting practice and policy that helps students rightly distinguish and not confuse the two kingdoms even as they must learn to live effectively for God in both, yet with a distinct inclination and direction toward the right-hand kingdom.

CONCLUSION

> But the Gospel and these ten Reformation insights about the Gospel remind us that we need multiple strategies in order to engage God's left-hand kingdom with the promises of His right-hand kingdom.

Our society no longer props up the Church and its education ministry, unconditionally supporting or at least consenting to the mission of the Gospel. As culture continues to change around us, Christians may be tempted to adopt a siege mentality and interpret their conditions as "Christ conflicts with culture." But the Gospel and these ten Reformation insights about the Gospel remind us that we need multiple strategies in order to engage God's left-hand kingdom with the promises of His right-hand kingdom. As Paul reminds us, "We do not wrestle against flesh and blood, but against the rulers, against the authorities, against the cosmic powers over this present darkness, against the spiritual forces of evil in the heavenly places" (Ephesians 6:12).

As you continue reading these essays, consider various strategies for your teaching ministry and your school. Lutheran schools are different—or they should be and need to be different. If, as Peter instructs us, the

Church is a holy and royal priesthood (1 Peter 2:5, 9), then our teaching and our schools are characterized by a priestly posture. The priest is a go-between, an intercessor for sinners and God's grace. Similarly, we mediate as a go-between. We need to make our education enough like the kind of education others expect so that they can recognize it and not regard us as weird and alien. But we also need to be different enough from the world and its educational institutions that others can notice the difference. We need to have something more to offer that cannot be found elsewhere. And that something else is not merely excellent education or morals or good discipline or an escape from other kinds of schools. That something else is our proclaiming and practicing the grace of God in Jesus Christ in all that we do.

2

THE ROLE AND IMPORTANCE OF LUTHERAN SCHOOLS[1]

Terry Schmidt

Why do we operate Lutheran schools? That is a question that perplexes Lutheran congregations, pastors, parish members, and at times, people in our community. Wouldn't our children be better served in public schools since we already pay taxes that support them? Why should we duplicate our efforts? It is my hope that in this short essay I will be able to make a case that Lutheran schools are worth the expense and effort.

From the very start, Lutherans in the United States have built schools. When Saxon immigrants, who later formed The Lutheran Church—Missouri Synod, arrived in Perry County, Missouri, a school was established within days of their arrival. The school was founded before the church was. When the LCMS itself was established in 1847, it began with twelve congregations and fourteen schools. After the first twenty-five years of the Synod's existence, there were 446 congregations and 472 schools. This was commonplace among our earliest arrivals. Schools were never an afterthought. The Lutheran Church—Missouri Synod and Lutheran elementary education have always gone together. We do not wish to lose this great heritage of Lutheran education, as it means so much to the future of our church body.

From the start, Lutheran congregations operated schools for two important reasons: (1) schools made disciples of all nations, and (2) our schools taught children to obey all that Christ had commanded. The

---

1   These sources were consulted throughout the essay: Rodney L. Rathmann, ed., *Integrating the Faith*, vol. 6. (St. Louis: Concordia, 1997); Kurt Taylor, "Christ's Commission and Lutheran Schools" (PhD diss., Ashland Theological Seminary, 2007); August C. Stellhorn, *Schools of The Lutheran Church—Missouri Synod* (St. Louis: Concordia, 1963).

earliest Lutherans in the United States understood the value of schools. Walther himself explained his rationale for making the harrowing journey from Germany to America: "Our only real object was to save our souls, to live faith over here, to establish here the true and correct public worship, and to maintain truly Christian schools for our children."[2]

Today, when a congregation operates a Lutheran school, it must be committed to a significant investment that has the potential for great reward. A quality school requires energy, money, staff, and prayers. This strong commitment of a Lutheran congregation demonstrates to its members and the community that the congregation is invested in its children. In our schools today, our most pressing priority is to do what Christ commissioned His Church to do. Therefore, our schools assist our congregations to carry out Jesus' command in the Great Commission: "Go therefore and make disciples of all nations, baptizing them in the name of the Father and of the Son and of the Holy Spirit, teaching them to observe all that I have commanded you" (Matthew 28:19–20).

Lives are being transformed in Lutheran schools. Change occurs because students are exposed to Jesus hour after hour and day after day. Our schools provide an inordinate amount of time and significant opportunities for teachers to share God's Word and witness. If a child enrolls in a Lutheran school from preschool through grade 8, that child is in the care of the school for a minimum of 13,869 hours. To receive that same amount of time in a church setting, the child would need to attend church every Sunday for 266 years.

> Lives are being transformed in Lutheran schools.

Our schools expose students to God's Word every day. The Holy Spirit works whenever the Word is shared in its truth and purity. In our schools, exposure to God's Word becomes a way of life. In the daily routine, students study the Bible, pray, and worship God. Teachers relate Jesus to all aspects of the curriculum. Teachers and students share Christ's love and forgiveness. Religious instruction is not limited to one class period per day. Through intentional integration and the power of the Holy Spirit, students grow in faith and in a sanctified life.

Our schools have a history of providing our congregations with the venue and opportunities to seek the lost. Some of the earliest LCMS schools were not established exclusively for the children of Lutheran families. While many congregations operated schools that were established solely

---

2   Stellhorn, 243.

> The early leaders of the LCMS saw the opportunity to nurture the faith of their own children while also sharing the Gospel with those outside of the Church.

for Lutheran families, others schools were founded with the distinctive purpose of outreach. The early leaders of the LCMS saw the opportunity to nurture the faith of their own children while also sharing the Gospel with those outside of the Church.

In Frankenmuth, Michigan, a school was established to educate children and conduct mission work among Native Americans. Records indicate that in 1846, three Indian children were baptized; in 1847, twelve were baptized; and in 1848, six more children joined God's family through the waters of Holy Baptism. One of the six baptized in 1848 was the son of the tribal chief. After the school was firmly established, the congregation was founded in Frankenmuth. Today, St. Lorenz Lutheran Church and School is one of our Synod's largest congregations and schools.

With rare exceptions, Lutheran parishioners who are invested in the life of their congregation want their church to grow. Most congregational mission statements reflect an evangelical focus. Growth of a church is often reflective of the vitality of a congregation. Today, excellent Lutheran schools provide mission opportunities for their congregations. In congregations supporting well-run Lutheran schools, a notable proportion of congregational membership growth is often a direct result of relationships that were cultivated through the school. Today, since more than 20 percent of the students attending our schools are not directly associated with a Christian church, there has never been a better opportunity to use the school for mission and outreach.

In the past three decades, Lutheran schools located in urban areas of the United States have experienced shifting enrollments and changes in their business model. Despite this fact, the world is coming to the United States. Many of these most recent immigrants are settling in urban areas of our country. As recently as fifteen years ago, many church members paid little or no tuition; today, the average cost to educate a child in a Lutheran elementary school exceeds $6,000 per year, according to data collected by the LCMS School Ministry. Families located in urban areas cannot afford tuition; in many cases, schools and churches located in urban centers have closed where they are most needed. Several alternative ways of supporting urban Lutheran education allow our schools to do what Christ commissioned His Church to do—reach the lost!

In the mission field of urban areas, parents want what most other parents want in a school. They seek a school that maintains high academic and behavioral standards and that teaches and applies values and moral standards. At a time when urban public schools are failing, Lutheran schools can meet the needs of families seeking quality educational options for their children. Our schools are often a tool to deliver the Gospel to those who might not already believe.

In Milwaukee and Racine, Wisconsin, Lutheran Urban Mission Initiative, Inc. (LUMIN) is setting a new standard for effective, Christ-centered, results-oriented urban education. Under God's provision, LUMIN has developed a network of urban Lutheran schools "that shares resources and expertise to create safe, high-quality Lutheran schools focused on educational success, leadership development, and spiritual growth."[3] LUMIN currently operates six schools throughout Milwaukee and Racine, representing more than sixteen hundred students. LUMIN schools participate in the Private School Choice program, which covers the cost of tuition for many students. This helps make a quality, Christian education a reality for many poor families residing in the urban community. As a result, the lives of urban students are being influenced with the love of our Savior, Jesus.

The mission field provided by our schools extends to suburban areas. In 2015, at St. Paul Lutheran School in Grafton, Wisconsin, twelve new adults became church members because of their involvement with the school. These adults have seven children who are enrolled at the school. In addition, one student was baptized during the school year.

Also in 2015, at St. Peter Lutheran School in Arlington Heights, Illinois, sixteen families (including twenty-one adults) transferred to the church as a result of their activity in the school. Two school children were baptized. In each of these congregations, pastors and teachers working together understand and value the potential for mission work through their school.

Over the past several years, teachers and staff at St. John's Lutheran Church and School in Orange, California, have become much more intentional about the topic of Baptism. They strive to conduct meaningful conversations with students and parents. To be effective in this effort, they must establish and develop authentic relationships with parents. This starts on day one with greetings, casual conversations, and familiarity

---

3 See www.luminschools.org/LUMIN-Schools.htm.

with each student's family—in other words, "nonschool" things. The topic of Baptism is facilitated in each classroom as it relates to religion instruction, chapel topics, and more. After discussion, students often go home and talk about Baptism with their parents. Then, as they approach the first parent-teacher conferences, there is a comfortable relationship that facilitates meaningful conversation about Baptism. As the year continues, the topic is revisited individually and collectively.

The school Baptism chapel service has become an annual tradition for St. John's entire school community. God is using this powerful tool for His kingdom. Everyone looks forward to the event that takes place during the school day on the last Wednesday of January. Statistics of the Baptisms associated with this intentional program show great results:

> 2011—Children 15, Adults 3
>
> 2012—Children 16, Adults 4
>
> 2013—Children 19, Adults 3
>
> 2014—Children 26, Adults 2
>
> 2015—Children 22, Adults 2

Lutheran schools provide their congregation with increased opportunities to actively engage Lutheran families in the support of their congregation. Weekly school chapel services help make God's Word and worship a part of the life pattern for students. At school chapel services, students experience the beauty of the liturgy that is connected to the rhythm of the Church Year. They experience how God speaks to them corporately, as a part of the community of believers. Church attendance by family members is encouraged by classroom teachers. On Sunday mornings, families are invited as children's choirs provide musical offerings. Students can also be used as ushers or greeters.

Our schools are a vital component of our church body.

Our schools provide quality educational options for their respective communities. Lutheran schools are places of intense activity and vitality. It is often difficult to find a time when the building and grounds are not in use. This provides the congregation with opportunities to connect with its community in unique ways. In addition, we reach out to the children and families of our community with the love of our Lord and Savior Christ Jesus. Our schools are a vital component of our church body.

Lutheran schools provide mission and mercy opportunities for students by serving the needs of their surrounding community and the world.

When church and school come together in service to others, they become the hands and feet of Jesus to those in need. In addition, our schools influence their community through the arts with music and visual arts; athletics, as they compete in a godly way with surrounding area school teams; and in connections with public, parochial, and private schools in their community as they work together to educate children. Through it all, our schools are a conduit for community connections that allows the congregation to reach out to others with the love of Jesus Christ.

Lutheran schools operate with the purpose of helping students grow in knowledge, skills, and love of Jesus. In this way, our schools have, through the Holy Spirit, become faith incubators, preparing and equipping students for life in this world and for eternity. There is no more noble institution than the Lutheran school. The operation of our schools is directly related to a sustainable future for The Lutheran Church—Missouri Synod.

> In this way, our schools have, through the Holy Spirit, become faith incubators, preparing and equipping students for life in this world and for eternity.

3

THE ROLE AND VALUE OF LUTHERAN EARLY CHILDHOOD PROGRAMS AND EARLY CHILDHOOD CENTERS[1]

Rebecca Schmidt

Jesus said, "Let the little children come to Me and do not hinder them, for to such belongs the kingdom of heaven." (Matthew 19:14)

RYAN'S STORY

Ryan stopped in the office one afternoon to ask if he could pick up some information about the preschool program in our church and school. He was researching and visiting several preschool programs in the area and had heard good things about our program from his neighbor. His wife had grown up Lutheran and also suggested that he visit our early childhood program. As we became acquainted, Ryan shared that he was a stay-at-home dad and provided the daily care for his three-year-old daughter while his wife, Amanda, worked full-time outside the home.

Ryan was attentive throughout the preschool visit and tour of the facilities. I asked him questions about his family, his interests, and what he was looking for in an early childhood experience for his daughter, Emma. I learned that Ryan was an avid bicyclist and musician. I also asked Ryan about his spiritual background. He responded, "Oh, I don't really have time for that. I play in a band in the evenings, and the weekend is the only time I can participate in the bike club I belong to." When we talked

---

1   For more information on this topic, see these resources: Janis Keyser, *From Parents to Partners: Building a Family-Centered Early Childhood Program* (St. Paul, MN: Redleaf Press, 2006); Julie Klopke and Judy Williams, eds., *In His Hands: A Manual for Beginning and Operating Early Childhood Development Programs* (St. Louis: The Lutheran Church—Missouri Synod, 2014).

about the religiously integrated, Christ-centered curriculum that Emma would experience in our preschool, Ryan nodded and said it was fine as long as Emma also received excellent academic preparation for kindergarten. I shared the specifics of the program, completed the tour, and invited him to consider our preschool for his daughter.

THOSE WE SERVE

Ryan is not atypical in the families who are enrolling children in our Lutheran preschools and schools today. The Pew Research Center describes the families we serve with data from a survey published in 2014, which states that "between 2007 and 2014, the Christian share of the population fell from 78.4% to 70.6%, driven mainly by declines among mainline Protestants and Catholics. The [religiously] unaffiliated experienced the most growth and the share of Americans who belong to non-Christian faiths also increased."[2] The drop in Christian affiliation is particularly pronounced among young adults such as Ryan. It was also reported that during the same period, the percentage of Americans who are religiously unaffiliated also increased from 16.1 percent to 22.8 percent. Additionally, the number of Americans who identify with non-Christian faiths increased by 1.2 percentage points.[3] Clearly, a great opportunity exists for Lutheran early childhood centers to share the Word of God and nurture the faith walk of children and families.

BUILDING RELATIONSHIPS

Confident that their child would receive an excellent early childhood experience in a caring environment, Ryan and his wife decided to enroll their daughter, Emma, in our preschool. Because effective communication between the family and the early childhood center is crucial to the success of building a program of family-centered care, the director shared regular and continuous information about the program with Ryan and Amanda. Throughout the summer, they received welcome letters and information about the preschool and the church, as well as invitations to a family orientation evening and a new family picnic. Additionally, a call from Emma's teacher requesting a time to visit Emma and her family before preschool classes started was an important component in

---

2   Pew Research Center, "America's Changing Religious Landscape," May 12, 2015. http://www.pewforum.org/2015/05/12/americas-changing-religious-landscape (accessed February 17, 2016).

3   Pew Research Center, "America's Changing Religious Landscape."

building a relationship and foundation of trust with Ryan and the members of his family.

From Ryan's Hand to Our Hand

On the first day of class, Ryan brought Emma to school; they were greeted by the director and personally welcomed by the teacher. The teacher showed Emma her cubby, and Ryan helped Emma hang up her backpack. Ryan signed Emma in and talked to the teacher about the lunch plan for the day. Soon Emma was settled in the classroom and joined a group of children at the block center. Ryan left with the confidence that his daughter would be well cared for in a safe and loving environment.

As the year progressed, the early childhood faculty and staff interacted several times each week with the families enrolled in the center. The Holy Spirit uses the staff members of an early childhood center to reach the unchurched, the dechurched, and the religiously unaffiliated who are attending their center. Teachers are equipped by God to reach family members who are not members of the Body of Christ by caring for them as Christ would and modeling His love. Pastors who greet families and are involved in the life of the early childhood center also have a significant impact. Both teachers and pastors are able to open doors to reach non-Christian family members by loving children, taking a deep interest in their families, demonstrating understanding, and freely extending grace and forgiveness to all who come to their centers and schools. Ryan's daily contact with the early childhood and church staff members continued to nurture and strengthen his relationship in the preschool community.

Special Events for the Whole Family

Special events for families and preschoolers—such as a harvest parties, trunk-or-treat events, family Christmas services, Easter egg hunts, grandparents' and special visitors' days, dads and donuts, Mother's Day activities, parent education meetings, and family literacy events—provided a variety of opportunities for Ryan and his wife to enjoy time with their daughter and become better acquainted with the staff and the parents of Emma's classmates. Pastors, directors of Christian education, and family ministry leaders also attended the events. As Ryan and Amanda became acquainted with the preschool, they also became acquainted with the church. The design of the events was intentional in supporting and nurturing a partnership with Ryan and his family and with other parents. Subsequently, parents and families often like to help create, coordinate, and develop new events; Ryan and Amanda found themselves volunteering their time in many of the tasks.

MINISTRY IS A TEAM EFFORT

One of the special events that occurred in Emma's first year took place during a worship service one Sunday morning. Ryan attended the service with Emma, whose preschool class was singing. In addition to hearing Emma's class sing, Ryan also listened to the praise team that led songs as part of the morning service. When Ryan dropped Emma off at school the following week, he asked Emma's teacher about the praise team. The teacher shared information about the team's ministry in the church and was able to connect Ryan to the team's leader.

Not long afterward, Ryan was invited to join the praise team. He thrived in this rich environment, where he was able to contribute his gifts and talents. It wasn't long before Ryan was regularly participating with the praise team in worship. Amanda and Emma attended the morning services when the praise team was playing as well. Additionally, the praise team was asked to participate in youth events, women's ministry events, and other activities in the community. Through his work with the praise team, Ryan experienced a variety of ministries in the church.

The pastor reached out to Ryan and Amanda and provided encouragement, prayers, and pastoral care. New member classes, adult Baptism, and adult confirmation ensued as Ryan's faith walk unfolded. When Ryan and Amanda learned that a new baby was on the way, they were surrounded with prayer and acts of caring throughout Amanda's pregnancy. After the birth of their new baby, they were showered with meals delivered to their home. They attended Baptism classes and celebrated the Baptism of their new baby. Emma's teacher and the director attended the service and continued to shower Ryan, Amanda, and Emma with care and affection. What a joyful day for the family of Christ when their son, Nathan, was touched by the Holy Spirit through Baptism, becoming a beloved child of God.

Ryan's story doesn't end here. As it happens with so many families, Ryan stopped by the office one day to share that his wife had accepted a new position in another state. Amanda would be leaving the family early to start her new job. Ryan and the children would stay behind through the end of the school year and until their house sold. Prayers continued for his family.

On the last day of school, Ryan once again stopped by the school office. This time it was to say good-bye. I noticed that on this day, Ryan was wearing a cross made of two nails on a leather strip around his neck. He thanked me for the great experience his children had at our school and for the preschool program where his experience began. He added, "I don't know if you remember when I came in to enroll Emma. I didn't really understand all that was involved with attending a Lutheran school. The Christian part was not important to me then, but I want you to know that I have been changed. I am growing every day. I had no idea what having a relationship with Jesus Christ could be. Thank you. I know that God will provide and that we will find a new church, but it's the school that I am really going to miss. I am forever changed, and I am thankful for our preschool, where it all began."

4

The Law and Gospel in Classroom Relationships

A Classroom Dedicated to Christ Is a Holy Place

Rodney L. Rathmann

For those who appreciate the privilege of teaching and learning in a Christian classroom, the environment they experience together is holy, for our Savior has promised that where two or three are gathered together in His name, He is there in the midst of them. Here it is that, before a backdrop of crosses, pictures of Jesus, and paintings of Bible scenes, dedicated Christ-centered teaching connects lesson goals and objectives with Christ Jesus and the Word of God. In these holy places, Christ-centered teachers, concerned about helping their students grow in faith and in a knowledge of the only true God, strive to prepare them well for the opportunities for significance, meaning, and fulfillment God continues to provide in lives lived for Him. Here, teachers evidence appreciation for their students as unique individuals created by God. Each has value because his or her life has been bought and paid for with the life and death of the very Son of God.

Appreciation for each student leads teachers to get to know them, their individual backgrounds, interests, and aspirations. Good teachers merge that appreciation and understanding of each student with both the content to be taught and time-honored, effective teaching strategies. Effective teaching and classroom-management strategies rest on the foundation of these relationships. In the best teaching/learning situations, relationships reign

> In the best teaching/learning situations, relationships reign supreme—first our relationship with God and then the relationships we build with one another.

33

supreme—first our relationship with God and then the relationships we build with one another.

Two Great Doctrines

We learn about the relationship God desires for us by reading and studying His Holy Word. Through the Word, God gives the all-important gift of faith and the blessings of forgiveness, salvation, and the desire and power to live a new life in Him. The Bible reveals God's action of gift-giving as the work of the Holy Spirit. The right understanding, teaching, and application of God's Word involves distinguishing each portion of the Scripture according to its two great doctrines—Law and Gospel. Achieving this distinction in understanding and application is also the result of the Spirit at work.

The Law of God at Work

Simply understood, the Law reveals God's design for us. It tells what we are to do and not to do and how we are to act. Since the fall of our first parents into sin, all of us find ourselves unable to keep God's Law. When effectively applied, the Law shows us that we are sinners, worthy only of punishment. This working of the Law is vital in preparing our hearts to receive the gift of the Gospel.

From God's Word, we learn the three purposes of the Law, each of which plays an important role in the classroom.

As a curb, God's Law channels student behaviors through the enforcement of the rules and routines that keep the classroom from disintegrating into bedlam. In efficiently run classrooms, these structures for living and working together are simply and clearly expressed and faithfully and consistently enforced. Offending behaviors are best met with immediate and precise intervening actions that may include consequences, fairly applied.

As a mirror, God's Law reveals to all, teachers as well as students, where we stand before God as we truly are. We have failed; we need help. Through the working of the Holy Spirit, we are led to repent, confess our sin, and place ourselves at the mercy of God.

As a guide, God's Law helps us understand what it means to be "salt and light" in a world many regard as apathetic and oppositional to God. It lays before us what God's Word calls "the narrow way." When taught in Christ-centered classrooms, it helps students to approach problems and difficulties with echoes of classroom conversations in which questions such as "How would Mrs. Wilson (my faith-filled teacher) handle this situation?" find their place.

The Power of the Gospel

Both Law and Gospel come from God and are given to us in God's Word for our good. Each person is very familiar with the Law because in addition to providing it in His Word, God has written it into each human heart. Because the Gospel comes to us only from outside ourselves—from God's Word—and because it motivates and empowers us for our new life in Jesus, effective teaching of the faith allows the Gospel rather than the Law to dominate.

God's Law tells what God expects of us. But the Gospel is all about love—God's love for us and for all people. It reveals a love that moved God to send His only Son to earth to be born human yet also fully God, to live a sin-free life in our place, and to take upon Himself the punishment we deserve. Stated in another way, as our substitute, Jesus took our sins upon Himself so that we can receive His holiness with its attending blessings of forgiveness, salvation, and the ability to begin anew. All of this we receive as a no-strings-attached gift, brought to us by the working of the Holy Spirit through the Means of Grace—God's Word and the Sacraments.

Studies repeatedly underscore that good teachers care about their students. At their essence, effective class instruction and class-management strategies are rooted in love. God's love is the heart of the Gospel. Christ-centered teachers have the power of God's love active in them and in the relationships they work to build with God and others.

> At their essence, effective class instruction and class-management strategies are rooted in love.

A GOSPEL-CENTERED LEARNING ENVIRONMENT

Gospel-motivated love is unconditional and unmerited. We express this type of love imperfectly and incompletely even in the best of human relationships. Still, with God's power, teachers can strive faithfully to deliver each day on the promise to let the Gospel dominate in the words they use to teach and instruct, in the classroom environment they create and maintain, and in the attitudes they project.

How does Gospel-dominated teaching present itself?

It is rooted in a teacher's consistent life of prayer, study of God's Word, and participation in the Sacraments. It speaks of a teacher's genuine faith that touches students' lives at the baptismal font and graveside, in common acts of folded hands and bowed heads, and in shared stories both old and new of God at work. It makes the classroom a "workshop in Christian living" as daily it celebrates a new and eternal life begun with faith and continuing in the resurrection hope into eternity.

Gospel-dominated teaching shows respect for students and all others as fellow redeemed people. As such, it responds to God's grace in a culture of servanthood and Golden Rule–style behaviors and courtesies and engages teachers in identity-celebrating activities of the observance of Baptism birthdays.

It presents Bible stories and devotions from a Law/Gospel perspective. Sin is identified and applied for the purpose of leading learners to repentance and the comforting assurance of forgiveness and life-changing power Jesus came to bring. For example, in teaching the account of Joseph forgiving his brothers, students can be led to see themselves in the hurtful actions committed by the brothers against Joseph. Then in Joseph's words of forgiveness, students can be brought to recognize God's forgiveness for us through Jesus' life, death, and resurrection.

Gospel-dominated teaching cares enough to confront wrongdoing for the sake of the individual—always with the goal of offering forgiveness and restoring and maintaining relationships. It works to connect with individual students, even with those most difficult to connect with. It exercises care to turn forgiveness into a teachable moment, not to review and elaborate on past offenses.

It pronounces God's forgiving, comforting, life-giving love after the realization, repentance, and confession of sins committed. Theologian C. F. W. Walther once referred to the Gospel as a rare guest in a person's conscience. In announcing words of forgiveness, Christian teachers usher in that rare and welcome guest!

Gospel-dominated teaching does not attempt to motivate using guilt or shame. Rather, it projects the Christlike qualities of love Paul describes in 1 Corinthians 13. It "is patient and kind; . . . does not envy or boast; it is not arrogant or rude. It does not insist on its own way; it is not irritable or resentful; it does not rejoice at wrongdoing, but rejoices with the truth." It "bears all things, believes all things, hopes all things, endures all things" (vv. 4–7). These qualities help make the classroom a warm, friendly place, conducive for learning.

It works to build Christ-centered relationships. This type of love can be seen in classrooms where teachers treat all students fairly while investing extra time and energy for the sake of individual students as situations and needs require. It extends the love of Christ beyond the classroom, into the home and community.

It "goes the extra mile," as it did when the teacher, mindful of a child's distress over a precious coat that accidentally became soiled at recess, arranged for the coat to go to the cleaners—and paid for the cleaning himself— so the child could happily go home at the end of the day with the coat (now clean and fresh) that she had only reluctantly been allowed to wear to school. In the face of difficult decisions affecting students, it leads decision-makers to conclude that if an error of judgment is made, it is made on the side of the Gospel.

> In the face of difficult decisions affecting students, it leads decision-makers to conclude that if an error of judgment is made, it is made on the side of the Gospel.

THE ART OF RIGHTLY DIVIDING LAW AND GOSPEL

Consider Law and Gospel at work in the following example of an actual classroom event. Two boys conspired together and carried out a minor act of theft from the classroom supply closet. Caught almost in the very act and confronted with their wrongdoing, they felt immediate contrition and received God's forgiveness from their teacher. Having felt true remorse and then the relief and comfort of the assurance that all was well again, they were more than willing to stay in for recess as the consequence of their offense. But, unwilling to let the matter rest there, the two asked the teacher if they might bring closure to the issue and respond to their forgiveness by using their forfeited recess time to clean and organize the supply closet, which they did with observable enthusiasm.

In the above example, confession neatly followed committed sin, which was then immediately followed by the assurance of forgiveness and actions expressing a desire to begin anew. Unfortunately, things don't always work out in every situation as neatly as they did in this case. In truth, rightly distinguishing and applying Law and Gospel is difficult most of the time. Luther says that he is willing to place him who is well versed in the art of dividing the Law from the Gospel at the head of all and call him a doctor of Holy Writ.[1]

---

1   See C. F. W. Walther, *Law and Gospel: How to Read and Apply the Bible* (St. Louis: Concordia, 2010), 9.

Still, we are called to apply both Law and Gospel in our life and teaching. We can take comfort in knowing that we don't have to do it alone, for we are taught by the Holy Spirit in the school of experience. And in His school, we are all lifelong learners.

5

TEACHING VOCATION

John T. Pless

In everyday speech, the word *vocation* has come to be equated with an occupation or job. It is tempting to confuse what we do with who we are. How do we sort things out so that this confusion is undone? The Lutheran doctrine of vocation is of great help here. Vocation is much more than a job; it embraces everything that the Christian is and does as a child of God. Lutheran teachers will seek to teach those entrusted to their care to think clearly about vocation in light of God's Law and Gospel. Two aspects of the doctrine of vocation are especially essential for this teaching. First, there is the duality of the Christian's calling to a life of faith and love. Second, there is the biblical truth that God works behind human "masks" to get His work done in the world.

The Christian life has a dual focus: faith and love. To borrow the language of Luther, Christians live outside of themselves in Christ by faith and in the neighbor by love.[1] Being comes before doing. We are not saved by our love but through faith in Jesus Christ. Our good works do not make us Christian but the Christian is busy and active in a life of good works. God does not need our good works but the world does. The life of good works is lived out in the place of our calling—in the family, congregation, community, and workplace (see the Table of Duties in Luther's Small Catechism). Freed by the Gospel, the Christian now lives a life of service not in order to gain salvation but to serve the well-being of the neighbor. The Christian life is one not of achievement and self-fulfillment but of servanthood. In every stage of life, the Christian is called to live by faith in Christ and in love toward the neighbor.

---

1 See LW 31:371.

It is God Himself who does the calling. The apostle Peter says that God has "called you out of darkness into His marvelous light" (1 Peter 2:9). This calling is the calling to faith itself. Therefore, Paul writes to the Thessalonians, "But we ought always to give thanks to God for you, brothers beloved by the Lord, because God chose you as the firstfruits to be saved, through sanctification by the Spirit and belief in the truth. To this He called you through our gospel, so that you may obtain the glory of our Lord Jesus Christ" (2 Thessalonians 2:13–14). On the basis of God's redeeming work in Christ, the apostle implores the Ephesians "to walk in a manner worthy of the calling to which you have been called" (Ephesians 4:1). Luther reflects the language and thought of Paul when he has us confess in the explanation of the Third Article of the Creed that "the Holy Spirit has called me by the Gospel." This is the calling to faith in Christ, and this calling gives us a new identity and status before God.

> It is essential that the distinction between being and doing, grace and works, faith and love be clearly articulated in our teaching.

For all of God's unmerited goodness to us, we "thank and praise, serve and obey Him."[2] It is essential that the distinction between being and doing, grace and works, faith and love be clearly articulated in our teaching. Only then will moralism—a severe confusion of Law and Gospel—be avoided and students will be firmly anchored in the Good News of Jesus Christ. We are called by the Gospel to faith in Christ, faith that is then active in a life of love in the places where God has put us.

Oriented by this understanding of faith and love, the Lutheran teaching of vocation will assist students in recognizing that God is served not by their self-chosen projects but in the responsibilities He gives each of them according to their place in life. For example, children have the responsibility to honor and obey their parents and others in authority according to the Fourth Commandment. The shape of this responsibility shifts when children become adults and take on a responsibility to care for aged parents. All people share in the responsibilities that come with citizenship. Those in public office have a particular responsibility toward those whom they govern to act with justice, integrity, and accountability. All Christians have the duty to hear and keep God's Word and live according to His Commandments. Pastors have the specific calling to preach and teach God's Word as servants of Christ ordained for this work, remembering that they are men who must give account to their Lord.

---

2   Small Catechism, explanation of the First Article of the Apostles' Creed.

Our callings in this world are not static. In some cases, they change as we move through life. The child marries and becomes a parent. The student completes her studies and becomes a teacher. An employee becomes an employer. A private citizen is elected to a position of governmental leadership. A layman completes seminary education and is called to serve as a pastor. In the modern world, one might retire from this or that occupation (something virtually unknown in Luther's day), but that does not mean that he or she is without vocation. The vocations of parent or grandparent, citizen, congregation member, and other responsibilities still remain and continue as the arenas for God-pleasing service to the neighbor.

A second aspect to the doctrine of vocation that will give shape to our teaching is the reality that God is at work behind "masks." God is at work in our work. God hides Himself behind masks to do His work in the world. God has created me in body and soul, but He did this through the instrumentality of my parents. He daily and richly provides me with all that I need to sustain and support this body and life, but He does this through farmers and workers who process, prepare, and deliver food. He guards me from danger and defends me from evil, but He does this through medical doctors, law enforcement officers, and soldiers. When God deals with us, He does so through creation.

Likewise, the Lutheran teaching of vocation recognizes that God receives our service behind the masks of other people. Luther could remark that when a mother and father hear the cry of their child in the middle of the night, this baby's voice is the very mouth of God saying "Come, and take care of me." Ultimately, it is God Himself who receives our service, though it is directed to Him through the mask of the neighbor. So we do our work, as Paul says in Ephesians 6:6–7, "not by the way of eye-service, as people-pleasers, but as bondservants of Christ, doing the will of God from the heart, rendering service with a good will as to the Lord and not to man." The catechism gets it right. For everything that God has given me in creation, purely out of His fatherly and divine goodness without any merit or worthiness in me, it is my duty to thank, praise, serve, and obey Him. We thank and praise God in prayer and confession, acknowledging Him as the benefactor of every gift (as we do in morning and evening prayer and mealtime prayers), and we serve and obey God in our various callings in the world. Luther identified these callings, or stations, in life in the Table of Duties appended to the Small Catechism as the congregation, the civil community, and the family (which in Luther's day, before the Industrial Revolution, was inclusive of one's occupation or daily work). In these places of life, God is at work behind His creaturely masks to give daily bread and also to receive our service born of faith in His name.

Perhaps the most overlooked and underutilized portions of the catechism are the Daily Prayers and Table of Duties. A more intentional focus on vocation in Lutheran teaching, using the resources that are already available to us in the catechism, is needed to counteract legalistic works-righteousness on the one hand and the assertion that one's work is simply a means of self-expression and self-fulfillment on the other. Our works in this world do not render us as acceptable to God or make us holy. Christ has accomplished that work, and faith receives it. Our works instead flow from faith and serve the well-being of the neighbor in this world.

This teaching on vocation serves as a lens through which to view every stage of the Christian's life from birth to death. Living from Baptism in repentance and faith, bearing the cross while trusting in God's promises, the life of discipleship is our vocation. It is a life oriented in faith and love, receiving all that God sends our way as an expression of His fatherly and gracious will and living lives of love according to His Commandments as His instruments for the blessing of other people both seen and unseen.

6

THE VOCATION OF LEARNER

John Oberdeck

If you are a Lutheran educator (commissioned or ordained), you no doubt have a strong commitment to teaching as your vocation, your calling. However, you are not the only person in the classroom with a calling connected to education. The people on the other side of your desk—whether playing on the carpet in preschool, mastering their multiplication tables, or manipulating test tubes in chemistry—also have a vocation: the vocation of learner.

The vocations of learner and educator exist in an intricate relationship—we might even call it a dance—as one influences the other in a whirl of cognitive, affective, and psychomotor skill acquisition. And what is the best outcome, the ultimate competency we look for as Lutheran educators for those under our care? Isn't our goal to aid students in becoming mature, competent, and faithful adults who trust in Jesus Christ for forgiveness and eternal life and who among their own many vocations maintain themselves as curious individuals ready to learn more in service to neighbor and to God?

Obviously, the vocation of learner extends beyond the classroom, embracing both the intended and the unintended curriculum. The vocation of learner is lifelong, as any baby boomer confronted by the digital age can testify. Scripture supports the enduring nature of learning across the life-span, especially when describing our relationship to God. Peter's admonition to "grow in the grace and knowledge of our Lord and Savior Jesus Christ" (2 Peter 3:18) provides for no graduation date. Moreover, Paul's encouragement to "attain to the unity of the faith

> Peter's admonition to "grow in the grace and knowledge of our Lord and Savior Jesus Christ" (2 Peter 3:18) provides for no graduation date.

43

and of the knowledge of the Son of God" involving "the measure of the stature of the fullness of Christ" (Ephesians 4:13) hints that the termination of learning in this life is the dawn of eternity in the next.

To describe the vocation of learner, we need clarity over the meaning of the term *vocation*, so that is where we will begin. Next, we will explore what it means for students to fulfill their learning vocation. Finally, we will offer suggestions as to how we can fulfill our calling as Lutheran educators by guiding our students in their vocations as learners.

What Is Vocation?

It's easy to think of vocation in terms of occupation, but that is far too narrow a definition. Likewise, the restriction of the term to church vocations, as has been done in some periods of history, is much too limiting. Our occupations are certainly included, but so are the roles that we fill in relationship to family, community, and church. By their very nature, vocations provide something of benefit to our neighbors; here, "neighbor" is defined in the broadest terms possible, from our spouse to our employer to the nameless person who receives the benefit of our labor.[1]

Martin Luther's contribution to our understanding of vocation is enormous. He redirects vocation away from a focus on our actions for God to how our actions benefit our neighbor. In fact, through our actions, God is caring for the neighbor.

> What else is all our work to God—whether in the fields, in the garden, in the city, in the house, in war, or in government—but just such a child's performance, by which He wants to give His gifts in the fields, at home, and everywhere else? These are the masks of God, behind which He wants to remain concealed and do all things.[2]

> Luther makes God the subject and the neighbor the object while we become the means God uses.

Seeing vocations as "masks of God" is a radical departure from looking at vocations as our service done for God or to God. Luther makes God the subject and the neighbor the object while we become the means God uses—very different from seeing ourselves as the subject with God as the object and our neighbor as the means to our ends. To be sure, serving our neighbor is certainly done as an act of obedience to God and is pleasing to God, but

1   Gustaf Wingren, *Luther on Vocation*, trans. Carl C. Rasmussen (Minneapolis: Muhlenberg Press, 1957), 4–10.
2   LW 14:114–15.

44

God doesn't need our service. Our neighbor does, as Luther explains. This means that at its root, all our vocations are the ways God is exercising His gracious care over creation—and especially His highest creation, humankind. We are God's masks behind whom God conceals Himself and accomplishes His goal of serving the needs of our neighbors.[3]

The Lutheran doctrine of vocation recognizes that our neighbors are not a means to our ends; rather, we are the means to God's ends as we serve our neighbors. In the same way, God is using us to serve our students. But if our students also have a vocation in the classroom, are they in some way serving us? How does this work?

LEARNERS FULFILLING THEIR VOCATION

Who is being served, or blessed, by the learners fulfilling their vocation? How does the vocation of learner serve as a mask of God that benefits the neighbor or me—the teacher? How can we recognize the vocation of learner in our classrooms? Let's consider these possibilities.

1. Learners give opportunity for teachers to exercise their vocation.

In a very direct way, learners are a blessing to their teachers. Just because this point is patently obvious doesn't mean it is recognized. Learners bless us all the time by their presence, giving us the opportunity to teach and challenging us to teach well, especially when the learners are failing in their vocation! We get to spend our time in the dance of teaching and learning with subject matter that we love and with students for whom we care. As a result, we receive the satisfaction of meaningful labor. Only when a school closes for lack of students do we become fully aware of this blessed mask of God.

2. Learners guide teachers in their application of Law and Gospel.

While we might think that the discipline problems we face fall under the category of curses rather than blessings, an honest appraisal of the situation reveals that we grow in our own understanding of judgment and forgiveness through the circumstances our students present. Without students being who they are, we could miss the subtleties of our own justification before God through Jesus Christ alone. As a result, we grow

---

3   Gene Edward Veith, *The Spirituality of the Cross: The Way of the First Evangelicals* (St. Louis: Concordia, 1999), 77. See also Gene Edward Veith and Mary J. Moerbe, *Family Vocation: God's Calling in Marriage, Parenting, and Childhood* (Wheaton, IL: Crossway, 2012). For a Bible study on vocation, see Chad E. Hoover, *Vocation: God Serves through Us*. The Lutheran Spirituality Series (St. Louis: Concordia, 2007).

in our own faith by teaching the faith. Next time your students are disruptive, consider the possibility that they are fulfilling their vocation of being a mask of God!

3. Learners serve their parents.

As with teachers, so with parents; the way we develop from childhood through adolescence into adulthood is filled with opportunities for parents to exercise their God-given vocation to care for and discipline their children. Naturally, we look at this relationship as one of parents serving their children's need to be brought up in the nurture and admonition of the Lord; but without those needs, the parents don't grow into their parental vocation. In the home, children are masks of God who bring the parenting role into clear view.

4. Learners serve their community.

Gaining knowledge, obtaining Christlike attitudes, and demonstrating competencies for the benefit of others—these are the marks of the learner's vocation. Through these behaviors, learners become blessings for their communities both in the present and in the future. We can express this blessing by saying that there is hopefulness for the future when students have learned lessons from the past and are applying those lessons in the present.

LUTHERAN PEDAGOGY AND THE VOCATION OF LEARNER

Korey Maas summarizes the Lutheran teaching on vocation this way: "Indeed, the distinctively Lutheran understanding is that God, rather than being served in vocation, is himself the one serving others in and through legitimate offices and individuals situated within them."[4] How can we inculcate a sense of God working through us among our students? Here are a few suggestions to stimulate our thinking.

1. Ask students to consider whom they are helping now through what they are learning.

Our students may not have the capacity to see their role as a blessing to their teacher, their parents, or their community. Development may not yet have opened the abstract awareness of the effect of the present

---

4   Korey D. Maas, "The Vocation of a Student," in *The Idea and Practice of a Christian University: A Lutheran Approach*, ed. Scott A. Ashmon (St. Louis: Concordia, 2015), 101.

or the past on the future. Help them to begin to think of themselves as masks of God now. They already have a vocation.

2. Ask students to consider whom they would like to help in the future.

Then follow up this inquiry with this question: "What will you need to know in order to be that kind of a helper?" Developing a learning plan in itself can be motivating especially when it is learner generated, and it certainly gives students opportunity to consider their interests and gifts.

3. Inform students that learning, like any vocation, involves rewarding work.

Accomplishing a task well brings satisfaction. Learning involves work, sometimes hard work. Let's let our students know that when they apply themselves to their vocation as a learner, they will work hard, but with working hard comes a sense of satisfaction. Performing well allows for a God-pleasing pride in God's accomplishments through us.

4. Remind students that the vocation of learner is not optional.

God has created us to learn. Learning is what our brains do, even prior to birth. Let's maximize inquisitiveness, curiosity, and imagination that creates a positive inertia and a desire to learn more. Passive learning is not as efficient or successful as active learning, and an interactive learning environment creates more pathways for memory.[5]

Let's help our students shift their attitude as they discover that their role in the classroom is not only to be a receiver of information but also a giver of meaningful service! Recognition of their role in the dance of teaching and learning can be a powerful motivator for the vocation of learner and can also bring fulfillment to those of us whose vocation is to teach.

> Let's help our students shift their attitude as they discover that their role in the classroom is not only to be a receiver of information but also a giver of meaningful service!

---

5   Holly J. Inglis, "The Nature of Learning," in *Sticky Learning: How Neuroscience Supports Teaching That's Remembered,* ed. Holly J. Inglis (Minneapolis: Fortress Press, 2014), 14.

7

GOD'S DESIGN OF THE BRAIN

Implications for Teaching the Faith

John Oberdeck

St. John Chrysostom, a fourth-century bishop of Constantinople, wrote this about children in worship:

> It is this very age that most of all needs the hearing these things; for from its tenderness it readily stores up what is said; and what children hear is impressed as a seal on the wax of their minds.[1]

Chrysostom would have had no knowledge whatsoever of the structure of the brain, how glial cells provide a framework for neuronal cells to fire electrically while synaptic gaps are jumped chemically by neurotransmitters, all taking place in microseconds. From his perspective, if he were familiar with what's beneath the skull at all, the gray matter might as well have been wax.

How much like soft, impressionable wax is the human brain? Not much, really. Nevertheless, the point made by Chrysostom through observation and the study of Scripture (see Deuteronomy 6:4–9) has been validated by neuroscience. Our brains are organic learning mechanisms of tremendous capacity and power, shaped not only by our environment but also by our own habits and choices. This finding brought one researcher to comment, "Our brains are programmable, and we are the programmers."[2]

---

1   John Chrysostom, "Homilies of St. John Chrysostom, Archbishop of Constantinople, on the Gospel of St. John," in *Saint Chrysostom: Homilies on the Gospel of St. John and the Epistle to the Hebrews*, ed. Philip Schaff, trans. G. T. Stupart, vol. 14 of *A Select Library of the Nicene and Post-Nicene Fathers of the Christian Church*, First Series (New York: Christian Literature Company, 1889), 10.

2   Daniel J. Siegel, *Brainstorm: The Power and Purpose of the Teenage Brain* (New York: Penguin, 2013), 17.

We can't help but describe information processing in this digital age using computer vocabulary. So let's use this to our advantage. Programmers are helpless without the hardware—a computer capable of accurate acquisition, precise storage, and exact retrieval—within which to load the software. From whence comes this computer—our brain?

In this article, I will share three implications for teaching the faith from what we know from brain research, not because these are necessarily the most important or recent, but because they are the ones I find most relevant for teaching the Christian faith.

GOD IS A CREATIVE GENIUS

First, the more we learn about our brains, the more evidence we have of our Creator's unfathomable genius. God is actually much, much more than a creative genius. Even a modest overview of the physiology of our brains is beyond the scope of this chapter, but consider these brief notes about what is going on inside our craniums:

1. The complexity of the brain as it operates alternatively by electrical charge in the cell and chemical reaction in the synapse

2. The sheer number of neurons in the brain, estimated at 100 billion, which create trillions of synapses

3. The specificity of function within the cortex of the brain—the occipital (visual), parietal (sensory), temporal (auditory), and frontal (motor) lobes

4. The interactivity and speed of entities in the brain—the hippocampus and amygdala, for example—in assessing the emotional significance of incoming stimuli[3]

What implication does this have for teaching the faith? The Bible encourages us to look outward for evidence of our Creator's power. "The heavens declare the glory of God, and the sky above proclaims His handiwork" (Psalm 19:1). We can also direct our students to look inward to find just as convincing evidence of the Creator's design. From the cosmic to the subatomic, God has left His fingerprint on all

> From the cosmic to the subatomic, God has left His fingerprint on all creation, including our own brain anatomy and physiology.

3   Holly J. Inglis, "How the Brain Works," in *Sticky Learning: How Neuroscience Supports Teaching That's Remembered*, ed. Holly J. Inglis (Minneapolis: Fortress Press, 2014), 23–26.

creation, including our own brain anatomy and physiology. We have ample reason to praise our Creator, for we are indeed "fearfully and wonderfully made" (Psalm 139:14).

GOD CREATED US TO REMEMBER

Second, God designed the brain with memory in mind, as evidenced by the variety of ways in which information is received, identified, categorized, stored, and retrieved by our brains. Are we using all the avenues by which our brains retain information, or do we tend to use one to the exclusion of other viable pathways? And what are those pathways? The five pathways actually make use of different parts of the brain; the hippocampus, cerebellum, and the amygdala are all governed to some degree by the decision-making center of the prefrontal cortex.

- Semantic Memory—Semantic memory is word based. Information is gained visually from the page as well as by hearing. Semantic memory tends to be the most difficult to recall and requires much repetition to create the neural pathways.

- Episodic Memory—Episodic memory deals with the context in which the learning event takes place. Content being learned is connected with the environment, and the environment reinforces our ability to retrieve the content.

- Procedural Memory—Procedural memory involves repetitive movements that, over time, become automatized, such as riding a bike. Once having learned something, we discover we have forgotten how we learned it, even when we can still perform the function, such as tying our shoes.

- Automatic Memory—Automatic memory involves actions or procedures that have become unconscious. Evidence of this memory pathway emerges when we find ourselves doing something unintentionally, such as singing along to a song on the radio.

- Emotional Memory—Emotional memory is the most powerful and is governed in the brain by the amygdala. Both good and bad memories with high emotional content are seemingly burned into our networks and are rapidly triggered by similar events.[4]

What implications does this information have for teaching the faith? The Gospel comes to us through the Word. We are word based in our

---

4   Holly J. Inglis, "How Memory Works," in *Sticky Learning*, 41–43.

approach to understanding God as our Creator, Redeemer, and Sanctifier. As a result, we have a predisposition toward semantic memory, which is necessary for a clear confession of our faith. But semantic memory is the most difficult to accurately store and retrieve. Strategies that emphasize place (episodic), movement (procedural), repetition (automatic), and feelings (emotional) assist learners to remember and provide more pathways for retrieval. For this reason, the arts—music, drama, painting, poetry, and literature—are especially helpful tools in communicating the Gospel.[5]

GOD CREATED US TO GROW

Third, since our brains are created to learn, we might think teaching the faith should be the most natural of processes. Why, at times, does it seem so hard? One answer that we receive from the Bible is that creation as we experience it now is not the way God originally created it to be, at least not since the fall of Adam. All of creation, including our bodies, was subjected to futility (Romans 8:20). Although our brain is a magnificent organ of incredible capacity and complexity, our brain does not have the perfection with which it was created; along with our other organs, it participates in the spiritual—and physical—death of humans apart from Jesus Christ (Ephesians 2:1–3). That there should be hesitancy to receive God's gifts for us shouldn't surprise us, since by nature we are enemies and are reconciled only through Jesus Christ (Romans 5:10).

Whether the manner in which brain development takes place in adolescence is part of the original plan of God or an aspect of the original sin of Adam is indeterminable. What we do know from brain research is that maturation of different parts of the brain are not synchronized in adolescence. The parts of the brain that govern emotions (the limbic system) mature before the parts of the brain that govern impulses (prefrontal cortex). This mismatch results in poor decisions, susceptibility to peer pressure, and dangerous risk-taking. And at the same time, the mismatch provides for positive risk-taking behaviors that adults would tend to avoid.[6]

What implication does this have for teaching the faith? The relevancy is in how we consciously attend to the developmental differences of our students, whatever age they happen to be. Educational theorists such as

---

5   Allen Nauss, *Implications of Brain Research for the Church: What It Means for Theology and Ministry* (Minneapolis: Kirk House, 2013), 114–18.

6   Jay N. Giedd, "The Amazing Teen Brain," *Scientific American* 312, no. 6 (June 2015): 33–37.

Piaget, Erikson, and Vygotsky based their findings on what they could observe. We now know from research on the brain the contours of what drives the changes. Particularly with adolescents, the pull toward peers and away from family can be understood as an aspect of brain development.[7] More attention, therefore, needs to be given to preparing for adolescence by both parent and child as well as to carefully choosing peers. On the positive side, recognizing the increased influence of the limbic system means that a strong, lifelong connection to Jesus Christ and commitments to a faithful vocation can also be made.

FINAL THOUGHTS

Knowing how the brain works does not provide the answer to the greatest puzzle for psychology and philosophy—consciousness. The mystery of the mind/body connection has not been, nor may it ever be, overcome by philosophy or science. As one researcher put it, "Knowing what is occurring at the level of neuronal function cannot tell us what the animal is experiencing."[8]

Of course, we are not animals. Instead, we are the unique creations of God who have both body and soul and are capable of self-reflection, relationships, and contemplation of our Creator. Neuroscience is doing a tremendous service as it reveals more and more about the brain. However, when addressing the concepts of selfhood, awareness, and what it means to be a person, neuroscience is at a loss. "What is mind?" Daniel Siegel asks. "There is no single answer to this question. And many science fields actually have no answer to this simple but challenging query. Odd as it might seem, it's true."[9]

This is where the faith community's competency comes into play. The mind is more than just the brain, and we are very much aware of this fact, for we believe ourselves to be creatures bound for eternity in one form or another. The brain along with the body returns to dust, and the soul returns to God (Ecclesiastes 12:7) to await the day of resurrection (1 Corinthians 15).

What is the implication for our pedagogy? Respect for our Creator means that we make every effort to use strategies that maximize our knowledge of the brain God has designed. Chrysostom called student

---

7   Giedd, "The Amazing Teen Brain," 34.
8   Robert A. Burton, *A Skeptic's Guide to the Mind: What Neuroscience Can and Cannot Tell Us about Ourselves* (New York: St. Martin's Press, 2013), 86.
9   Siegel, *Brainstorm*, 45.

learning the "seal on the wax of their minds." We who teach the faith do so with the knowledge that we are holding the seal and that how we press that seal into the wax makes a difference.

8

A FAITH DEVELOPMENT PRIMER

Becky Peters

It can't get much more basic than this: "For by grace you have been saved through faith. And this is not your own doing; it is the gift of God" (Ephesians 2:8). If there would be only one bit of information we need about faith, the apostle Paul summed it up nicely in his Letter to the Ephesians. Other verses tell us that this gift of faith comes from the Holy Spirit. Faith is not earned; we could never do enough to deserve it. Neither is it a possession or a condition that one might force on another whether that other person wants it or not. Faith is a gift given by the Holy Spirit. Yet Romans 10:14 reminds us, "How are they to believe in Him of whom they have never heard? And how are they to hear without someone preaching?" In other words, how can people hear about God unless someone tells them? This verse calls us to share our faith using words the listeners can understand and actions that illustrate the truth behind the words.

So now you have the essentials; however, there is so much more we can learn about sharing our faith in a way that the learner can understand. Just as most rookie readers aren't satisfied stopping at the basic phrase "The cat sat on a rat," you probably want to know more about how we can effectively teach and share our Lutheran Christian faith. This is a broad field encompassing biblical literacy, theology, learning theory, and more. This essay focuses on faith development theory as it pertains to teaching the faith.

THE WORK OF JAMES FOWLER

James Fowler (1940–2015) investigated faith and how it changes in people over time. Although he was a Christian, he applied his studies to all belief systems, including those of agnostics and atheists. He believed faith to be a lens through which individuals view the world. People may not subscribe to a particular religion to have a worldview or something in which they trust. For many, that trust is focused on their god whom they identify as the god; for others, that trust is located in their love of power and possessions or a belief that their own viewpoints are all that matter. Fowler believed that faith is universal in that everyone has some type of faith regardless of the object of faith.

Fowler also contended that humans go through various stages in the ways they perceive their faith. People move through these stages in a specific order. Although one might go back to an earlier stage, it is not a haphazard progression; it is ordered consistently and sequentially.[1]

In Fowler's more recent work, he emphasized that faith stages are not the only piece of faith to be understood. One must also consider the content of faith as well as reactions to life as people live in faith.[2] Not all researchers agree with Fowler's vision of faith stages, but his work has set the path for those who study this field.

Fowler drew on the work of several foundational human development theorists. Piaget studied cognitive, or intellectual, development. He identified four stages of thinking, or problem solving, that people use starting in infancy and moving through adolescence and adulthood. Piaget believed that his stages were universal and sequential as well. Erickson's work focused on psychosocial or personality development. He devised eight stages of sequential and universal human development, although he allowed for deviations within the stages. Kohlberg was another influence in Fowler's work. Kohlberg was fascinated by moral development and how one determines right from wrong. He identified six stages through which people move, although not everyone achieves the higher stages.

It's important to note that not everyone agrees with the work of these theorists. In the years since they did their original work, others have followed who continue to develop the theories or even challenge them. However, the work of each of these researchers has been foundational. It is helpful to be familiar with their work to better understand faith development theory.

---

1   James W. Fowler, *Stages of Faith: The Psychology of Human Development and the Quest for Meaning* (San Francisco: Harper & Row, 1986).

2   James W. Fowler, "Faith Development Theory and the Postmodern Challenges." *The International Journal for the Psychology of Religion* 11, no. 3 (2001): 159–72.

Fowler's Stages

Although Fowler identified six faith stages, this essay will focus on the three that most relate to teaching children and adolescents. The ages described as relating to each stage are not absolute but rather generalities; nevertheless, in a typical classroom of students, you will find that a majority will fall into the same category.

Stage 1: Intuitive-Projective Faith

Children ages 2 to about 6 are typical of Intuitive-Projective faith. In this stage, children's impressions of God are closely aligned to their perception of their parents. When parents show affection and care to their child, the child thinks of God as loving and caring. When a parent is emotionally cold and distant, the child sees God as not wanting to be involved with people. And when a parent is harsh, God is seen as a harsh judge. When loving parents demonstrate an active faith life, the child begins to value faith and a relationship with God as well. Yet it is difficult for young children to differentiate between reality and fiction, which might lead to confusing God with Santa Claus or a superhero.

Strategies for teaching this age include lots of storytelling that emphasizes God's love. You can actively involve children with pantomime, echo prayers, songs with motions, and even dressing up as characters from the Bible. Don't worry if they don't have all the facts right. Understanding comes with time and repetition. Remember that young children do not have long attention spans, and change activities frequently.

Stage 2: Mythic-Literal Faith

Fowler places children ages 7 to 11 or 12 (primarily elementary-age children) in the Mythic-Literal stage. They see the world as literal, and faith is considered in concrete terms rather than the abstract. A major concern of younger elementary students is the concept of fairness, although their idea of fairness might not coincide with an adult's understanding. Students often reason that if they "keep God happy" by their words and behavior, good things will happen to them. When life doesn't treat them as they would desire, they may believe that they have brought misfortune on themselves. Because of this, they tend to be moralistic and believe that they can earn God's love. This can lead to works-righteousness and a reliance on the Law, which makes more sense to them.

One of the biggest complaints of older elementary students (fourth through sixth graders) is being treated like babies. They desire to move beyond the Bible stories they've heard for years, or they want to approach familiar stories in new ways. They like being challenged to learn new things as long as it doesn't lead to frustration. They are learning to grasp the concept of Law and Gospel. They understand that they make poor choices that can lead to sin. Peers are growing in importance.

While there are different developmental aspects to consider within this age range and a teacher needs to design lessons with his or her specific students in mind, we can identify useful teaching strategies for this stage. Opportunities to pray both memorized and impromptu prayers; drama, from simple pantomime to role-playing with costumes and props; and experiential learning and activities all support age-appropriate faith development. Primary-age children need simpler activities with teacher support. Older elementary students love active involvement with making their faith visible through assisting younger children and service projects. They appreciate having options in deciding what they want to do to demonstrate their learning.

Stage 3: Synthetic-Conventional Faith

Most middle school students move into the Synthetic-Conventional stage and remain in this stage through high school. Once again, there will be some differences between younger and older students in this stage, but there is no fixed timeline for their movement and maturity. Younger adolescents tend to be conformists in slang, fashion, and beliefs. If friends and family are important to them, they conform to their beliefs and practices without analyzing why they believe as they do. They usually begin thinking in Piaget's Formal Operational Stage, which means they develop their ability to think abstractly. They are able to take the perspective of others (sometimes too much so). They desire to be accepted by others and display understanding of the fact that God isn't fair because He loves them despite their imperfections.

Middle school teachers need to get to know their students—to care about, listen to, love, and value them. While teens crave this, they often need reminders to love and value their classmates in ways that demonstrate God's love. Building a sense of community within the class is essential as relationships (with peers, adults, and Jesus) are a primary concern. They enjoy being involved in projects that reach beyond the church or school in ways that support the larger community. Because they are learning to think abstractly, they need to be challenged to higher-level thinking.

Older teens experience emotional roller coasters as do younger ones, but older students tend to have more mastery over their emotions. While they still accept the same faith as those who are important to them, they often question and talk about faith differences more. Issues of sexuality become more prominent in their lives, and beliefs don't always meld with actions. For many teens, life is all about college decisions and the achievement required to get into the college of their choice. Others look at vocational goals on the horizon and stress over their options. Some are beginning to question their long-held belief system as they move on to the next chapter of their lives. Most appreciate the hard questions of faith, and higher-level thinking builds greater spiritual maturity.[3]

Active involvement in the life of the congregation, mission trips, and in-depth discussions appeal to older adolescents. They need to know they are the church of today and are not just relegated to the future church. Teachers need to accept teens' honesty when they disagree with the status quo, letting them know they are trusted even when they question the Bible and theological truths.

THE BENEFIT OF FOWLER'S FAITH DEVELOPMENT THEORY

Some may question why it's important to understand theories. We may not agree with all of Fowler's presuppositions and findings, but his work can provide direction for the way we teach and share the faith. Fowler himself saw value in using his theory to better understand how to teach various ages and to better communicate with those who are in a different stage of faith than we are. He stressed that the goal of his theory is never to urge a learner to move to the next stage; rather it is a guide for what we do as teachers.[4] When we look at faith development theory in conjunction with human development and learning theories, we increase the opportunities for the Holy Spirit to use us as His conduit in bringing a student to faith and nurturing that faith. What greater opportunity is there?

---

3   Eugene C. Roehlkepartain, "The Thinking Climate: A Missing Ingredient in Youth Ministry?" *Christian Education Journal* 15, no. 1 (1994): 53–63.

4   James W. Fowler, "Faith Development at 30: Naming the Challenges of Faith in a New Millennium." *Religious Education* 99, no. 4 (2004): 405–21.

9

USING FAITH INTEGRATION
TO FOSTER LEARNING SKILLS

Kim Marxhausen

In Martin Luther's "A Sermon on Keeping Children in School," he praised congregations that support a Lutheran education for children:

> *But praise and thanks be to God, who has long since countered the devil's intentions and put it into the heart of an honorable and wise council to found and equip such a splendid and excellent school. . . . For in this they have shown generous Christian consideration of their subjects, contributing faithfully to their eternal salvation as well as to their temporal well-being and honor. God will assuredly strengthen such a work with ever increasing blessings and grace.[1]*

At a time when few people saw the benefits of children learning more than the minimum of reading and math, Luther saw that Christian education was important for the communities that would benefit from doctors, lawyers, and teachers who lived and worked in the faith. Luther had a vision for the potential of Christian education. God's vision goes beyond that. His plan includes a way for parents and teachers to help children develop successful learning by integrating the faith into every part of the day.

To see the connection between teaching the faith and academic success, we start with an understanding of the scope of intelligence. For many years, researchers were concerned only about intelligence in terms of academic learning and general problem solving. Recently, psychology has broadened the definition of intelligence to include other areas of

---

1   LW 46:213.

giftedness as well as a realization that social and emotional skills play a significant role in the expression of intelligence.[2] Some refer to this as social, emotional, and intellectual (SEI) skills. The SEI concept is an understanding that we cannot separate intellect from the skills that support it. Intelligence is impractical if we cannot control emotions or work in a social setting.[3] Among other things, SEI skills include the ability to self-regulate and develop self-understanding. These skills manifest themselves as trust, persistence, and resilience—characteristics fundamental to academic and personal success.[4]

Educators and researchers have long noted the relationship between self-understanding and performance. However, many have incorrectly assumed that the creation of a positive sense of self-understanding will promote better performance. This is a classic example of assuming that correlation (a statistical relationship) equals causation. In this case, it is the assertion that praise will create confidence for future performance. Most experienced teachers will affirm that constant praise will not create good performance; it will instead create a need for more praise. What researchers now understand is that a strong sense of self-understanding comes from succeeding at something difficult.[5] In other words, self-understanding is related not to performance, but rather to the effort put into problem-solving and recovery from failure.

> Through our relationship with God, we learn that we cannot separate understanding of self from our faith.

When parents and teachers integrate the faith into everyday teaching, children develop more than faith. They develop a proper self-understanding as they learn their place in God's world and His plan. There are many aspects to self-understanding, but the three most commonly mentioned are self-concept (Who am I?), self-esteem (How good am I?), and self-worth (How valued am I?). Children learning in a secular setting focus on labels and self-evaluation. God blesses children learning in a Christian setting with a different perspective. Through our relationship with God, we learn that we cannot separate understanding of self from our faith.

---

2   Robert Sylwester, *A Child's Brain: The Need for Nurture* (Thousand Oaks, CA: Corwin, 2010).
3   Daniel Goleman, *Emotional Intelligence: Why It Can Matter More than IQ* (New York: Bantam Books, 1995).
4   Ellen Galinsky, *Mind in the Making: The Seven Essential Life Skills Every Child Needs* (New York: HarperCollins, 2010).
5   Galinsky, *Mind in the Making*.

Without faith, the answer to the question "Who am I?" consists of labels that identify characteristics as well as perceived strengths and weaknesses: I am a girl, I am smart, I am athletic, I am a friend, and the like. These labels become part of a child's idea of self and work well until a major change or crisis occurs. For example, a child who applies the label "friend" must find a way to explain being the victim of bullying. However, for a child of God, the first label and the one most often mentioned in everyday teaching is the one that declares, "I am a child of God." This label is a reminder that God is each child's Creator and Protector—regardless of what happens in day-to-day life. Being a child of God is an aspect of self-concept that does not depend on the self. It is an expression of grace.

Without faith, the answer to the question "How good am I?" is fraught with potential trouble. The student may think, "Today, I may be good at math, but what about when I take an algebra class?" Or, "Today, I may be a fast runner, but what about when I come across someone who is faster?" As is true with self-concept, the understanding of self-esteem for a child of God does not depend on the abilities of the self. The answer to this question is "I am forgiven by my Savior." With this understanding, a failure does not have to mean the destruction of self-esteem. When we are not good enough, we are forgiven. In fact, our faith teaches us that we are never good enough, so we must place our trust in God and not ourselves. Such thinking encourages the development of resilience, or the characteristic that allows students to continue after failure and to learn from every situation.

Without faith, the answer to the question "How valued am I?" rests on the perception of being able to make a difference in a given community. Here, self-understanding becomes more interactive with the environment than a matter of description or competition. The secular view of self-worth is dependent on the reactions and acceptance of others. When others ignore us, we do not feel valued. If we cannot make a difference in the lives of others, we are not valued. However, for a child of God, the answer to this question is "I am powered by the Holy Spirit." In faith teaching, we learn that we grow through the work of the Spirit—not by our own efforts or skill. With the understanding that "I am" because of God, the great I am, children learning in faith increase their emotional competency. Every failure can bring learning, every disappointment can be a cause of thanks, and every event in life can be seen through the understanding of a triune God who is a part of every aspect of life.

In Lutheran schools, teaching the faith is about so much more than Bible stories and doctrine. When we integrate the faith, the lessons from religion class and chapel are seen in every aspect of the day. Students learn *about* God's love in Bible study and learn to *understand* God's love as it is modeled. Students learn to *feel* God's love in relationships and learn to *share* God's love with others. The concept of unconditional love grows from the awe-inspiring story of Jesus' death and resurrection to an understanding that is part of each student's life and living. Each student can live and learn, knowing he or she is unconditionally loved. This knowledge creates a safety net. Students can take the kinds of risks that produce good learning because forgiveness and unconditional love will catch them when they fall. Additionally, unconditional love develops empathy. Empathy is as important to learning academics as it is to developing relationships with others. Empathy is the ability to take on a perspective other than your own, which is an abstract thinking skill essential to developing cognitive skills.

Faith integration teaches learners to build their understanding of self as being God's child and gives them the peace of knowing they are unconditionally loved. These are two ways to encourage resilience in learners, which in turn works to produce strong academic achievement. Integrating the faith also builds strong self-regulation skills and the ability to trust.

The proper application of Law and Gospel creates a training ground for students to strengthen self-regulation skills. Self-regulation is the ability to control attention, emotions, and behavior in ways that promote learning. The development of self-regulation requires both discipline and encouragement. An environment that gives only encouragement will not show the student how to direct attention or behavior. Likewise, an environment that spends all of its time in rules and consequences will eventually create discouragement. However, rules, consequences, encouragement, and forgiveness work together to teach control. A child with the ability to direct attention can use emotions appropriately and can behave in a manner that promotes learning. This child will succeed far beyond a child who has a high IQ but lacks these skills.

Trust is essential to learning. Babies who develop a healthy bond with parents begin to learn from them. Students who trust their teachers will feel comfortable trying new things, knowing that help is available when learning presents a challenge. Faith integration is a constant reminder that God is in control, and He makes it possible for us to trust in Him. This trust reduces anxiety and creates an environment conducive to optimum learning. Many children come to school from less than ideal home environments. They may not trust members of their family to keep them safe and to provide for their needs. When they come to their Lutheran school, they find people they can trust who continually remind them of a God who loves and cares for them. Integration of faith provides them with a necessary condition for learning.

As Lutheran teachers consider the blessings of integrating the faith, we are reminded of Jesus' encouragement to "seek first the kingdom of God and His righteousness, and all these things will be added to you" (Matthew 6:33). God knows His children and our needs. He encourages us to put His kingdom—and the teaching of His Word—first in all we do. We can trust that He will provide what our students need to be happy, healthy, successful children of God.

10

INVITING YOUNG PEOPLE INTO GOD'S WORD

John T. Pless

The apostle Paul confidently wrote that Timothy had known the Holy Scriptures from childhood. We cannot so surely assert the same of many young people today. Biblical illiteracy is quite common in the larger culture, as the basic storyline of the Holy Scriptures is unknown to many. The Bible is seen as an antiquated book, irrelevant to life in the twenty-first century at best or, at worst, repressive to human desires for liberation and fulfillment. In public education, sensitivities to rigid lines of church-state separation have made teachers cautious of references to biblical events and characters, lest they be accused of showing favoritism to Christianity. Where the Scriptures are considered, they are approached with a "hermeneutic of suspicion" as to their historical veracity. Add to that the assumptions of pluralism as exhibited in the "Coexist" bumper sticker. Readings of the Holy Scriptures governed by the First Commandment are seen as exclusive and judgmental and are therefore dismissed.

But the problem is not only with the culture; Christians themselves bear some responsibility as well. The older practice of having a Sunday School curriculum centered on the use of Bible stories collapsed under pressures for approaches that would be more relevant, stressing relationship-building rather than biblical knowledge. Gracia Grindal has noted that much mainline-denominational curricular material excludes the biblical stories because of their violence (Cain and Abel, the flood, etc.), making it impossible to speak of Jesus' death and resurrection and thus leaving children and youth with moralism and ethical principles devoid of God's Law and Gospel.[1] The Scriptures and the Small Catechism are rarely taught in the context of family devotions. Adult Christians who themselves are bored with the Bible and give the impression that the Bible has little significance for life will hardly be able to teach it with authentic clarity and conviction to youth.

Fundamental for helping young people read the Bible is a right understanding of the nature and authority of Holy Scriptures and, in light of this, a way of reading them that is coherent with their character as the Word of the triune God. Given the challenges to the truthfulness of the Christian faith and the Scriptures that young people are likely to face in the academic community, a careful apologetic should be part of Christian education in confirmation instruction and throughout the high school years. Youth need to know not only what we believe about the Bible but why we believe it.

The father of modern liberal theology, Friedrich Schleiermacher (1768–1834), spoke of the Holy Scriptures as a mausoleum of the Spirit in that they give evidences of the Spirit's work in the past. In the twentieth century, Karl Barth (1886–1968) compared the Bible to the Pool of Bethesda. Just as an angel would occasionally stir the waters so that the lame were cured, so the Spirit would stir the pages of the Bible so that the reader might encounter God there; hence the Scriptures would become the Word of God in this encounter. Fundamentalists, on the other hand, give the impression that the canonical Scriptures are given from heaven in a way that differs little from the Islamic version of the origin of the Qur'an. Lutherans, by way of contrast to the above-mentioned views, receive the Holy Scriptures as the Spirit's Word, which delivers Christ sent from the Father to reconcile the world to Himself through the blood of the cross. The Scriptures are true and trustworthy because Christ is the truth, and His Spirit, the Holy Spirit, is the Spirit of truth (John 16:13; 17:17). Lutherans trust the Holy Scriptures because they trust Christ.

The Bible is neither an artifact of the Spirit's past work nor a place where, under proper conditions, the Spirit might be expected to drop in from time to time. The Holy Scriptures are inspired—that is, God-breathed—and the Spirit continues to breathe on us through them. The Spirit who inspired the prophets and apostles to put God's Word into human language has guided and guarded its transmission in the course of human history, preserving it for the sake of the Gospel. Because the

---

1   See Gracia Grindal, "The End Is Everything," *Dialog* (Spring 1997): 91–99.

Scriptures are His Word, they alone are the "rule and norm" for Christian believing, confessing, and living.

We receive the Scriptures as the Word of God, not because the Church has made them such, but because they *are* the Word of the triune God. Martin Chemnitz, a Lutheran church father of the sixteenth century, put it like this: "The church does not have such power, that it can make true writings out of false, false out of true, out of doubtful and uncertain, certain, canonical, and legitimate."[2] Or as John Webster has more recently stated, "Scripture is not the word of the church; the church is the church of the Word."[3] The process of "canonization" was not so much the Church deciding that some books are the Word of God and others are not, but rather the Church confessing that these books inspired by the Spirit (see 2 Timothy 3:15–17; 2 Peter 1:16–21) are the Word of God.

While the Holy Scriptures stand in service of proclamation, they are not robbed of their normative character because they are written. They are no less the Word of God because they are written rather than oral. Hermann Sasse helpfully explains, "All proclamation that is to be preserved must be written down. The written Word may lack the freshness of the oral proclamation, but its contents remain the same, and it gains the advantage of remaining unchanged and being preserved for future generations."[4]

Where the Scriptures are not recognized as the Word of God, there can only be what Luther, in the Smalcald Articles, called "enthusiasm." The enthusiasts cannot help but seek some other authority in one's reason, experience, or a selective reading of tradition for "they boast that He [the Spirit] has come into them without the preaching of the Scriptures."[5] They will look behind, beneath, or above the text for an answer to the question "What does this *really* mean?" But we are to be content with the Holy Scriptures in the way God has given them to us, for they give us Christ Jesus in whom we have certainty and confidence.

What, then, does this mean for the way in which we teach the Holy Scriptures to youth? First, we approach the Holy Scriptures as the book in which we hear the voice of the Good Shepherd, recognizing that they

---

2   Martin Chemnitz, *Examination of the Council of Trent,* trans. Fred Kramer (St. Louis: Concordia, 1971), 181.

3   John Webster, *Holy Scripture: A Dogmatic Sketch* (Cambridge: Cambridge University Press, 2003), 44.

4   Hermann Sasse, "Luther and the Word of God" in *Accents in Luther's Theology,* ed. Heino Kadai (St. Louis: Concordia, 1967), 71–72.

5   Smalcald Articles, Part III, Article VIII, paragraph 6.

were written that we might believe in Him and have life in His name. We do not apologize for the Scriptures or treat them as something that must be made relevant. Because the Bible is the Word of God, it is eternally relevant. The question is not whether we, the readers of Scripture (young and old alike), are relevant to God's plan and purposes revealed through the Scriptures. In other words, do not be afraid to let the Scriptures stand on their own claims and so use them for the purposes that God gave them: for teaching, reproof, correction, training in righteousness, and supremely for making us wise to salvation through faith in Christ Jesus, as Paul says in 2 Timothy 3:15–17.

> We do not apologize for the Scriptures or treat them as something that must be made relevant. Because the Bible is the Word of God, it is eternally relevant.

Second, in teaching youth the Scriptures, we learn to ask the right questions. The question is not "What does this mean to you?" but "What is God saying in this text?" How does God give me knowledge of myself, that is, how does He expose my sin (Law), and how does He promise and deliver forgiveness of sins (Gospel) so that I might live as His child? Without the right distinction between the Law and the Gospel, we inevitably will ask the wrong questions of the Scriptures and therefore get the wrong answers. Scripture then remains a closed book, and youth will seek some other code by which they can crack its contents. Unfortunately, this means that they create their own meanings and find in the Bible the building blocks for their self-made gods, not the crucified and risen Lord Jesus Christ.

Third, in teaching the Scriptures, our aim is not merely to outfit youth with a bunch of data about the Bible or information about biblical events or characters. The goal is not that they become better Bible trivia players, but that they think and live in the logic of the Scriptures themselves. That means they live with faith in Christ and with love toward the neighbor, not being squeezed in the mold of this world, to

> The goal is not that they become better Bible trivia players, but that they think and live in the logic of the Scriptures themselves.

paraphrase Romans 12:2. Shaped by God's Word, they are not pressured into conformity with the patterns of sin, death, and the devil but renewed to live in the promise of Baptism as those who belong to Christ. We live in the midst of a culture of religious diversity that is skeptical of Christian claims to truth and populated by communities who self-identify as Christian but have forsaken the apostolic faith and wandered into postmodern mythologies. Therefore, our aim is to help youth know and trust the Scriptures as the only sure and certain foundation for faith and life.

11

CHRISTIAN SCHOOL LEADERS AND THE MIT (MOST IMPORTANT THING)

Jim Pingel

There is nothing more important than the Most Important Thing (MIT). For Christian school leaders, the MIT is building a school culture dedicated to the teaching and learning of God's Word and the biblical faith. Encouraging students to love God with all of their heart, soul, and mind (Matthew 22:37) is a daunting objective today. The demands of funding, advancement, relationship building, new programs and government regulations, changing demographics, educational fads and reforms, curriculum development, recruitment, retention, strategic planning, professional development—to name a few—seemingly dominate a school leader's to-do list. And, of course, you want your school to measure and achieve brilliantly on these scorecards.

The drive for secular achievements and accolades, however, can crowd out and overwhelm the MIT. In *The Screwtape Letters*, C. S. Lewis depicts Satan bent on distracting Christians with busyness so that they might fall away from the faith. Might our tempter and adversary be deploying the same strategy against our Lutheran school leaders today?

More important than secular success, Christian leaders are to be faithful to the Word of God and to teach it. As the Bible notes, students who receive a Christ-centered education are equipped and prepared "ten times better" in their learning, skill, and wisdom, because their learning comes from God (Daniel 1:17–20).

If Lutheran schools are to "train up a child in the way he should go" (Proverbs 22:6), Christian school leaders should worry less about keeping up with the Joneses and more about lifting up Jesus. Deuteronomy 6:5–9 commands Christian leaders to love God with all their heart, soul, and might; to "diligently" teach the Bible; and to pass on the faith so that God's Word and Christ's love can boldly be proclaimed on "the doorposts" and "gates" of Christian homes and schools everywhere. Nothing is more important than building a learning culture where young people will know and love Christ crucified and risen.

LEAD BY EXAMPLE

The construction of an effective, faith-driven school community begins with you. Faithful divine worship attendance and regular Bible and devotional study remain the chief spiritual cornerstones and habits of a Christian school leader. Before faculty and staff will buy into any message, they want to buy into the messenger. More important, *you* need to hear and receive God's grace daily for your own spiritual good. Satan loves to target those who love their Lord and are prominent, visible ambassadors of the Christian faith. So get in the Word and stay in the Word. Be richly fed each and every Sunday morning. Put on the "whole armor of God, that you may be able to stand against the schemes of the devil" (Ephesians 6:11).

In addition to an active church and Bible study life, here are some other helpful habits:

- Find a prayer partner—someone who will lovingly hold you accountable in your faith life and spiritual growth.
- Start or join a Christian book club so you can have fellowship with other believers and routinely study God's Word.
- Take one area pastor out for breakfast or lunch each month. Build strategic relationships that benefit your school, but also learn and grow spiritually from an enriching and expanding faith network.
- Make sure your teachers can answer these two questions affirmatively about you, their leader: (1) Did he help me become a better instructor and minister of the Gospel? (2) Did she help nurture and encourage my faith life and growth in Christ?

Your colleagues will remember many things about you and your leadership legacy, but none more important than these two features.

How to Lead Your Team and Constituents

Marcus Buckingham conducted extensive research on leadership and concluded two things about successful leaders:

1. They have a positive, uplifting vision of the future.

2. They clearly and relentlessly articulate the vision.[1]

As a leader, how would you grade yourself on these two components?

Lutheran schools have a splendid and uplifting vision to share: thanks be to Jesus, heaven is our home and destination. As the leader, impart and ingrain the MIT in your school with the gifts, talents, resources, relationships, and leadership skills God has provided you. "How beautiful are the feet of those who preach the good news!" (Romans 10:15).

As a Christian school leader, you need to get off the dance floor and get up in the balcony to examine the big picture[2] and monitor the MIT. *You* are the mission and vision keeper of your school. Like Esther, you have been particularly placed by God "for such a time as this" (Esther 4:14). Mission is *why your school exists*, and vision is what *mission accomplished* looks like. Make no mistake: no one else is going to concentrate on the MIT with your intensity and devotion.

So here are some simple ways to impart the MIT to your faculty, staff, and other circles of influence:

- Give frequent BBMV (Big, Bold Mission and Vision) presentations to your team. Encourage and celebrate their efforts in bringing mission and vision to fruition.

- Celebrate "Christian Leadership Sightings" or "Teaching or Learning the Faith" moments at *every* faculty and board meeting.

- Mandate weekly Bible study for your team. Do more than a five-minute devotional. Time allocation reveals priorities. Dive deep into the life-saving Word of God. Let your faculty talk and dialogue. These will be the best minutes of your week.

- Require team members to identify one personal and one professional faith-teaching goal. Hold them accountable.

- Recruit guest presenters, alumni, and community leaders to speak to your team about their faith journey, stewardship, and witness.

---

1   Marcus Buckingham, *The One Thing You Need to Know . . . About Great Managing, Great Leading, and Sustained Individual Success* (New York: Free Press, 2005), 59–71.
2   Ronald A Heifetz and Marty Linsky, *Leadership on the Line: Staying Alive through the Dangers of Leading* (Boston: Harvard Business School Press, 2002).

- Frequently fill teacher in-boxes, or mailboxes, with devotional literature and professional articles on faith teaching and evangelism.

- "Catch" team members teaching the faith in an exemplary, inspirational, or creative manner, and publicly praise them in your board reports.

- Every "Warm Fuzzy Friday," write two personal notes to team members, or other supporters, who are teaching the faith or enhancing your faith culture.

- Develop a Faith Integration or Christian Leadership Assessment Catalog. Have each teacher submit one artifact for each unit taught. Make it accessible on the school's website. No secular school will have anything like this!

- Give your team summer "homework" and reading materials that encourage faith development and intentional strategies for teaching the faith.

- Measure faith integration and learning in formal observations. Encourage teachers to have at least one learning objective (accompanied by an assessment) on a faith-related issue or component. What gets noticed, and rewarded, gets done.

- Demand that teachers take advantage of the "two-for-one" opportunity by teaching higher learning and critical thinking skills through *intentional*, faith-based instruction. Require *faith* applications; analyze content from a *biblical* perspective; synthesize and evaluate material from a *Christian worldview*; design projects and create solutions that build a platform to witness and share the *Good News*; inspire servant leadership through *God's Word* and *Christ's love.*

- Feature team member faith journeys or unique contributions in teaching the faith in your regular publications and social media. Simply ask, "How are you sharing or teaching the faith?" Their public pronouncements will make them more cognizant and reflective of the MIT.

- Ask team members to provide data and evidence that answers the question "How do you really know students are learning and growing in the faith?"

- Have each teacher explain how his or her classroom is $10,000 (or current tuition) better than the government-run classroom down the street.
- Feature students—who are living the mission—on the school's website, newsletters, and social media. Ask them to specifically articulate how their school is nurturing their spiritual growth.
- Conduct a focus group of a diversified sample of your senior or upper-grade students. Ask them what your school should keep doing, stop doing, and start doing in terms of the MIT. You can do the same focus group effort with parents too.

Noted education scholar Michael Fullan argues that skill development and expertise leads to, or builds up, one's passion.[3] In other words, the better you become at something, the more you like it and live it. The more you can encourage and equip your team in teaching the faith, the more passionate, inspirational, and creative they will become in their pursuit of the MIT. What a wonderful cycle to embrace!

When parents and constituents gather for school functions, welcome and seize each opportunity to uphold and reinforce the MIT of your school:

- Tell a short story or have a testimonial delivered on how faith learning is making a difference in your students and alumni.
- Praise faith teaching and learning prominently on your website, in social media, and in *every* major publication.
- Feature a "Donors Deliver" section in publications to highlight those who—through monetary gifts, volunteerism, or expertise—give to make the MIT come to fruition.
- Conduct a Faith Audit. Invite and assemble an outside group of community movers and shakers to visit and scrutinize your school, particularly on the MIT. Receive unvarnished and unbiased feedback, impress audit members with your conviction and desire to improve, and make some new "friends of the program."

Enjoy the Journey

Jesus Christ did not give mediocre blood on the cross to save us from our sins: He shed perfect, innocent blood—the very best. Inspired by His

---

3   Michael Fullan, *The Principal: Three Keys to Maximizing Impact* (San Fransisco: Jossey-Bass, 2014), 125–27.

sacrifice, Lutheran schools, if they are to exist deep into the twenty-first century, must be exemplary and stand out from a crowded field of competitors. Unfortunately, Lutheran school leaders often shoot for excellence by chasing the latest educational fad or focusing their energies on outperforming the local public school on secular scorecards.

Shun the fool's gold, and embrace the real treasure. "Press on toward the goal for the prize" (Philippians 3:14) in Christ Jesus, and set your mind "on things that are above" (Colossians 3:2). "Commit your work to the LORD" (Proverbs 16:3), and relentlessly focus on teaching, learning, and living the faith. A school dedicated to the MIT will be "ten times better" than any other school in the area. "Do you not know that in a race all the runners run, but only one receives the prize? So run that you may obtain it" (1 Corinthians 9:24).

God will bless your devotion to the MIT. Indeed, the Holy Spirit knows no bounds and will spur you and your school to achieve and excel in other areas too. After all, each student inspired by the Gospel will live a life of purpose, stewardship, and good works (Ephesians 2:8–10).

God put you where He did for one thing—to focus on the MIT. Just do it.

12

REACHING EXCEPTIONAL AND DIVERSE LEARNERS: THEIR FAITH MATTERS TOO!

Amanda Geidel

The methods used for teaching the faith to exceptional students, including those who have disabilities and those who come from diverse cultural backgrounds, should be no different than teaching them math or science. We are blessed to have the freedom in our Lutheran schools to teach religion every day, share chapel time together regularly, pray together, and nurture the faith of our students, just as we teach them the academic subjects. However, the value of their growth and learning in a religion class, at chapel, or through shared prayer will reach into eternity, therefore making our efforts to reach every student necessary and worthwhile. Each student has his or her own potential for growth, and our job as educators is to help each of them reach it, no matter how small or infinite their potential may be.

Teaching exceptional students can be challenging and difficult. It requires forethought on the teacher's part and the ability to plan ahead in order to meet the needs of all students. Your purpose for teaching in a Lutheran school is to share God's love with all who enter your classroom, but this mission can be frustrating at times, especially if you lose sight of the purpose. Remembering that children are growing and developing at different rates and in different areas will make your classroom atmosphere more comfortable and accepting for all. Remembering that you, their teacher, are fearfully and wonderfully made will help to remind you that God can use each of us, no matter how great our gifts or challenges may be.

When we consider teaching the faith to exceptional students, the initial challenge will come in getting to know them, understanding their unique family situations, and discovering their struggles and strengths. The value of observation cannot be ignored. It may take some time for you to understand each of your students, but through careful observation of social behaviors, emotional maturity, academic progress, behavioral choices, and spiritual maturity, a teacher can identify the unique level of development of each student. Observation also includes listening. What are you hearing your students say about their families, about God, about their Sunday activities, about friends, about faith? Sometimes what we hear can be as powerful in getting to know our students as what we see.

> It may take some time for you to understand each of your students, but through careful observation of social behaviors, emotional maturity, academic progress, behavioral choices, and spiritual maturity, a teacher can identify the unique level of development of each student.

Once you've gotten to know your students better, and you understand their background and unique strengths and needs, you can begin making some simple, routine classroom accommodations. Perhaps you already have. For example, when you discover that a student is a good reader, you may ask him to read a Bible passage or devotion aloud in class, without warning. But for the struggling reader, you've started to let her know ahead of time what verses you will call on her to read, and when, so that she will have time to prepare. If a student is having social troubles, you have likely already moved his seat to be away from a peer who isn't helpful to the situation or to be next to a peer who is a good social role model. If you have students who struggle to remember directions, you may write the directions to multistep activities on the board as a reminder. For those who have trouble seeing the board, you have probably moved their seats closer to the front; for those easily distracted, you have moved them away from the pencil sharpener or window. These are all examples of simple classroom accommodations that you are no doubt making each day, without much thought.

In the same way, we can make accommodations that support the faith development of every student. For example, if you learn that a student cannot make it to church on Sunday because Mom is working, can you help find him a ride, either from a friend or yourself? If you discover that a child hasn't been baptized, let your pastor know, and then you can begin the conversation with the family, introducing them to the idea and the importance of Baptism. Instead of making the children call their church attendance out loud in front of everyone, is there a way you can privately collect that information so that none will feel judged when they have not attended week after week? For the student who struggles with reading, locate a Bible that is written at her own reading level. If you have a child who cannot read at all, can you secure an audio version of the Bible, or portions of it, for the child to listen to? Most important, teachers need to help all children, no matter their strengths or needs, make connections to their faith journey in the everyday happenings of school life.

In order to accomplish this task, simple classroom accommodations may not always be enough. When a student's struggles keep him or her from learning and from developing a stronger faith in Christ, a teacher will need to make modifications to lessons, activities, conversations, and assignments. The following questions will help you plan for meaningful modifications.

Lesson Plans

- The core of your lesson preparation will focus on the developmental level of most learners in your class. Once you have written your lesson plans, you will want to ask yourself two questions. (1) Which students will need modifications—changes made to the lesson goals, presentation style, or requirements—in order to participate in a meaningful way? (2) What specific changes will be most helpful or necessary?

Activities

- In activity planning, you may want to ask these two questions. (1) What types of supplies will be needed by which learners? (2) Who can work well with whom, and which learners need a partner or group that will support them during this activity?

Conversations

- When thinking about conversations, ask yourself these two questions. (1) Does a student need visuals to better understand my words? (2) Will the student better understand my words if explained by a peer?

Developing Assignments

- Finally, in developing assignments, be sure to consider the following. (1) Is this assignment going to be meaningful to all students? (2) Will it help to deepen their understanding of the Lutheran religion and deepen their faith?

In answering all of these questions as you plan, you will better be able to reach all learners.

For continued learning in religion and growth in faith development to occur, and in order to meet the needs of every student in your class, using the following types of modifications can be very helpful.

Size: Reduce the length of the lesson, assignment, or conversation. If it is memory work, one student may learn one line or a few words while others recite several verses.

Time: Increase the amount of time you give a student to complete an assignment. Spend more time with students who are struggling with the work or their faith walk.

Level of Support: Offer extra support or help to those who struggle. If you cannot always be that helper, assign classroom peers who are eager to help or able to support your students who are struggling. Sometimes a community volunteer can also be a great classroom helper. If students are completing a worksheet, providing a word bank is one example of assignment support that does not require another person's involvement. Note outlines or study guides are another example of support.

Input: Change the way you present information. Use visual aids and hands-on activities as often as possible so that the information becomes real for the students. Allow students to learn by listening, reading, watching, or doing.

Output: Allow students to choose from different options to show you what they have learned. Examples might include drawing, acting, speaking, singing, presenting, or writing. When it comes to faith, watch for them to show it throughout the day and also during extracurricular activities. Students will demonstrate their faith in many different ways, not always through their words.

Difficulty: Change the skill level required in an assignment, lesson, or task to fit the various levels of learners. One student may write two pages and another one sentence. One may take a twenty-item test and another answer four questions orally to the teacher.

Goals: Alter goals for students who are unable, either because of developmental level or family background, to achieve those of their typical peers. Center their goals on what is essential for them to achieve or understand in each lesson.

Participation: Allow learners to be involved in any given activity or lesson in different ways. Some will write the script, some can act, and others can collect props or provide sound effects.

When it comes to matters of the faith, can we as Lutheran educators afford not to make accommodations and modifications for our exceptional learners? Regardless of whether their abilities and family background allow them to master all the grade-level religion materials and write or speak eloquently about their faith, what is essential is that they believe that Jesus Christ is their Savior and are baptized children of God. We can be creative and flexible in our efforts to teach them our Lutheran doctrine and in helping them grow their faith, so that they continue to grow spiritually. Every teacher will face the challenges of accommodation and modification, and all students will vary in developmental progress. All children deserve the opportunity to learn the most important lesson we can teach them—that our God loves them and sent His Son, Jesus Christ, to save them.

13

THE TIP OF THE SPEAR: TURNING THE MISSION ON FOR OFF-CAMPUS EMPLOYEES

Jim Pingel

"I am the vine; you are the branches. Whoever abides
in Me and I in him, he it is that bears much fruit, for
apart from Me you can do nothing." (John 15:5)

Picture the moment: Your school has a packed auditorium, and attendees are thoroughly captivated by opening night of the classic *Romeo and Juliet*. So far, the directing and acting have been superb. The whole production, in fact, has been one terrific showcase for your school. With cuteness and innocence aplenty, the actors and actresses have all performed in an exemplary fashion.

At the climactic moment, however, a loud crash and thud crudely interrupt the magnificence and serenity of the moment. Directly behind the audience, your hardworking, nighttime, part-time custodian has just fallen off a ladder in the foyer while attempting to dust some pictures. The sound of the impact is so obnoxious, everyone—*everyone*—jumps in their seat and turns around to see what the intrusive commotion is all about. Romeo and Juliet flinch onstage and take an unrehearsed pause in reciting their lines. Attendees twist, turn, and stand up as they survey the chaos. The annoyance of the piercing crash morphs into concern for the injured custodian. As the scene offstage unfolds, a new reality becomes clear onstage: the custodian's fall has ruined the magical moment that had been building for over an hour—actually for over three months. The entire night, which started out so promising, has been irreparably tainted and tarnished.

80

The Tip of the Spear: Turning the Mission On for Off-Campus Employees

There is nothing more harmful to the reputation of a school than words, actions, moments, or behaviors—intentional or unintentional—that spoil or run counter to the mission. Mission infractions puncture a school's persona. When the varsity basketball coach relentlessly berates officials, cusses, and takes God's name in vain during the big game, the image of the school suffers. When the forensic coach fails to return an email or phone call to a concerned parent in a timely fashion; when a teacher posts lewd pictures or passive-aggressive rants on social media; when student athletes talk and laugh throughout the singing of the national anthem; when students taunt the opposing team's star player; when a director fails to choose an appropriate script or does not carefully edit the coarse language or brazen sexual innuendo in a drama production; when the athletic director offers a crude, sexist, or racy joke for cheap laughs at a seasonal athletic meeting; when your school's internal and external publications laud and praise athletic achievements far more often than sportsmanship, servant leadership, and gratitude to God—the mission and vision of your school writhes with hypocrisy and disappointment. Reputation redemption comes hard when trust and promises are broken.

Thus, making sure that every aspect of your school is on mission, and stays on mission, is the most important thing (MIT), the greatest charge, of a Lutheran school leader. To be sure, keeping full-time teachers and support staff focused on the mission is a formidable task for any administrator or school leader. Perhaps even more challenging, however, is keeping the MIT front and center for part-time, off-campus employees, who often lead your school's all-important, and very public, extracurricular activities.

Make no mistake: athletic coaches, drama and music directors, forensics and student council mentors, to name a few, are the tip of the spear in terms of your school's public identity, visibility, and community perception. The reality is that the boys' varsity basketball coach is often more well-known in the community than the principal or upper-level math teacher. Your band and choir directors often find themselves leading and performing in churches, senior-citizen centers, and community events, which provide great opportunities and platforms to promote your school's mission and students. If "all the world's a stage," as William Shakespeare once insisted, then Lutheran school leaders must insist and ensure that their extracurricular activities and organizations represent, display, and live the mission in a compelling and God-pleasing manner.

HIRE TO INSPIRE

Since many Lutheran schools must hire from outside to fill their coaching and other extracurricular vacancies, administrators often find themselves contracting mediocre applicants. To be fair, the pool of candidates can often be thin or nonexistent for a particular sport or activity. Moreover, even if you find and hire a qualified off-campus individual, he or she will miss out on important "insider" training and spiritual development opportunities. Full-time faculty and staff receive many ministerial benefits—weekly Bible studies, mission and vision reminders, spiritual development seminars, chapel services, praise and feedback from Christian peers—that outside hires are not able to participate in or experience.

> Even more than your called and synodically trained workers, off-campus employees need coaching, reminders, and encouragement on the MIT.

While serving as executive director of a school, I had some of the most meaningful and intimate ministry moments with coaches and other extracurricular leaders after tough losses or setbacks. Often I would find them the next day and commiserate with them over their tough loss or stumble. Eventually, however, I would thank them for their work and leadership and remind them of the goals beyond winning a conference title or performing a classic, exemplary concert. I genuinely wanted each coach or director to know how I cherished his or her efforts in sharing God's Word and teaching a Christian worldview to students throughout the entirety of the extracurricular experience. All extracurricular participants, after all, were winners in Christ. These everyday, cup-filling moments, I believe, truly made a difference in shaping the outlook, values, and daily practice of our coaches and directors. When you hire off-campus personnel, you must be intentional and make it a priority to have everyday ministry conversations. Even more than your called and synodically trained workers, off-campus employees need coaching, reminders, and encouragement on the MIT.

When recruiting off-campus personnel, school leaders should hire employees based on the three Cs—competency, character, and Christian leadership. Competency is fairly easy to assess compared to the other two requirements. In addition to reviewing someone's résumé, administrators can certainly uncover someone's experience, expertise, and readiness to coach or direct with a few phone calls and a deep-dive interview.

Evaluating a candidate's character and Christian faith are, of course, more difficult to discern. Nevertheless, here are some simple interview questions and concepts to ask your off-campus candidates:

- How faithful are you in church attendance and Bible study?
- What kind of daily devotions would you use or share with your team or group? Why?
- What are some biblical themes you would implement as core values of the team or program? Why?
- What are your favorite Bible passages? Why?
- Do you plan to send your kids to our school? Why or why not?
- What are some favorite devotional materials that you have used in the past?
- How would you coach differently here compared to the school down the street?
- What does the mission statement mean to you? How would you integrate it in your program?
- What does the Bible say in terms of handling conflict?
- What are your secular scorecard goals and your faith-focused goals for the students in your program?

Of course, few people, including your full-time faculty and staff, could answer all of these questions to perfection or even to your satisfaction. Competent coaches and directors are difficult enough to find, let alone ones who are also strong in their faith. Moreover, you might find someone who truly wants to grow spiritually and be part of a vibrant, Christ-centered community. Praise God for these witnessing and evangelistic opportunities. A candidate who fails to convincingly answer even just a few of these questions, however, should make you pause in hiring someone who will be in daily contact with your students, parents, and community at large.

Faithful Follow-Through

Once you have hired an off-campus employee, you must assist the individual with mission and vision implementation in his or her sport or activity. Your faithful follow-through of the MIT will speak louder than any words you shared in the interview process.

Here are some ways to encourage your off-campus coaches and directors to embrace, own, live, and reflect upon their own faith walk, Christian leadership practices, and the MIT as they lead students in their respective extracurriculars:

- Pray with them every time you meet with them. By God's grace and the power of the Holy Spirit, model the faith community you and your staff are trying to build.

- Host an evening meal at your house with all the various extracurricular leaders. Enjoy Christian fellowship, and show your off-campus employees that there are others who share the same vocational joys and challenges. After the meal, give a personal presentation on the MIT and why their roles are so crucial to mission and vision fruition at your school.

- Invite them to regular faculty and staff Bible studies, Christian leadership workshops, and faith development seminars. Schedule some of these faith-building experiences when they can attend.

- Give devotional materials and books that pertain to their craft and extracurricular activity. Oftentimes, off-campus personnel want to be solid spiritual leaders for their teams, but they are not properly equipped or aware of the resources available to them.

- Go over your school's mission and vision statements during and after the hiring process. Be clear with your expectations for faith integration and application.

- Have them set goals directly related to the MIT. Provide solid feedback, encouragement, and challenges where necessary.

- Set up biweekly meetings with your hires and ask them to specifically grade themselves on their goals and the MIT. Offer constant feedback and encouragement. Remind them that faith integration is a major component of their job performance evaluation.

- Ask them about their church life. If they have not found a church, invite them to attend yours. Show them you truly care about their spiritual growth and faith walk.

- Send a card or write an email every time you catch them doing something positive in mission implementation or faith integration.

The Tip of the Spear: Turning the Mission On for Off-Campus Employees

There are surely other things you can do to turn the mission on for off-campus hires. The main point is that you must be committed and intentional in immersing, leading, and encouraging all of your coaches and extracurricular leaders in mission integration and fruition.

There is an adage that a team is only as strong as its weakest link. When it comes to your athletic coaches and extracurricular leaders, you ain't got a thing if they don't make the mission sing.

14

TEACHING THE FAITH TO YOUNG CHILDREN

Patti Hoffman

Recently, a five-year-old performed before a live television audience. She sang and danced with great energy and was exceptionally composed for her age. When her performance concluded, one of the judges told her that she must have Shirley Temple inside her. The child did not hesitate. Even though she had no clue who Shirley Temple was, she responded, "No, I have Jesus in me!" The stunned judges had no response. What gave this child the confidence to respond in this way? Obviously, it was her childlike faith. But from where does that faith come? How is it that a small child has such an unshakable faith?

Another young child, even younger, visited her aunt. She asked to read "her" book. Naturally, her aunt was pleased with the young girl's love of books. The girl went straight to the bookshelf and selected the same book she always chose. The child was not yet a reader; however, she carefully turned each page of the book, clearly narrating the story as it unfolded on the page. She was reading the Easter story. While she was not reading the actual words on the page, she was reading the pictures and telling the complete story with amazing detail. How is it that this child went beyond just reading the pictures in this story and added details that were not there? The more interesting question is this: Why did the girl choose this story? Why did she choose this story over and over? Why did this story mean so much to this child? Could it be because of her faith?

These two examples of young children provide us with insight into the faith of young children. As teachers in Lutheran schools, our first and foremost priority is the faith of the children with whom we live and work. It is essential that we provide our students with the best in all areas of the curriculum. We owe our students nothing but the best, but planting the seeds of faith is why we are Lutheran teachers. Having responded to the call from God, our priority must always be to plant the seeds of faith and then to nurture the growth of that faith. As Lutheran teachers, we get to be the tool of the Holy Spirit in this process. So, how do young children come to faith? What is our role in that process?

The obvious answer to the question of how children come to faith is that the Holy Spirit creates faith in the heart of a child through the water and Word of the Sacrament of Holy Baptism. Jesus commanded Baptism when He told us to "make disciples of all nations, baptizing them in the name of the Father and of the Son and of the Holy Spirit" (Matthew 28:19). When Jesus referred to all nations, we, as Lutherans, believe that He was including children. This becomes one of many references that support infant Baptism.

Martin Luther wrote the Small Catechism to support the head of the household in teaching his children how to live a godly life. Clearly, Luther believed that the head of the household was also responsible for the faith life of the children. Today, we still believe that it is the role of the parents to bring the child to Baptism and then to nurture the faith of the child as he or she grows. Parents are the child's first teachers.

It is important to understand that our role in the child's life is not to supplant the parents, but to support them in nurturing the faith of their children. The key issue, however, is that often parents do not have the background or knowledge about what to do to nurture faith in their children. Too many parents did not receive faith nurturing as young children and therefore have no idea how to proceed in nurturing the faith of their own children. These parents often bring their children to us because they recognize their own lack of ability.

Other parents enroll their children in our schools or centers simply because they have heard we are good at what we do. They are correct; however, families receive something much more important than a good education. Their children are introduced to the saving love of Jesus.

What and how do young children learn about Jesus? This process can be summed up in one word: relationships. Many religious concepts can be considered developmentally inappropriate for young children. For example, the Trinity, a God whom they cannot see, and grace itself are not concrete ideas and therefore would not be considered developmentally appropriate for young children. Some years ago, while speaking to a group of teachers who were not all Christians, one of them brought this very point to my attention. "Why," she asked, "should we introduce these Bible stories to young children when they are not developmentally appropriate for the age group?" This teacher had a point. These are abstract concepts that even adults cannot explain. This is one of the great mysteries of faith. Young children believe with all their heart that Jesus is their friend, that He loves them and takes care of them, and that He will never leave them. And yet, they have never heard or seen Jesus. What is the answer? It is the answer I shared with that teacher—it is the work of the Holy Spirit. How do we, then, become the tool of the Holy Spirit? It is in the relationships that we build with young children, as we learn from Paul's example in 1 Thessalonians 2:8: "So, being affectionately desirous of you, we were ready to share with you not only the gospel of God but also our own selves, because you had become very dear to us." We are to become "Jesus in skin" to young children. When a young child knows that we will listen, he or she learns that Jesus listens. When young children learn that we love and care for them, they learn that Jesus loves and cares for them. When we are happy to see the child enter the room in the morning, the child learns that Jesus welcomes him or her into His family. When young children learn to trust us, they learn to trust Jesus. But is that all there is to our role? As Lutheran educators, we must be highly intentional about the relationships we develop with young children. It is our role and responsibility to connect young children and their life experiences to Jesus.

Let's revisit the little girl who "read" the Easter story to her aunt. How is it that she was able to read the story and even fill in the details that were not in the pictures? This little girl is surrounded by a family who nurtures her faith. The intentionality of those around her provide this child with daily examples of the love of Jesus. Specifically, the family prays together before meals and at bedtime. In addition, the family worships together on a regular basis. During worship, this child is taught how to behave in church as well as what different parts of the worship service mean. The family talks about the beauty of God's world and makes connections between daily events and the love of Jesus. The extended family is all part of these conversations. Supported by the family, this little girl attends a Lutheran preschool where her teacher also makes the intentional connections between everyday occurrences and Jesus. Nurturing the faith of her students is a priority for this teacher, and she takes every opportunity to integrate faith nurturing amid the daily curriculum. Day in and day out, this child learns to trust people because she can trust in the love of Jesus. Every day, she learns about Law and Gospel in the way both her parents and her teacher guide her behavior. Daily, she learns that because of her Baptism, she can start over as a for-

> She is surrounded by a conspiracy of faith nurturing in her family, school, and church. This child has it all.

given child of God. The Bible stories that this child hears that tell about the love of Jesus become familiar. She is surrounded by a conspiracy of faith nurturing in her family, school, and church. This child has it all. Faith theorists such as John Westerhoff and James Fowler believe that faith is "caught more than taught."[1] We know that little ones observe and imitate adults and their behavior.

What about the child who does not live in this faith-nurturing conspiracy? This is why it is so important for us to be intentional about integrating the faith into our everyday curriculum. Children who are not brought up in the faith at home are still children created by God and for whom His Gospel message is intended. Every day we have the opportunity to share Jesus with children and families who may not have heard the Gospel message. As Lutheran educators, we are the ones whom these little ones will be watching and imitating. It is from us that they might "catch" their faith. If we treat children with love and kindness and tell them that we love them because Jesus loves them, they learn that Jesus is kind and loving. When we teach young children Bible stories and songs about Jesus, these children share them at home. It is no secret that many young children, through the work of the Holy Spirit, have brought their parents to faith.

In summary, as Lutheran educators, we have a great responsibility and a great privilege in nurturing the faith of young children. Whether we are supporting parents who desire to surround their children with faith-nurturing experiences or whether we are the child's introduction to the love of Jesus, we must take our privilege and responsibility seriously. We must develop relationships with young children that will show them the love of Jesus every day, and we must be intentional about how we develop and grow those relationships. We stand on the shoulders of the giants of our faith, but it is the work of the Holy Spirit that brings each child to Christ.

---

1   John H. Westerhoff III, *Will Our Children Have Faith?* rev. ed. (New York: Morehouse Publishing, 2000), 83.

Teaching
and Learning

Ultimately, as indicated by the title, this is a book about the pedagogy of faith. Pedagogy is concerned with the methods and the practice of teaching. It is focused upon that which results in student learning. While theory and foundations are important, even critical, it is not pedagogy until we build upon those foundations to teach the faith. This section takes us to that point, helping us explore many important questions, practices, methods, and strategies for teaching the faith.

In this second section of the text, you will find fifteen essays to begin or expand your thinking about the *how* of Lutheran education. As with the first section, we start with a few essays to address some foundational issues. Russ Moulds starts us with an important piece about "Christ and Curriculum," an essay that reminds us of the distinctive way we think about and approach teaching the faith, whether it is in a theology class or any other content area. I follow that with a practical essay about how to design teaching-the-faith lessons, whether it is a chapel message, a short devotion, a theology class, or integrating the faith across the curriculum. Laurie Friedrich introduces us to recent literacy research and how that can be incredibly helpful in nurturing the faith, even addressing insights into selecting Bible translations for diverse students. Then, Lorinda Sankey writes about designing the Christian classroom, establishing a culture and context that is conducive to teaching the faith.

From there, the essays venture into the exploration of specific practices and considerations. Paul Buchheimer helps us examine how to respond to the challenging questions posed by students and offers an essay exploring the value and role of memory work. Kenneth Kosche, an accomplished church musician, composer, and teacher, is our tour guide as we think through the important role of music in teaching the faith. Jill Hasstedt provides suggestions on when and how to make use of intergenerational approaches to teaching the faith. Matthew Bergholt introduces us to the good and bad of using technology to teach the faith. And Mark Blanke gives us a fresh look at a long-standing practice in Lutheran education: confirmation. I also offer an essay that helps us look at the familiar practice of grading and assessment in view of our core beliefs and convictions in Lutheran education. These essays serve as a means of examining many long-standing practices in Lutheran education, reconsidering them in view of our Lutheran theology and also with the hope of challenging us to discover or rediscover them in ways that draw us even deeper into our foundations of Lutheran education.

While some traditional practices are explored, we have also focused on essays intended to help you think through the affordances and limitations of a variety of contemporary approaches to teaching and learning. As such, Dave Black provides a helpful guide for approaching the modern concept of personalized learning, and Tim Schumacher introduces us to the benefits and limitations of inquiry-based learning when it comes to teaching the faith. Randall Ferguson explains the practice of service learning, making a case for its value in teaching the faith. And I offer a guide for thinking about the widespread and growing practices related to blended and online learning.

The selections in this section are not exhaustive, nor are they a recipe book for teaching the faith. They do, however, offer examples of how Lutheran educators strive to apply Lutheran theology and God's Word to consider different approaches to teaching the faith. They are insights from a dozen Lutheran education practitioners across diverse settings.

15

CHRIST AND CURRICULUM

A Two-Kingdoms Intersect Approach

Russ Moulds

A very capable colleague—an innovator in the classroom praised by students and an effective academic manager appreciated by peers—had expressed discomfort about curriculum and the Lutheran tradition. In our conversation, this colleague gently but plainly repeated three times that the idea of including biblical or theological themes in teaching "makes me uncomfortable." This colleague was at a loss as to how religion—a potentially controversial matter—could or should inform classroom instruction.

We have reasons to share that discomfort. Here are four:

1. The Gospel is not a natural part of this world and is, Paul reminds us, an offense (1 Corinthians 1:18).

2. Students and families who come to our schools for reasons other than Christian education have expectations that may conflict with our aims.

3. Bringing together the curriculum and the things of faith demands additional preparation and practice.

4. We have seen or tried approaches to Christ and curriculum that are less than successful.

> However, if Lutheran schools and universities sidestep Christ and curriculum and merely replicate what other schools do, then we have no reason to exist.

However, if Lutheran schools and universities sidestep Christ and curriculum and merely replicate what other schools do, then we have no reason to exist. Schools that teach only matters of God's left-hand kingdom abound, and many do excellent work,

94

often at less cost (at least for families and students). What's more, the Lutheran ethos and its two-kingdoms framework endorses and supports worldly institutions by which God's left-hand kingdom sustains temporal peace and order.

But the world's cultures shift and change. The Church cannot rely on the world's institutions to bring together the promises of Christ and His kingdom with the present kingdom of this world. The Church, then, has always developed and redeveloped its ministry of teaching as a blessing both to the Church and to the world: *Ecclesia semper reformanda est*. By means of some amiable conversation and some reading, my colleague came to realize that our teaching calls for more than textbooks and effective instructional practices—but was still uncertain about how to proceed.

Those of the Lutheran persuasion are often rightly cautious about Christ and curriculum. We have seen assorted proposals come and go, seeking to bring together the Christian faith and the academic disciplines. In the late twentieth century, American evangelicals promoted an integrating-the-faith approach. In this view, all truth is God's truth, human rationality reflects God's own rationality, and we can locate content in the disciplines that integrates with the truths of the Bible.

For example, the beauty and symmetry of mathematics reflects the order and coherence of God's creation. The narrative form of the world's literature is an echo of the story that God is telling in His themes of creation, fall, and redemption. And the social sciences contain and illustrate the biblical pattern of sin, judgment, and grace played out across human affairs.

Another approach to Christ and curriculum is allegorizing, a method that recognizes that "the earth is the Lord's and the fullness thereof" (Psalm 24:1). Thus, everything we study must in some way correspond to the mind and work of God. In examining the activity of electrons and valence levels in chemistry (*valentia*, L., power, competency), we can analogously glimpse the valence shift of the Second Person of the Trinity from the right hand of the Father to our level of being and consider His state of humiliation and state of exaltation. A study of human political systems corresponds, however approximately, to the spiritual powers and principalities about which the Bible testifies (e.g., Ephesians 6:12).

This approach strikes many of us as the stuff of Bible colleges or even Sunday School. But before we sniff or wince, note that the Church used this method for study and teaching for more than a thousand years prior to the Reformation and still managed to be the Church. Note also that, in the end, all our words in all our disciplines are finally simile, metaphor, and allegory. The Church's scholarly work today does not much rely on allegorizing; nevertheless, we employ allegory in our instruction in many ways whether we notice this or not.

A third view of Christ and curriculum is the personalized approach. By this view, curriculum content remains standardized by its academic discipline without reference to biblical or religious concerns. The spiritual component is adjacent but intentionally present by virtue of our Christian format for the course and our Christian character as an instructor. Those not especially pious by temperament are often uncomfortable with this style and tend to dismiss it as religious window dressing with a Bible verse in the syllabus and prayer at the start of class. We have seen this done superficially and poorly.

However, we also know teachers who are expressive in their faith and have developed a style that effectively communicates God's love to others—even to those of us who are not very pious. Respected authors such as Richard Foster and James K. A. Smith have written extensively on how to apply the Church's traditions in piety and spiritual disciplines to instruction. And biblical themes of welcoming the stranger (Deuteronomy 10:19) and the gift of hospitality (1 Peter 4:9) need not be foreign to the classroom.

Yet integrating, allegorizing, and personalizing still make many of us uncomfortable. Despite their possibilities, we detect the potential artificiality in these approaches.

What, then, sets Lutheran education apart and makes it worth sustaining? An instructional approach to Christ and curriculum selects and features points of intersection between God's two kingdoms, an approach that

- affirms the goodness of creation and our study of it;
- avoids either the conflation or compartmentalization of God's right-hand and His left-hand kingdoms; and
- sustains meaning in all temporal studies by locating them in service to God's ultimate aims in Christ.

By this approach, the aim of the instructor is to include meaningful examples and incidents of these two-kingdoms intersections within course content. These examples exhibit the subject matter in pedagogically sound ways but also—sometimes directly, sometimes indirectly—draw the students' attention to the context of God's larger purposes in Christ's coming kingdom.

What would this approach to Christ and curriculum look like? And would we be uncomfortable with it? Unlike integrating, allegorizing, and personalizing, this approach has no formula and is course- and content-specific. It is not simple and artificial. And it actively applies those several practical themes of the Gospel articulated in the Reformation. For example, in a technical course, the intersections may have to do with biblical themes of social justice, stewardship of creation, or a biblical anthropology. In a humanities course, the themes often involve Christian liberty and vocation. And in the arts, the themes of incarnation and the hiddenness of God provide many opportunities.

An intersection approach means that the instructor needs to have a working grasp of the Reformation's several insights about the Gospel. In other words, to teach within the Lutheran tradition (or, for that matter, any of the Church's other rich traditions), we have to know and understand that tradition. Perhaps this homework is also part of what makes us uncomfortable.

Our changing culture, like all times in history, presents a stream of events and opportunities to identify intersections of what is happening in God's world and what God is doing in Christ. To suggest one example from recent news (at this writing), a laboratory at Newcastle University in England has received government approval to create the first embryo from a DNA combination of three human beings. Doing so may eliminate severe hereditary disorders but will initiate a hereditary line that has never before existed. Issues at stake include the nature of personhood, the second Great Commandment, science and ethics, the accountability of vocation, and the concepts of Christian liberty and Enlightenment liberty. This intersection example is one that will shape our students' future and is worthy of study through courses in social studies, science, or business.

We do have reasons to be cautious about putting Christ and curriculum together in contrived and superficial ways. But my colleague gets the last word here, after some conversation and reflection: "While, yes, this subject did make me a bit uncomfortable, I now not only better understand the approaches, but am also excited about the possibilities of

trying some intersections in class. This is an approach that is both coherent with the Lutheran tradition and versatile across many subject
areas."

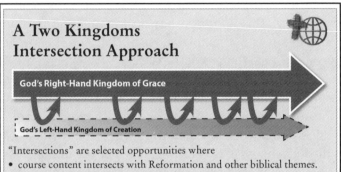

A Two Kingdoms Intersection Approach

God's Right-Hand Kingdom of Grace

God's Left-Hand Kingdom of Creation

"Intersections" are selected opportunities where
- course content intersects with Reformation and other biblical themes.
- speech acts serve as efficacious promises, words of hope, indicators of
  grace, etc., and intersect with student receptiveness, drawing the student
  toward the right-hand kingdom.
- community events, practices, and incidents in harmony or tension with
  God's word of Law or of Gospel can function as "spiritually loaded
  incidents."
- a decision or action (individual or community) publicly alerts us to the
  distinction and tension between the two kingdoms—sometimes costly.

Moulds, 2014

Christ and Curriculum: Four Approaches

Integration	Allegorizing	Personalizing	Intersections
Selects discipline content that matches biblical truths, themes, and content: beauty and symmetry in math integrates with order and structure of creation; social patterns of error, penalty, and progress integrate with the Bible's sin, judgment, and grace.

Course content and Bible are integrated. | All truth is God's truth—thus, all truth that we teach corresponds at some level to God's Word. Energy levels in physics are analogous to spiritual dominions; empires rising and falling are allegories of creation and the fall.

Course content provides similes and metaphorical comparisons. | Uses relationships, interpersonal style, role model, personal testimony, and appropriate devotional practices of opening prayer and biblical course themes. Koinonia and community create opportunities for witness.

Course content remains focused on conventional subject area. | Selects and creates course content that intersects with biblical themes (grace, justice, covenant, etc.) and our tradition (incarnational theology, *simul*, vocation, 2K, etc.).

Discipline content remains conventional; standard biblical themes inform content, critique, application, etc. |

Moulds, 2014

98

16

DESIGNING ENGAGING LESSONS TO TEACH THE FAITH

Bernard Bull

How can we design teaching-the-faith lessons that engage learners? I'm not referring to simple entertainment, but rather to deep engagement. There are many factors to consider when seeking to answer this question. Guidance from Scripture can help us as we seek answers to this question. We can also learn from recent educational practice and research.

When I was taking a research class in graduate school, the professor told the story of someone who conducted research on why students fall asleep in class. Was it because they worked all night, they stayed up too late playing video games, or perhaps they were generally bored with the class? After conducting a series of interviews with students who did indeed fall asleep in some classes and not others, the researcher came up with a simple but profound two-word answer to his research question: "perceived meaninglessness." People fell asleep when they considered whatever was being taught to lack meaning for them. The students might have been completely wrong in their judgment about what was valuable, but this research finding seemed to suggest that the student perception of meaning makes a huge difference.

Notice that this is not about what the teacher considers to be meaningful. It is the perception of the student. What are the potential implications for teaching the faith? In Isaiah 55:11, God reminds us about the power of His Word. "So shall My word be that goes out from My mouth; it shall not return to Me empty, but it shall accomplish that which I purpose, and shall succeed in the thing for which I sent it." Then, in 1 Corinthians

99

2:13, Paul explains to the Corinthians that he did not preach with wise and persuasive words but with a demonstration of the Spirit's power. Combined, these two passages remind us that the Holy Spirit works through the Word and that the effectiveness of sharing the Gospel does not rely upon the eloquence or persuasive speech of a teacher. Our goal is not to be the most entertaining, but we do want students to be engaged and see meaning in what they are learning. It would be a misreading of the two passages to assume that language and communication do not matter. For example, sharing the Gospel in German to a person who only speaks English is unlikely to communicate meaning to him or her. The same thing is true if we are using words, examples, and illustrations that students do not understand. Given these realities, following are four simple ways to design lessons that are more likely to engage students and help them see the meaning in what they are learning.

GET TO KNOW THE STUDENTS

When it comes to matters of the faith, students do not come to us with blank minds. They come with a lifetime of experiences along with a variety of beliefs and convictions that they have developed. They come with passions, fears, interests, gifts, and challenges. They come with a mind full of memories about lived experiences, the literature and films that they have consumed, and the faith stories that were shared with them. Each time students encounter a new person, idea, or experience, they compare those things to their own memories and stories. As a result, learners do not enter a learning experience as a blank slate. They come full of beliefs, convictions, attitudes, interests, and stories.

Effective teaching and learning involves testing these internal stories, comparing and contrasting them with other stories. It is rare that a learner will instantaneously abandon an existing story for one that is shared by a teacher or classmate. In fact, the stories that students bring to a class sometimes make it difficult even to understand a new lesson or story that you might teach them. The more we get to know the ideas and stories in our students' minds, the better we are able to design lessons that help build upon or replace them.

Early in my career, when I was teaching middle and high school religion, I had a young lady who came to class happy and interested but quiet. I often noticed the pensive look on her face when I taught lessons. On occasion, she would ask questions that showed her deep curiosity about what we were learning. At the end of the school year, I asked the students to give me a written reflection about their learning and experiences in the class over the year. When I read the first paragraph in her essay, my heart sank. "You probably already know this about me, but in case you didn't, I am a Mormon." How could I possibly have gone the entire year without learning something so important about her? I thought back about all the examples that I used in class about Mormon beliefs and teaching, contrasting them with Christian theology. How would I have taught that class differently if I had known this about her? I would have certainly been unswerving in teaching the content of the faith, but how I did it would have been different.

Take the time to learn about your students. What do they already know about what you are going to teach them? What fears, joys, interests, and experiences do students bring to the topic that you plan to explore with them? Use this knowledge to come up with teaching strategies, examples, and illustrations. This doesn't mean that you have to talk like students or know everything about their favorite bands, television shows, websites, and video games. It is not necessary to turn every lesson into an opportunity to display your knowledge of popular culture. However, understanding the world in which they live will help you guide them toward seeing the meaning in what they are learning. Ultimately, this involves learning about what is meaningful to the students (individually and collectively) and asking how you can help them connect the lesson to those things.

> What fears, joys, interests, and experiences do students bring to the topic that you plan to explore with them? Use this knowledge to come up with teaching strategies, examples, and illustrations.

REMEMBER THAT *PLAYFUL* IS NOT A BAD WORD IN TEACHING

Learning takes time and discipline, but the most effective learning environments are also engaging, at times even playful. A Christian educator who understands the importance of designing or facilitating engaging learning experiences does so to the benefit of his or her students. As Martin Luther wrote in the Large Catechism:

> *We could train our youth this way [Proverbs 22:6], in a childlike way and playfully . . . with kindness and delight. For children who must be forced with rods and blows will not develop into a good*

generation. At best they will remain godly under such treatment only as long as the rod is upon their backs [Proverbs 10:13].[1]

This principle applies to all people and all ages.

From the earliest years, children learn through play. They experiment, explore, pretend, imagine, create, and enjoy games of all kinds. Why not use these tendencies in our teaching? Use riddles. Add a little adventure into a lesson by having them engage in role playing. Come up with fun but effective ways to help them remember important facts, figures, and lessons. Set up simple experiments for students to test out how something you are teaching looks in the world. Don't be afraid to use humor, to smile, to show that you enjoy spending time with them. You will be delighted at how these efforts will capture the interest of students enough for them to discover the rich meaning and wonders in God's Word.

CONNECT LEARNING TO THE REAL WORLD

What you teach students will affect how they think, speak, feel, and live in the world. That means that we are not designing lessons with the goal of students doing well on a quiz or exam. We are preparing them for faith, life, and learning in the world and beyond. As such, consider how you can help students make connections between the lesson and what is happening in their lives, the lives of their friends and family, their community, and the world. How might you help them transfer what they have learned in the classroom to real-world challenges, opportunities, and situations? This is modeled for us in the very form of the New Testament Epistles, where many portions are written in response to current events, false teachings, and issues in the lives of Christians in a given community.

One way to aid with life application is to provide authentic and simulated learning experiences and to plan authentic assessments that seek to determine how students might perform in a real-world situation. Consider reviewing the examples that Martin Luther uses in the Large Catechism when he teaches about the Ten Commandments. His teaching is rich with examples on how these Commandments look in real-world contexts.

As you create assessments or ways to measure what students learn, consider how you might check their understanding of how a lesson looks

---

1   Large Catechism, Part I, paragraph 75.

and feels in a real-world context. This does not mean that traditional quizzes and tests lack value. They can be helpful sources of formative feedback for the learner and tools to help the teacher determine whether students require more guidance. However, it is one thing for them to learn the meaning of the Sixth Commandment and provide a general answer about its meaning on a quiz question. It is yet another to understand how the Sixth Commandment informs our thoughts and actions in new contexts, such as on social media or in some other fully or partially digital context.

SET CLEAR GOALS AND LET STUDENTS KNOW HOW THEY ARE DOING

What do you want students to learn? Setting goals or learning objectives for lessons is a basic skill of the modern teacher. By clearly communicating those goals to students and making sure that each student understands the goals, you will be helping them find meaning in what they are learning. You can also use this as a chance to help them discover how achieving these goals has meaning for them, now or in the future.

This goes back to why it is important to get to know your learners. If you set a goal that is too simple for one student or too much of a stretch for another, you are likely to lose their interest. The student who already knows it may be less likely to find meaning. Why pay attention to it if I already know it? The student who is overwhelmed by the goal will likely become frustrated, experiencing despair or disinterest. Why try if there is little to no chance that I will succeed? This is a common challenge when teaching the faith to a diverse student population. Some students may have grown up in the Church and a Christian family, while others may never have stepped into a church, or they might come from a different religion. This will affect the goals that you set or the pace at which they will be able to progress toward meeting a goal.

At the same time, if we have goals, we can increase student motivation by making sure they know how they are doing. Consider the nature of video games. How many teachers are able to keep students focused and hold their students' attention for hours on end? Not many; yet video games manage to do so all the time. Why is that? There are entire books written about what teachers can learn from video games, but I will offer one simple concept to keep in mind: video games give lots of frequent and meaningful feedback about how you are progressing toward a goal. This feedback keeps you motivated and engaged. Consider how you might make sure students get lots of frequent and meaningful feedback on their progress toward the learning goals in your lesson. Also note that not all feedback needs to be graded. Feedback itself can be an effective motivator because it helps students see when they are making progress, and people tend to enjoy making progress. As a useful exercise in learning how to give effective feedback, consider reviewing the Gospels, paying special attention to the many times and ways that Jesus gives feedback to people.

CONCLUSION

Keeping students engaged is important. If they are not attending to what you are teaching, they are less likely to learn. And even when they are paying attention, engagement will decline if they do not understand the lesson, see meaning in what they are learning, or know why they are learning it. You don't have to compete with the flash, sound, colors, and actions of the video games and media that students often consume daily, but it is nonetheless important to consider simple ways to keep them engaged in each lesson.

17

LITERACY RESEARCH, PRACTICES, AND POSSIBILITIES FOR FAITH FORMATION

Laurie Friedrich

What does it mean to be a literate person in the twenty-first century, and how does this affect pedagogy and curriculum in Lutheran schools? To put this in a biblical perspective, we begin with some stimulating thoughts about literacy shared by Rev. Dr. Dale Meyer in his online devotion. Bible stories were shared orally through the first century AD as the New Testament was being written. At that time, only 10 percent of the Roman Empire could read, and people learned by hearing. With the invention of the printing press around AD 1440, the general population could access printed materials and slowly learned to read. At this time, literacy was defined as the ability to get information from a book. Today, we are experiencing the digital revolution, where most of the world has access to multimedia materials via the Internet.[1] Traditional definitions of reading and writing as decoding and encoding text have expanded to include use of images, video, audio, and hyperlinks to convey meaning. Already in 1996, the International Reading Association (IRA) and National Council of Teachers of English (NCTE) added viewing and visually representing to the traditional literacy skills of listening, speaking, reading, and writing.[2] As the Internet rapidly defines information, reading, communi-

> As the Internet rapidly defines information, reading, communication, and learning, teachers must incorporate new literacies into the curriculum to prepare students to be literate in today's world.

---

1   Dale Meyer, "The Meyer Minute for May 7, 2015," The Meyer Minute, posted on May 7, 2015, accessed February 19, 2016, http://www.themeyerminute.typepad.com/meyerminute/2015/05/the-meyer-minute-for-may-7-2015.html.
2   International Reading Association and the National Council of Teachers of English, *Standards for the English Language Arts* (Newark, DE, and Urbana, IL: International Reading

cation, and learning, teachers must incorporate new literacies into the curriculum to prepare students to be literate in today's world. In this essay, we will examine current literacy research, defining best practices for the classroom and implications of use for faith development.

RESEARCH-BASED LITERACY PRACTICES

God has blessed us with many resources to meet the learning needs of each student. The National Reading Panel convened in 1997 found that teachers should use a combination of strategies, including phonemic awareness, phonics, comprehension, vocabulary, and fluency when teaching children to read.[3] Renewed emphasis on reading informational text in light of the Common Core State Standards compels teaching these literacy skills across the content areas.[4] For example, we can teach cause and effect as we read the Book of Proverbs or sequencing as we read the Holy Week account. An excellent website for literacy ideas that can be applied across the curriculum is readwritethink.org, which provides timelines, Venn diagrams, trading cards, and poetry ideas to communicate learning. Comprehensive literacy instruction provides a variety of experiences students need, beginning with motivation. Teachers motivate students by including choice, collaboration, and relevance in learning activities. Supplying a variety of materials at individual reading levels empowers students to select texts they can understand that help them find answers to their questions. Whenever possible, allow students to consult both print and digital resources to evaluate and synthesize information in the inquiry process.[5] Teachers also need to provide time for self-selected reading and writing.

SELECTING A BIBLE VERSION

Selecting an appropriate version of the Bible matched to reading ability can empower learners to read with understanding as God creates and strengthens faith through His Word. BibleGateway.com is a helpful online resource that allows biblical searching by passage, keyword, or topic

Association and the National Council of Teachers of English, 1996), 1.

3   National Reading Panel, "Teaching Children to Read: An Evidence-Based Assessment of the Scientific Research Literature on Reading and Its Implications for Reading Instruction," National Institute of Child Health and Human Development, accessed February 19, 2016, https://www.nichd.nih.gov/publications/pubs/nrp/pages/smallbook.aspx.

4   "English Language Arts Standards," Common Core State Standards Initiative, accessed February 19, 2016, http://www.corestandards.org/ELA-Literacy/.

5   CCSS.ELA-LITERACY.RI.5.7

in fifty-three English versions and in over sixty other languages and audio versions. Teachers can select the appropriate version of the Bible for their class by entering the lesson verses into Microsoft Word to calculate the readability level for various translations. To do so, enable readability statistics and then run a grammar check to see the Flesch–Kincaid readability level by grade. (Tutorials for enabling this feature can be found online.)

> Selecting an appropriate version of the Bible matched to reading ability can empower learners to read with understanding as God creates and strengthens faith through His Word.

It is important to remember that marketed readability levels are an average across all books of the Bible, and different books are written at higher levels. For example, in the English Standard Version (ESV), John's Gospel is written at a fifth-grade level, whereas Paul's Letter to the Ephesians is at an eleventh-grade level, so the publisher averages these results and markets its ESV translation at eighth-grade reading level, the level recommended for the general population.[6] The Easy-to-Read Version (ERV) is written at a fourth-grade level and works well with children. This version uses shorter words and sentences to increase comprehension. For English language learners of all ages, the New International Readers Version (NIrV) uses concrete words in shorter sentences and reads at a third-grade level.[7] With any version of the Bible, it is important to discuss concepts with learners to ensure understanding.

When sharing Bible stories with preschool children who are not yet reading, use a short text with engaging pictures. Three- and four-year-olds generally have an attention span of approximately three to six minutes, so short is good. Involve children in the story with actions, questions, activities, pictures, and repeating lines of a prayer after you. Two examples of Bibles that engage young children in this way are *The Story Bible*[8] and *The New Bible in Pictures for Little Eyes*.[9] Individual Bible story books such as Concordia Publishing House's Arch Books capture the interest of five- to nine-year-olds and are written at the third-grade comprehension level (fourth- to fifth-grade reading level).

6   Crossway Staff, "ESV Readability (Grade Levels)," Crossway, blog posted August 8, 2005, accessed February 19, 2016, http://www.crossway.org/blog/2005/08/readability-grade-levels.
7   Christianbook.com, "Translation Reading Levels," accessed February 22, 2016, http://www.christianbook.com/page/bibles/about-bibles/bible-translation-reading-levels?event=Bibles.
8   Edward A. Engelbrecht and Gail E. Pawlitz, eds., *The Story Bible* (St. Louis: Concordia, 2011).
9   Kenneth N. Taylor, *The New Bible in Pictures for Little Eyes* (Chicago: Moody Press, 2002).

BIBLE RESEARCH TOOLS

Encourage students to write questions they encounter as they read God's Word. Providing a variety of print and digital resources allows students to seek answers to their questions. Study tools such as the *Complete Bible Discovery Guide*[10] provide visual text filled with engaging pictures and helpful information for children of all ages, while *Concordia's Complete Bible Handbook*[11] has more text in smaller font along with pictures for upper grades. Online sites allow students to access additional information in multimedia formats. For example, OpenBible.info provides Bible geocoding using Google Earth to open every location in the Bible with pictures, and it also has a "Labs" section that analyzes online data to produce visualizations of verses, stories, and versions of the Bible. YouTube also houses Bible movies to build background knowledge before teaching Bible content.

COMPREHENSION STRATEGIES

Teachers can model the following strategies to help students increase comprehension. *Before reading*, have your students complete a graphic organizer using an app such as Popplet, or take a picture walk to activate prior knowledge. Teach vocabulary by developing a semantic web around the story and clarifying difficult words. Also make sure your students learn how to navigate digital text so that they can read ebooks, search key words, evaluate websites, and create digital projects. *During reading*, ask students to visualize the characters and setting. Focus on using strategies, asking questions, setting purpose, predicting, inferring, and interpreting graphics and media. *After reading*, involve students in critical thinking by having them make connections to other texts and personal experiences, look for evidence in the text to support claims, and reply to others' responses. Engage students' metacognition by having them demonstrate the strategy they used by recording their procedure in a screencast such as Educreations. Students can engage with Bible texts through praying, singing, storytelling, journaling, acting, and creating multimedia to demonstrate learning. In so doing, students make faith their own by applying biblical truths to their own lives.

---

10 Abigail Genig, Cynthia Schilf, Susan Schulz, and Julie Stiegemeyer, *Complete Bible Discovery Guide* (St. Louis: Concordia, 2012).
11 Edward A. Engelbrecht, ed., *Concordia's Complete Bible Handbook*, 2nd ed. (St. Louis: Concordia, 2013).

Student Response to Reading

The read-write connection. Writing can help students think deeply and express their reflections while reading. Research encourages writing routinely using a variety of print and digital formats, including journaling and blogging.[12] Students can summarize reading and apply it to their lives through writing prayers and blogging about ways God is answering those prayers. Research is showing that students write more and better when utilizing the immediate feedback provided for spelling and grammar that is available when writing online.[13] Online writing today is often called composing because students can incorporate multimedia. Students can create multimedia projects that witness their faith to the world by inserting pictures, songs, video, audio, and hyperlinks into online compositions and sharing them.

Collaborating to communicate learning. Collaboration is one of the twenty-first-century skills that students need in order to participate in a global society. Collaborating within the classroom and with other classrooms provides an authentic audience and feedback as students demonstrate learning. When students read and comment upon one another's blogs, they receive feedback from a variety of people. They can email a missionary with words of encouragement as a way of sharing their faith while adding relevance to the writing task. Students can also create digital stories to share using a variety of apps and websites, such as storyjumper.com and HaikuDeck.com. The project will vary based on age: young children can create retellings of stories they know; students in middle grades can make life applications with a story; older students can be challenged to make a difference in the world with their stories. Students can practice fluency through repeated readings and then act out a Bible story with puppets using an app such as Bible Buddies.[14] Or students can act out stories themselves, perhaps videotaping their play to share in chapel or with parents.[15]

---

12 Linda B. Gambrell and Lesley Mandel Morrow, eds., *Best Practices in Literacy Instruction*, 5th ed. (New York: Guilford Press, 2015).

13 Virginia W. Berringer and William D. Winn, "Implications of Achievements in Brain Research and Technology for Writing Development, Writing Instruction, and Educational Evolution" in *Handbook of Writing Research*, Charles MacArthur, Steve Graham, and Jill Fitzgerald, eds. (New York: Guilford Press, 2006), 96–114.

14 See http://www.polishedplay.com/apps/bible-buddies.html. There is a paid version called Director's Pass that gives access to many more stories and allows you to put in your students' pictures.

15 Here is an example of a dramatization of Jesus praying in the Garden of Gethsemane enacted by a second-grade class in a Lutheran school: youtu.be/WeVo6NtSiZo.

Faith Development

Faith grows by the power of the Holy Spirit working through the Word. John H. Westerhoff's view of faith development emphasizes the importance of the community of faith.[16] Experiences within this community help children value the variety of people God uses to support us, and fruits of faith become visible as we demonstrate acts of love in helping others. In addition to our church and school communities, today we can join online communities that support learning and faith development. Consider connecting with an international school or missionary as students tell the story of their faith, discuss a shared reading, or create projects jointly without leaving the classroom. By integrating email and video-chat technologies, teachers expand students' ways of communicating their faith and making a difference in people's lives at a distance. Online communities also support teachers with ongoing professional development, shared resources, and faith support. Consider joining Twitter and following other Lutheran teachers at #LuthEd, #LEA, or #TEC21LCMS.

Teaching Literacy in the Digital Age

Teachers today have a wealth of materials to prepare each student to become a productive Christian citizen in the twenty-first century. God is opening doors for our students to be missionaries today right from our classrooms and planting the seed for them to affect the world in the future. To be literate today, we need to communicate multimodally in meaningful ways. We can present God's Word in a version that can be understood by each learner. Students can then respond in ways that make learning personal as they receive God's Word and apply it to their lives. The Holy Spirit working through the Word will develop faith in each learner. Some of the literacy tools have changed in our digital society, but God reaps the same harvest of faith. What an awesome time to be a teacher and a learner!

---

16 John H. Westerhoff III, *Will Our Children Have Faith?* (San Francisco: Harper & Row, 1976).

18

TEACHING CHRISTIAN HABITS IN THE CLASSROOM

Lorinda Sankey

The Christian classroom engages students in the daily habits of Christian life. Teachers plan for these Christian habits to be prominent parts of their classroom procedures so that students learn how a Christian lives in response to God's salvation, grace, and mercy. Classroom procedures are the everyday routines that are planned and practiced in order to accomplish daily needs, such as distributing materials or transitioning from one activity to another. Educational literature about classroom management accentuates the need for procedures in order to establish classroom environments that are safe, predictable, and smoothly run. Wong and Wong, widely considered as experts in the area of classroom procedures, state that "procedures result in PERMANENT behavior changes."[1] When procedures for daily actions are planned, taught to students, practiced regularly, and reinforced throughout the school year, behaviors do change. The procedures become the new behaviors.

Consider this idea of procedures, or habits, changing behaviors in Christian classrooms. When teachers plan, teach, practice, and reinforce the habits of faithful Christians, students' behaviors may be permanently changed. What a powerful opportunity teachers in Christian classrooms have to influence the lives of their students! Devoting time to God, Bible reading, praying, memorizing, bringing offerings, and serving others are integrated into the daily procedures of Christian classrooms at all age levels, so that students learn about these habits and are empowered to continue them beyond the classroom.

---

1   Harry K. Wong and Rosemary T. Wong, *The First Days of School: How to Be an Effective Teacher,* 4th ed. (Mountain View, CA: Harry K. Wong Publications, 2009), 196.

DEVOTING TIME

Teachers in Christian classrooms teach, practice, and reinforce the devoting of time to focus on God and His Word. These classroom "devotions" include Bible reading, singing, and praying. Devotions may also include a reading that applies the Bible verses to students' lives. Devotions are regularly scheduled for a specific time of the day (or class period in middle and high school) when teachers and students set aside all work.

Devotions typically begin with the Invocation, teacher and students making the sign of the cross over their heads and hearts while speaking, "In the name of the Father and of the Son and of the Holy Spirit" as a remembrance of their Baptism. Many teachers include singing a hymn or Christian song in classroom devotions. Some teachers lead the singing themselves; others use digital recordings or other professional resources to lead singing.

Some teachers plan and lead devotions all year. Others assign students—or ask for volunteers—as individuals, pairs, or small groups to lead devotions. Most classrooms use published devotions with Bible readings, applications, songs, and prayers from the religion curriculum or other resources. In some classrooms, students write and lead the devotions with teacher guidance.

It is important for teachers to plan the order or contents of devotions and lead the devotions for at least the first few weeks of school and intermittently throughout the school year in order to model the structure of devotions for students. The habit of devoting time to God and structuring that time for Bible reading, singing, and praying is important for teachers to teach, practice, and reinforce.

A classroom altar provides visual support for Christian habits in the classroom. A small table, desk, or shelf may be used as an altar that displays a cross and holds the materials for devotions. Often a cloth in the color of the Church Year is included on the altar. The teacher or student who leads devotions stands by the altar so that the altar provides a visual support for the habit of devoting time to God and His Word.

READING THE BIBLE

Reading the Bible every day is one of the habits of the Christian life that teachers can teach, practice, and reinforce during devotions and religion lessons. Young students see the teacher reading from the Bible or Bible story book. Students who are of the age to read independently have their own Bibles from which to read. Students also need guidance from their teacher for how to find Bible verses and how to read them. When students are listening to the Bible read aloud, they can be directed to follow along in their own Bibles or to listen for specific words or actions. Then the teacher leads a class discussion asking and answering planned questions or ones that arise from students.

Students should also be taught the habit of reading the Bible for themselves. Choral reading (reading aloud in unison) is an effective classroom habit and can be used at all ages. Choral reading bridges the transition from listening to reading for oneself, and it is a habit that is used in Sunday worship services to read the Bible and liturgy. Other transitions from listening to reading for oneself include reading aloud with a partner or small group and reading aloud for the whole class while peers follow along.

Teachers should be cautioned against Bible reading for devotions or religion lessons in which the Bible is opened, read aloud, and then closed with no explanation or guiding of students' understanding. It is true that the Holy Spirit works faith through God's Word. However, the habit of reading the Bible as a mindless routine, just to say that it was read, is not the desired habit of a Christian. Instead, teachers who teach, practice, and reinforce the habits of actively listening to and reading the Bible instill these habits in their students for life.

> Instead, teachers who teach, practice, and reinforce the habits of actively listening to and reading the Bible instill these habits in their students for life.

PRAYING

Praying is a vital Christian habit that teachers in Christian classrooms should teach, practice, and reinforce with students. A teacher in a Christian classroom teaches students to pray at various times of the day: beginning of day, lunch, end of day. The Lord's Prayer, Luther's Morning Prayer and Evening Prayer, and mealtime prayers may be prayed at these times. Just like reading the Bible, cautions must be taken so that praying does not become mindless routine. Students' active participation in these group prayers is important in establishing the habit of praying.

In order for the habit of praying to be authentic, students need to have opportunity to pray about people and circumstances in their lives. The act of going to God in prayer about concerns and needs and in thanksgiving to Him takes time and is a habit that is worth the class time. One method teachers can use to teach students how to pray is to place a prayer request box on the classroom altar where students can leave requests and thanksgivings so the teacher can speak the prayer for the whole class to pray.

Another method is to post a prayer list in a visible place in the classroom. Students or the teacher may write prayer requests on the list. Then, at a designated time of the day, the list of prayer requests is read aloud and prayers are spoken aloud. Teachers should demonstrate how to speak prayers in an age-appropriate manner in order to teach students the model of beginning the prayer by addressing God, then speaking the requests and thanksgivings, and ending with a closing such as "In Jesus' name. Amen."

After days, weeks, or months of modeling, as is age appropriate, the teacher may organize students into small prayer groups of three or four; each person in a prayer group can then choose a prayer request and/ or thanksgiving from the class prayer list and take turns speaking the prayer. Other methods include silent prayer or an individual student speaking the prayer for the whole class. It is important that teachers model how to pray and designate time in the daily classroom schedule for prayer.

One influential method to model praying is when teachers pray for their students. For example, teachers may systematically choose one student to pray for each day and tell that individual student, "I am praying for you today." Teachers know their students personally and pray for them based on what they know about students' needs and blessings, or teachers may ask students for specific prayer needs. When teachers pray for their students, they teach, practice, and reinforce the Christian habit of praying by providing a personal model for students.

MEMORIZING

Memorizing Bible verses, Luther's Small Catechism, hymns, and songs is a Christian habit that should also be taught, practiced, and reinforced. One method that teachers use to empower students' memorization is oral repetition; regularly using specific prayers helps one to eventually memorize them. Hymns and songs may be memorized in the same way. Additionally, teachers may post Bible verses on the classroom walls, refer to them, ask students to read them aloud, and the like.

Many Lutheran schools and teachers require memorization as part of the curriculum, assigned for students to recite to the teacher. For young children, the memorization of the week is repeated orally several times a day and sent home for families to read and review. Older students may be assigned memorization twice a week and recite it to the teacher on specified days. Longer assignments need to be broken into parts so they are attainable for students. Some teachers challenge students to memorize longer passages or give them choices about what to memorize and the time frame for completion. Whatever the method, it is important to teach, practice, and reinforce memorization of the Bible, catechism, hymns, and songs as one of the habits of Christian life.

Bringing Offerings and Serving Others

Christians respond to God's salvation, grace, and mercy by regularly bringing offerings and serving others. Teachers can teach, practice, and reinforce these habits with a variety of methods. Students may research organizations, choose where to donate their offerings, and then bring offering money for that designated organization. When students are engaged in bringing offerings, they learn the value of offering their money to God in service to others.

Similarly, when students have opportunities to serve others directly, they learn the value of service. Teachers lead their classrooms in serving others in the school, congregation, and community. Examples of these service projects include ushering for school chapel or cleaning the pews afterward, making birthday cards for shut-ins, collecting coats for homeless people, or collecting money for an international mission. Lutheran schools and teachers involve their students in a wide variety of short- and long-term projects that serve others. For mission resources and ideas, visit the LCMS website. The habits of bringing offering money and serving others are important to teach, practice, and reinforce in Christian classrooms.

Conclusion

It is the Holy Spirit who works and strengthens faith in the hearts of teachers and students. As teachers and students live together in Christian classrooms, they practice the habits of faithful Christians. Teachers

> Teachers intentionally integrate these habits into the everyday procedures of Christian classrooms so that students learn these habits and integrate them into their lives outside of classrooms.

intentionally integrate these habits into the everyday procedures of Christian classrooms so that students learn these habits and integrate them into their lives outside of classrooms. As students practice these habits in their own lives and carry them forward into their futures, they have opportunity to influence family and friends to do the same.

19

THE ROLE OF QUESTIONS IN TEACHING THE FAITH

Paul Buchheimer

It was the fall of 2008. My pastor and I were returning from a conference when he received a phone call from a parent in our school. Soon he received several more calls, and I also began to get calls. All the parents were upset about the same incident that had just taken place in our eighth-grade classroom. During religion class, one of the students had asked the teacher if Jewish people will go to hell. The teacher's response was "Yes"—because they don't believe that Jesus is our Savior, they will not be saved. The school is located in South Florida in an area that is predominantly Jewish. Many of the students in our Lutheran school had family members who are Jewish. It was easy to understand why the teacher's answer to a difficult question had caused such a strong negative reaction. What was the teacher to say?

I have learned from experience that many of the problems that arise are not due to any part of the formal teaching curriculum. They come from teachers trying to answer those tough tangential questions that students ask during the lesson. What is a teacher to do?

First of all, I think we realize that there are many mysteries of God that we cannot fully understand. Telling the students that we just don't have an answer for their questions makes sense. As we question many matters of God, I am reminded of what my father, a Lutheran pastor, once said about this. He compared our understanding of God to our explaining the Internet to an ant. We cannot possibly grasp the answers to so many questions our students and we will have.

Now, back to the opening situation. When I returned to the campus, I had to deal with some damage control. I was able to calm everyone down by using a very simple approach. When asked difficult questions, I referred the students back to Scripture. What I have to say on a topic is not important, but what the Bible says *is* important. My response would be, "Let's turn to God's Word and see what His answers are."

I believe it is very important that we guide and direct students through their explorations of faith and belief in God. On major faith issues, we must stand strong and be clear. As we learn in 2 Timothy 3:16–17, "All Scripture is breathed out by God and profitable for teaching, for reproof, for correction, and for training in righteousness, that the man of God may be complete, equipped for every good work." We have the opportunity to help our students understand that we are all sinners and each fall short of God's Commandments. In this regard, we are no better than anyone else and cannot earn our way to heaven. Good works are our response to God's love, and we cannot use them to earn eternal salvation. But God loves us so much that He sent His Son, Jesus, to pay the price of our sins with His innocent blood on the cross. The Holy Spirit works within students' hearts to believe this most important truth. We can treat other issues that are confusing and puzzling to our students with a focus on God's Word and prayer for the Holy Spirit to guide our learning.

I have found that the safest and best way to deal with the difficult questions that students ask is to refer these issues to the pastor. He will normally welcome the chance to interact with our school classes and use his training and experience to guide young people through difficult doctrinal issues. His support and awareness of questions brought up by our classes are also very important for us. When the pastor and principal are able to work together, it results in a very strong and effective team ministry.

I truly believe that we must encourage our students to dig deep into the Bible and what God is telling us. I have met some parents and church leaders who felt that to question anything is wrong. They believe that if we truly have faith, we will accept everything we read and hear without any doubt or wonder. I have been told that Scripture interprets itself. While that is an important principle of biblical interpretation, other church leaders and students of the Bible point out another important perspective. They explain that as we "wrestle" with what the Bible is telling us, we will find deeper meanings in God's Word, and the Holy

Spirit will better reveal to us many things that are not obvious on a first reading. We pray as the psalmist prayed in Psalm 119:18, "Open my eyes, that I may behold wondrous things out of Your law." We certainly will not understand everything that we read and hear from God's Word, but isn't that what faith is all about? Unlike Thomas, we can believe without seeing, or in this case, without everything making perfectly logical sense to us. We know that God's wisdom extends far beyond our human understanding. Once our students can recognize this truth, they can be open to truly studying and getting into the Bible.

It is only when we really delve into the Word of God that we find true applications of the Bible and apply them to our lives in today's world. Hopefully, our students can appreciate how the words of the prophets and disciples written so many years ago remain just as true today as they were back then. Do they not realize that the questions they are asking us today have been asked by so many throughout history? Why did God allow sin in the world? Why do good things happen to bad people and bad things to good people? Why are some people born into extreme poverty and others into wealth? Why did God make me the way I am? Why does life seem so unfair? Will my pets be with me in heaven? I'm sure you can go on and on with questions, many of which we cannot fully answer. We must realize that it is our human nature to ask these questions. When we and our students stop wondering and asking questions, then that is the time for us to be concerned.

In summary, God's blessings to you as you field the tough and challenging questions that your class will ask. But remember to let God be God. We must not tell God how He should act and behave. We cannot be the all-knowing and ever-powerful ruler of heaven and earth—the job is already taken. At times, our answer to students should be "I don't know. I can't answer that. We'll pray about your concerns now, and one day we can ask God in heaven."

20

PERSONALIZED LEARNING
AND TEACHING THE FAITH

Dave Black

In the previous century, industrial-era one-size-fits-all educational delivery was the norm in all types of schools. The lecture delivery and test methodology met the needs of a society seeking order and advancement for its citizens. Lutheran education and theological training applied this approach in classrooms and catechesis instruction to the benefit of the student and the church. Students always possessed strong academic and thinking skills upon graduating from Lutheran schools and after completing catechism instruction at Lutheran churches.

But some students benefited from this experience more than others. The learning process and activities connected well with a subset of students, while others were challenged by this process. In the past, we simply categorized children as "good students" or "poor students" and encouraged them to pursue career opportunities based on this label.

Although this may have been a successful model for the 1900s, it really is not a model that is at the heart of Lutheran theology. The instructional delivery of that century was the same for each student. However, we see clearly in Scripture that God has gifted each of us in unique and various ways for service in His kingdom.

While there are several Bible passages that speak to the varied gifts we have been given by God, perhaps the best verses on this topic are from the great chapter on the Body of Christ in 1 Corinthians 12, which uses the body metaphor to explain how each person has been given a different set of gifts by our Creator. These gifts serve to complement the larger Body of the Church to ensure that no gift is lacking among God's people. Our God is intentional about how He has blessed us. No two of us have been granted the same gifts, for the kingdom of God would not be able to carry out its purpose fully with redundancy. The unique variety of gifts each of us is given is designed to make our work as God's people complete. The kingdom of God comes indeed without our asking. God doesn't need us to carry out His purpose, but He does give us His Spirit and enables us to use these gifts for service in this world.

This raises the question: If everyone, including students, has been given unique gifts, why have we been teaching everyone the same way in our classrooms? As noted earlier, the basis of our educational system is rooted in the industrial era, when we prepared students to take their place in this world by teaching reading, writing, history,

> If everyone, including students, has been given unique gifts, why have we been teaching everyone the same way in our classrooms?

and math. Children were evaluated on their ability to memorize facts on these topics. They were then encouraged to enter a field that was matched with their success in this endeavor. Unfortunately, this process was most beneficial for those who possessed the gifts to succeed academically. As we see in 1 Corinthians 12, there are many gifts our Creator gives. Yet these gifts were not acknowledged, celebrated, or nurtured in a system where education was approached through only one method.

As we are now well into the twenty-first century, it is clear our country and world have moved past the industrial era to an age that is known either as the information age or the digital age. The employment needs of organizations are extremely varied. In addition, the world is changing at such a breathless pace that success for our students is measured in different ways. The skills they needed five years ago may be very different from the skills needed today. How will students be prepared to pursue new learning if their entire educational experience has been scripted for them?

This is where the approach known as personalized learning is playing an increasingly significant role in education. A standard Wikipedia definition, which is suitable for our purposes, states that personalized learning "is the tailoring of pedagogy, curriculum and learning environments by learners or for learners in order to meet their different learning needs and aspirations."[1] Since God has seen fit to gift each of us uniquely with talents and aptitudes, a personalized learning approach fits effectively

---

1   Wikipedia, "Personalized learning," accessed February 22, 2016, https://en.wikipedia.org/wiki/Personalized_learning.

with Lutheran theology. This approach honors an individual's unique gifts and seeks to enhance them through a learning process that nurtures each student in a different manner.

Teaching the faith in Lutheran schools and catechism classrooms has historically been carried out through the standard industrial-era classroom model, with good reason. First, the truths of Scripture are so significant that we want all our children to have a thorough knowledge of who God is and what He has done for us through Christ Jesus. Second, teachers tend to teach the way they were taught. The vast majority of Lutheran school teachers (and pastors, in the case of catechism classes) were taught in traditional classrooms. There is a comfort level there for those seeking to instruct students.

While the efforts of Lutheran teachers and pastors are admirable and effective with the enabling and guidance of the Holy Spirit, it is also remarkable that the model for personalized learning of the faith is found in the Bible. As Paul wrote to the Christians in Corinth, he was aware not everyone was prepared to receive the Gospel message in the same way. In 1 Corinthians 3:2, the apostle writes, "I fed you with milk, not solid food, for you were not ready for it. And even now you are not yet ready." Paul was attuned to the reality that the spiritual readiness to accept the Gospel message varied greatly. Therefore, he sought to share the Good News of Jesus Christ in a manner that met the spiritual needs of the hearer.

We see in the Book of Acts that Paul shares the message of Jesus to different people in different ways. In Athens, he appeals to the worldly wisdom of the Greeks. Then he reveals that the unknown god to whom the Athenians built an altar was the true God (Acts 17:16–34). But when Paul is in Antioch and speaking to Jews, he invokes the history of Israel as he points to Jesus as the true Messiah (Acts 13:13–43). In this way, Paul carries out his version of personalized learning as he shares the Gospel with the people of the first century.

The transition from the traditional educational model to a more fluid approach is challenging for educators. This may be an even more difficult transition for those whose primary responsibility is teaching the faith, since the truths of Scripture are unchanging. Yet, we can plainly see that a personalized approach to faith instruction has value, as it is modeled in the Bible.

Thus, what does personalized learning look like in the teaching of the faith? Perhaps the most significant element in this process is the opportunity to give the student choices—choice of assignment output, choice of assessment process, and sometimes choice of content or topic. Personalization does not take place without choices. This does not mean choices may not be guided by a teacher, but ultimately the learning decisions made are mindful of individual needs and aptitudes.

While the application of personalization and choice may seem daunting to a teacher or pastor using this method for the first time, many ways exist in which choice may be implemented. Below are two examples of teaching the faith using personalized learning to jump-start creative thinking about applying personalization for faith development. These examples are listed in no particular order and may not apply to all classroom environments. However, they provide a look into what is possible for personalized learning and teaching the faith.

Personalized Questions and Answers

According to the Barna Group research organization, one key reason why people disengage from faith in traditional settings is they no longer feel the church is a safe place to ask questions.[2] They are bombarded with all kinds of messages about life and culture and tend to view answers from classroom and church leaders as "slick" or "half-baked." In other words, they often do not feel their questions are answered in a manner that respects their deep queries as an important step in faith development.

Each student has different faith questions in mind. Hence, personalization is helpful—and in many instances essential—for answering these questions. Here are some strategies from a personalized learning perspective:

- Establish God's Word as the ultimate source for answering faith questions. If the understanding of the inerrancy of Scripture is not present, share some key facts that support inerrancy.
- Gather questions in some way that meets the needs of your students. I like to use technology and service called Padlet—an interactive bulletin board where questions may be posted anonymously through the website or app—to gather these deep questions.

---

2   David Kinnaman, *You Lost Me: Why Young Christians Are Leaving Church . . . and Rethinking Faith*, with Aly Hawkins (Grand Rapids, MI: Baker, 2011).

Others use polling technologies such as Socrative (socrative.com), which allows posters to choose whether to be anonymous or to share their name.

- Allow students to research questions of interest as an individual or in a group. It may be helpful to have them look at sites you have chosen (such as the LCMS website), but also to let them encounter what others are saying about the topic. This is a good time to remind students to seek godly and biblical wisdom rather than human wisdom.

- Provide choices for how learning is shared—whether with the instructor individually or with the entire group through a paper, a video, a presentation, an audiocast, or some other method.

- Share feedback with the students in a personalized method that applies biblical perspectives and also opens the door for continued conversations on the topic.

SOCIAL MEDIA

What would Bible characters say if they had present-day social media available during their time? How would they express their faith and challenges? Allow students to choose the social media service (e.g., Facebook, Twitter, Instagram) and Bible character they want to use as they seek to connect with a character from the past to better understand faith in the present.

This process can provide some insightful but also humorous creations. One student, using Twitter as the Old Testament character Jacob, created the following tweet: "First I stole my brother's birthright. Then I got a Twitter account. #BestDayEver." Who knows—perhaps Jacob would have spoken this way if he could have broadcasted his thoughts to the world!

What other personalized learning ideas for teaching the faith might you consider? These ideas are limited only by the instructor's creativity and willingness to engage students in the partnership of learning more about our gracious God. While the challenges of teaching the faith in this digital age are many, so also do we have many new opportunities to connect the Christian faith with our students, especially when we leverage the resources we have available to personalize the educational experience for students. Teachers should be encouraged to explore, experiment, and share! Enabled by the Holy Spirit, we seek to lead students into a greater understanding of who God is, what He has done, and what He is doing for us (head knowledge); we also seek to lead them into a closer relationship with their Lord (heart knowledge) and a deeper desire to share Him.

21

LEARNING TO SERVE VIA SERVICE LEARNING

Randall Ferguson

Jesus charged His first-century followers to "go therefore and make disciples of all nations" (Matthew 28:19). Today, followers of Jesus Christ invest in that same charge; empowered by God's Spirit, we seek to transform lives via faith and action. Indeed, the most precious thing we can teach our students (or anyone, for that matter) is the life-changing, life-saving message of the Gospel. But then, almost in the same breath, we will want to teach them how to live the Gospel as well, teaching them to be disciples of Jesus Christ in a world that seems to spin further and further away from Calvary every day, which is why living the Gospel is so important. Accordingly, it is terribly insightful for the apostle Paul to write, "So now faith, hope, and love abide, these three; but the greatest of these is love" (1 Corinthians 13:13). The greatest is love? Why not faith? Well, perhaps because love is our witness to the world of the faith within us. We can love others in many ways, but none more tangible and impactful than a life of servanthood that reaches out to people in need at home and around the world. This essay will briefly explore some key distinctions, benefits, and practical suggestions for teaching others to be servants of Jesus Christ via service learning.

DISTINCTIONS

Service learning takes participants beyond the common one-day, in-and-out service project. One-time service projects are important endeavors, but they typically do not provide the meaningful faith development that service learning can create. Service learning brings together the server and the served in a communal relationship where each learns from the other; interaction between the two is critical. Furthermore, service learning usually extends over a period of time that can run from weeks to months before the end result is accomplished. Finally, service learning involves reflection; servers should be given carefully crafted opportunities to reflect upon and publicly share the personal impact (faith formation) that their service had on them.

BENEFITS

One end goal here is faith enrichment; we want our students to think more deeply and feel more strongly about what it means to belong to the Body of Christ. We want to provide inspiration and a vision for Christians to embrace their role in God's kingdom here on earth. We must teach and model a faith that extends far beyond sitting in our favorite, comfortable pews on Sunday morning! Indeed, we want believers to embrace their calling as ambassadors of Jesus Christ, gifted and purposed for "works of service" (Ephesians 4:12 NIV) in order to "walk in love, as Christ loved us" (Ephesians 5:1). Service learning can lead participants down this path.

Ted Engelbrecht offers seven reasons why Lutheran educators should enhance the social conscience of their students. His justification for service learning can be summed up in the third reason: "When social conscience education is Spirit-directed and Scripture-based, it describes the sanctified life of Christians, and gives students a sense of their vocation and calling to minister to the world."[1]

Educators at public schools have long touted the benefits of service learning. For example, when the University of Rhode Island dove deep into this endeavor, they established the following goals for their students. They wanted students to (1) attain a better understanding of themselves and their importance to the community, (2) develop a sense of responsibility for learning and addressing issues facing their community, (3) be exposed to diverse communities and dialogue about the preconceived notions they had about those populations, and (4) discuss their plans for future civic engagement.[2] These are all great reasons for doing service learning, but now frame those reasons within the Christian message of

---

1 Ted Engelbrecht, preface to *Christ, Conscience, and the Curriculum: ALEA Schools in Mission*, by Marty Schmidt and Mike Kersten (Hong Kong: Asian Lutheran Education Conference, 2011), accessed February 22, 2016, http://www.ln.edu.hk/osl/conference2013/output/6D/4.%20ALEA_Booklet_OnlineVersion_final.pdf.

2 Jayne Richmond, "The University of Rhode Island's New Culture for Learning," in *Service-Learning and the First Year Experience: Preparing Students for Personal Success and Civic Responsibility,* ed. Edward Zlotkowski (Columbia, SC: University of South Carolina, National Resource Center for the First-Year Experience and Students in Transition, 2002), 68–69.

the Gospel and the charge from the apostle John to "not love in word or talk but in deed" (1 John 3:18), and we begin to see the impact that service learning can have on the faith development among believers of all ages.

Mike Kersten, whose teaching ministry in Taiwan was greatly enhanced by a service learning trip to a state-run orphanage in Foshan, China, describes his own transformation this way: "Not only did that first orphanage trip open up avenues for sharing the Gospel with my students that never existed before in my classroom, it also helped my own faith transcend beyond something bookish and learned to something breathing and living."[3] Service learning can be a powerful way for educators to facilitate the work of the Holy Spirit in brandishing the cross of Jesus Christ unto the hearts and lives of Christians so that the Gospel might have all the more impact, which is what faith formation should be all about.

PRACTICAL SUGGESTIONS

> We don't serve to make a name for ourselves or to feel good about ourselves or to find favor with God. We want to help the needy because of what Christ has done for us, with the hope that those served will be drawn to the Gospel because of our actions.

Service learning takes time and resources, so be sure to consider both up front when embarking on this journey. What follows are some practical suggestions for two possibilities: (1) enhancing a single-event service project with service learning, and (2) engaging in a full-blown service learning experience over an extended period of time. Whichever endeavor you choose, it begins with education. Spend time talking with your students about why helping others is such a vital component of the Christian walk. Engage your students in Scripture and in discussion. Work through the life of Jesus and note how important it was for Him to minister to others. Motivation is important. Lutherans believe that we should be motivated by the Gospel, not by the Law. We don't serve to make a name for ourselves or to feel good about ourselves or to find favor with God. We want to help the needy because of what Christ has done for us, with the hope that those served will be drawn to the Gospel because of our actions. For Lutherans, service is much more than a kind, humanitarian act; it is an act of faith!

---

3   Marty Schmidt and Mike Kersten, *Christ, Conscience, and the Curriculum: ALEA Schools in Mission*, 13. Booklet published for the Asian Lutheran Education Association conference in Hong Kong, October 21–22, 2011.

You can make **single-event service projects** more impactful and thus transformational by doing the following:

- Facilitate a better understanding of the broader issue at hand. For example, if you will be visiting a soup kitchen, have your students research and report on various aspects of the worldwide issue of hunger.

- Facilitate a better understanding of the organization you will be helping. For example, if you will be visiting a homeless shelter, have your students research and report on the shelter's history, values, accomplishments, and challenges.

- Facilitate personal reflection. Consider assigning each student to write a paper reflecting on how the service project affected him or her. What did you learn? What did you feel? How was this endeavor an exercise of your faith? Why is this particular service important? Would you like to do this again? Having students share their reflection papers in small groups or with the entire class can help the value of this endeavor to hit home.

When committing to a **full-blown service learning experience** that extends over an entire class term, here are some helpful hints:

- Identify a community partner early on. Meet with the community partner (by yourself or with your students) to determine what need could be addressed during the term. Don't assume you know what they need or want!

- Divide a big task into smaller tasks. For example, if you will be improving the physical plant of an elementary school, you could assign painting to one group, playground enhancement to another, and landscaping to another.

- Provide opportunities for your students to interact with those they will be serving. This is very important! Even better, organize times when both groups can work together to bring about the desired change.

- Make connections between class concepts and your particular service. This is where service learning gets its name. For example, if you are wedding a social studies class with helping a neighboring nursing home, examine the politics and economics of providing care for our senior citizens.

- Have students keep a journal in which they chronicle their personal journey and make connections to course ideas.

- Celebrate. Organize an event that brings everyone together to recognize what was accomplished. Be sure to recognize the purpose of this endeavor by framing it within the context of our Christian faith.

- Debrief. Bring closure to your service learning at the end of the term with small-group presentations and/or plenary discussion.

ARE WE PAYING ATTENTION?

A large crowd followed Jesus on His way to heal the daughter of Jairus when a woman who had been sick for twelve years reached through the masses to touch Jesus; she hoped that by merely making contact with Him, she, too, would be healed. Upon her advance, Jesus turned and asked, "Who touched Me?" The disciples were puzzled that He would single out her presence among the hundreds of people who were pressing in against Him (Mark 5:21–34). But here's the thing: Jesus was paying attention! He literally felt someone's desperate need and attended to it. As those who follow Jesus today, do we give that same kind of attention to those in need around us? Service learning is a powerful way for educators to impress upon their students that all of us should be paying attention. Accordingly, what a wonderful way to teach Luther's understanding of vocation, which proclaims God is present in everyday human labor and uses people like you and me to serve the needs of others; this means that our various jobs or vocations are channels of God's love. Gene Edward Veith puts it this way: "Thus, God is graciously at work, caring for the human race through the work of other human beings."[4]

The beauty of the pedagogy in service learning is twofold. First, it's effective because of its experiential nature (doing versus telling). And second, it can be used among students of nearly every age; elementary, secondary, and higher education students can all grow in their faith and walk closer with their Savior as they exercise their membership in the Body of Christ via service learning.

---

4   Gene Edward Veith, "The Doctrine of Vocation: How God Hides Himself in Human Work," *Modern Reformation* 8, no. 3 (1999): 5.

22

INQUIRY-BASED LEARNING
AND FAITH FORMATION

Tim Schumacher

Lutheran education in the twenty-first century is challenged by the tension resulting from living in a rapidly changing world while trusting in a never-changing God and the absolute truth of His Word. In a proper perspective, this situation is no different from the past century or the century prior to that. The gift of Lutheran education has long been its ability to prepare students to be grounded in God's eternal promises and prepared to live and serve in a world that is always evolving in its blindness to those promises.

So, when the content of what Lutheran schools are expected to teach expands and the so-called "best practices" for teaching and learning evolve, the Lutheran school has the blessing of unchanging truths that guide its continual efforts to provide for the best education of its students. Malcolm Bartsch, an Australian Lutheran pastor, emphasized what never changes about Lutheran education:

> The gift of Lutheran education has long been its ability to prepare students to be grounded in God's eternal promises and prepared to live and serve in a world that is always evolving in its blindness to those promises.

> While Lutheran schools must respond to the findings of disciplines such as educational philosophy, educational psychology, sociology, and pedagogy and be sensitive to insights from the history of education, all of these must be read in the light of the beliefs and values which define an authentic approach to Lutheran schooling.[1]

---

1   Malcolm I. Bartsch, *A God Who Speaks and Acts: Theology for Teachers in Lutheran Schools* (Adelaide, Australia: Openbook Howden, 2013), 5.

This authentic approach is critical in the teaching in and across all disciplines in Lutheran schools, but especially so in the context of faith formation. Much good can be gleaned from the world's collective knowledge of how students learn and grow, but Lutheran educators also need to be aware of educational practices based on worldviews that can be in conflict with a Lutheran understanding of faith formation. Inquiry-based learning is one such practice.

TEACHING THE FAITH

In one sense, we cannot "teach" faith. The faith in Jesus Christ that saves us comes to us in Baptism as a gift from God through His Word and by His Spirit. Neither can this type of faith be "formed" by us. Faith can be described as "trusting the promises of God,"[2] but as we know from Martin Luther in his explanation of the Third Article of the Apostles' Creed, this trust is not something we can initiate. For Lutherans, this emphasis on God's act alone to save us is central to our understanding of the doctrine of justification; it is also often at the heart of what separates Lutheran theology from many other Christian denominations that suggest that each of us participates in acquiring faith through good works and/or our decision to believe.

"Faith formation" in the context of Lutheran education is more often referring to another dimension of faith, that is, the lifelong Spirit-guided process of strengthening our trust in God's promises and working out how we can live freed from sin and in service to Him. This is explained in our Lutheran doctrine of sanctification and derived from Bible passages such as Colossians 3:1–3:

> If then you have been raised with Christ, seek the things that are
> above, where Christ is, seated at the right hand of God. Set your
> minds on things that are above, not on things that are on earth.
> For you have died, and your life is hidden with Christ in God.

Sanctification is progressive and participatory. As the faith gifted to us in Baptism takes root, the Holy Spirit works in us and with us to strengthen our trust in God's promises as we study them in God's Word and learn to live out His will in our lives.

Effective Lutheran education considers this pattern of faith development through childhood in its choice of appropriate teaching and learning strategies. In the earlier stages of faith development, Lutheran

---

2   Thomas A. Droege, *Faith Passages and Patterns* (Philadelphia: Fortress Press, 1983), 25.

teachers share the stories of the Bible that communicate to the child his or her identity as a child of God. As faith grows, we teach the Church's basic truths of faith and doctrine, traditionally through direct instruction and memorization. According to Thomas Droege, at some point, typically late in the middle school years, a shift happens as the promises of God are internalized and faith understanding increases:

> But over a period of years mature students are able to assume the responsibility for making their own judgments. There is a movement from conformity to individuality, from strongly felt but unexamined trust and loyalty to objective reflection on different points of view, from being what others want them to be to being the person they are and can become.[3]

Later in the context of confirmation instruction, Droege identifies a phase that calls for a different learning strategy than direct instruction:

> But a distinction needs to be made between two phases of development alternating back and forth in the life of a growing child. One is a dependence on learnings (the Catechism), sources of authority (the pastor), and institutions (the church). The other is a phase characterized by independent action, problem solving, involvement in life, and a general attitude of experimentation.[4]

It is this latter phase that seems to have learning goals that could be accomplished through the application of inquiry-based learning in the middle school and high school years, and beyond.

INQUIRY-BASED LEARNING

Inquiry-based learning is a student-centered learning strategy from the family of constructivist learning theories that have also produced related strategies such as discovery learning, project-based learning, and experiential learning. There are many varieties of inquiry-based learning used across multiple disciplines. Student-generated questions are at the core of this strategy, which employs a student-driven cycle of inquiry typically consisting of (1) asking, (2) exploring, (3) analyzing, (4) communicating, and (5) reflecting (and possibly acting).[5] This cycle can be repeated as the questions are refined and new models of knowledge are constructed. Inquiry-based learning requires a shift in

---

3   Droege, *Faith Passages and Patterns*, 58.
4   Droege, *Faith Passages and Patterns*, 90.
5   Mollie Crie, "Inquiry-Based Approaches to Learning," accessed July 10, 2015, http://www.glencoe.com/sec/teachingtoday/subject/inquiry_based.phtml.

the teacher's role from that of knowledge-transmitter to questioner and facilitator. The students become researchers investigating authentic, meaningful problems—building on knowledge from their personal experiences and social collaborations.[6]

Applied to faith formation, inquiry-based learning has much to offer. It is quite capable of leading students through the shift described by Droege from "unexamined trust and loyalty to objective reflection."[7] Foundational understandings from the earlier stages of faith development can support a personal exploration into life applications. The inquiry-based approach encourages a cross-discipline approach, which suits our need to integrate the faith in all aspects of learning. The use of questions to challenge students to deeper understanding is very Lutheran (recall the "What does this mean?" and "How is this done?" questions in Martin Luther's catechisms) and very Christlike (refer to the questioning He used with His disciples). Indeed, the Bible calls for us to "test the spirits" (1 John 4:1), and in our current age of overwhelming amounts of information, students are incredibly challenged to divide the godly from the worldly.

RELATIVISM VS. ABSOLUTE TRUTHS

However, to "read" inquiry-based learning "in the light of the beliefs and values which define an authentic approach to Lutheran schooling" as Bartsch calls us to do,[8] Lutheran educators should acknowledge the underlying relativist philosophy that is not compatible with God's Word and essential Lutheran teachings.

Inquiry-based learning in its pure, constructivist form does not acknowledge absolute truths. The inquiry process is designed to lead students to temporary, personalized models of reality that are neither universal nor eternal. Beyer explained the expected outcome of student inquiry in his book *Inquiry in the Social Studies Classroom*:

> *A good inquirer knows that what is touted as knowledge—as fact— is only someone's opinion of reality and that that opinion is colored by a frame of reference or background of experience unique to that individual. This means that different people can have very similar experiences or work with the same data and legitimately*

---

6   Nancy Fichtman Dana, Jamey Bolton Burns, and Rachel Wolkenhauer, *Inquiring Into the Common Core* (Thousand Oaks, CA: Corwin, 2013), 45.

7   Droege, *Faith Passages and Patterns*, 58.

8   Bartsch, *A God Who Speaks and Acts*, 5.

arrive at different—but equally reasonable—answers. There can be many sides to the same question.[9]

Clearly this is in conflict with the Lutheran understanding of the normative authority of Scriptures. The cycle of student-led investigations in the setting of a Lutheran school needs to be directed back through the Word of God, guided by the Scripture-tested big ideas of our Lutheran Confessions that we directly teach our students. Our reliance on Scripture is explained well in *Lutheranism 101*: "Lutherans are not anti-reason or anti-tradition or anti-experience. We simply use the Scriptures to judge the validity of these things and not the other way around."[10]

> The cycle of student-led investigations in the setting of a Lutheran school needs to be directed back through the Word of God, guided by the Scripture-tested big ideas of our Lutheran Confessions that we directly teach our students.

EQUIPPING STUDENTS

In order to be able to validate their investigations based on Scripture, students in Lutheran schools need to be equipped with common Bible study tools and skills. From the early stages of faith development, students should expand their ability to navigate the books of the Bible, memorize key verses, and identify important themes. In time, as they progress through their elementary and high school years, students need to be introduced to study notes, concordances, cross-references, and parallel translations while expanding their access to supporting resources such as commentaries and the Lutheran Confessions. They should be taught the principles of biblical interpretation and the differences between Christian denominations. In the end, students should know how to search the Word for the promises of God and the evidence of the fulfillment of those promises, confident in using Scripture as their "lamp" and their "light" (Psalm 119:105).

FRUITFUL QUESTIONS AND THE ROLE OF THE TEACHER

As the student takes on the role of questioner and investigator, the teacher becomes a facilitator who guides the inquiry process. The definition of this teacher role presents another issue for Lutheran educators.

---

9   Barry K. Beyer, *Inquiry in the Social Studies Classroom: A Strategy for Teaching* (Columbus, OH: Merrill, 1971), 16.

10 Scot A. Kinnaman and Laura L. Lane, eds., *Lutheranism 101*, 2nd ed. (St. Louis: Concordia, 2015), 23.

As McTighe and Wiggins explain, their role is to be helpful, yet "to almost never answer questions; to almost never evaluate an answer."[11] To provide an answer or a judgment of an answer would be to suggest there are overriding truths that bound the students' investigation—a notion that is incompatible with the relativist theory.

In the Lutheran school setting, the teacher as facilitator has three important functions that affect the inquiry process. The first is to choose or guide the students to fruitful questions. The best questions will accomplish one or more of the following: (1) be linked to essential teachings of the Church, (2) lead to a strengthening of trust in God's promises, (3) bring to light false or misleading teachings, (4) expand the students' understanding of their identity in Christ, and/or (5) clarify their vocations and their relationship to the world. We know from the example of Job that there are unfruitful questions, as some questions simply cannot be answered or merely lead to further misunderstandings of God's will.

The second function of the Lutheran teacher is to model the inquiry process itself. Students will benefit from being aware of some of the questions that test their teacher's faith; they will also benefit from observing that teacher's own process of praying and working through the Scriptures to find the absolute truths with which the Holy Spirit sustains us.

Third and most important, the Lutheran teacher uses inquiry-based learning activities to continually point students back to the Scriptures and, ultimately, the cross. We point to the testimony of Job, who, in the midst of great personal turmoil and a failure to find comforting answers to his and his friends' questions, triumphs in the objective truth of God's promises to him in Christ. Unlike the relativists, our search for faith understanding begins and ends with this absolute truth from Job 19:25–26:

> For I know that my Redeemer lives,
>
> > and at the last He will stand upon the earth.
>
> And after my skin has been thus destroyed,
>
> > yet in my flesh I shall see God.

---

11 Jay McTighe and Grant Wiggins, *Essential Questions: Opening Doors to Student Understanding* (Alexandria, VA: ASCD, 2013), Kindle edition, Kindle locations 1795–98.

23
THE ROLE OF MEMORY WORK IN FAITH FORMATION

Paul Buchheimer

In today's world, many past practices that were taken for granted are being questioned. Do students need to learn to write in cursive? Can students use calculators in their math lessons? Should students be given recess? When students have such easy access to information, is there really a need for them to learn history facts and dates? In our Lutheran classrooms, the value and benefits of requiring students to memorize Bible verses can also be included in this list.

In this essay, we will look at whether memory work is still worth the effort. We will then explore some dos and don'ts of memory work and finally consider some tips on how memory work can be implemented in your classroom. I have used a 1943 publication, *General Course of Study for Lutheran Elementary Schools*,[1] for some background on the topic.

Through informal talks with Lutheran educators in some Lutheran schools in the Texas District, I have sensed that there are Lutheran schools that believe memory work is still an important part of their program. Whether this opinion is fueled by a resistance to change in general or not, I tend to agree with them. Memory work still has value in our classrooms, and our students will be shortchanged if we remove it. God's Word is more than simply some verses that can be repeated to impress our friends and elders. As students learn and recite Bible passages, they are using a tool to help them move the Word of God from their heads to their hearts. Memorizing is a great vehicle to help students really understand God's message.

---
1   St. Louis: Concordia, pp. 45–54.

Memorizing Bible verses provides students with a lifelong tool they can turn to when they are being tested in difficult times. As the psalmist wrote in Psalm 119:11, "I have stored up Your word in my heart, that I might not sin against You." Reciting Bible verses can bring great comfort and peace to those who face a challenging situation. The reassurances that God is with them will help bring them strength and comfort.

If we decide that memory work does indeed have a place in our schools today, then we must implement it effectively.

Weekly assignments are important. The lesson should be of reasonable length, and the teacher should be sure that the students understand the meaning of the verses. If the memory assignments are not given in the religion book, there are many other resources available that have weekly suggestions. Having the students recite the verses, as opposed to writing them down, is a more effective method of testing the students, and it is not always necessary for the student to repeat the lesson perfectly on a first attempt. It is reasonable to help a student with some prompts and hints, but there are limits as to how much help he or she should be given. Some students will just need further practice. After all, the goal is not simply to grade them and move on; rather it is to help each student achieve the desired goal of learning God's Word. Finding the time to hear each student recite individually may be a challenge, but a creative teacher can listen to recitations while the rest of the class is working on other individual or group activities.

How should the students be graded? In many schools, the memory work is a part of the religion grade; in others, the memory work grade is separate. We have to realize that there will be some students who might have a hard time with memorization. As with other subjects, it might be necessary to modify what and how some students are given their memory assignments. Remember that while memory is important, understanding is even more important.

The next question we might consider is which grade levels should use memory. Even the youngest children can learn some songs and basic phrases. As they get older, children should be more challenged each year. Ideally, the memory assignments should match with the religion lessons and the seasons of the Church Year. I see no reason to stop memory work when students get to high school. The benefits are the same regardless of age.

Here is an example of how one Lutheran school handles memory work in the fifth grade. On Friday, the class is introduced to the memory assignment for the next week so that they have time over the weekend to get a head start. On Monday, the teacher discusses with the class the meaning of the assigned verses or phrases, especially going over any words that might not be familiar. On Tuesday, the teacher has the class say the verses in unison. At this time, the class might also break down the lesson and learn at least the first part of it. Then on Wednesday, the class finishes the rest of the verses and puts it all together. As time allows, the teacher finds it helpful to have students recite their memory work to a peer; they then take turns providing help and feedback to one another. Finally, on Thursday, each student individually goes to the teacher's desk and recites the lesson while the rest of the class works on another assignment. If a student has not learned the verses satisfactorily, he or she has a second chance on Friday. Since the objective is to have the student memorize the verses, the teacher gives those students who need it additional time to learn the verses during the next week.

Teachers should provide opportunities throughout the semester to go back and review lessons covered previously in order to assure that students remember verses in the long-term. It would also be beneficial for the class to have some opportunities to demonstrate to other classes, parents, and church members how well they have learned their Bible verses. As with other subjects and lessons, we want to make the memory process as positive and enjoyable as we can. Mixing up the routine and finding new and fun ways to carry out the lessons will prevent the class from getting in a rut. The memory verses can even be incorporated into a game at times.

Memory work still has significant benefits for the students. However, it must be done in a manner that brings out the value of studying and learning the Word of God, which thereby helps the students move the words from their heads to their hearts. As the apostle Paul writes in Colossians 3:16, "Let the word of Christ dwell in you richly, teaching and admonishing one another in all wisdom, singing psalms and hymns and spiritual songs, with thankfulness in your hearts to God." In a world full of many messages, how much more important is it for our minds to be filled with God's Word? May each student in our schools join in the words of Proverbs 6:21–22: "Bind them on your heart always; tie them around your neck. When you walk, they will lead you; when you lie down, they will watch over you; and when you awake, they will talk with you."

24

Blended and Online Learning
for Faith Formation

Bernard Bull

Welcome to the blended and online learning revolution. Every year, millions of people go online to
learn everything from fifth-grade language arts to
graduate-level advanced statistics. Some of these
are fully online learning experiences, meaning that
students are not required to meet with the teacher
or other classmates in person. Others are blended

> What are the
> implications of this
> blended and online
> learning revolution
> when it comes to
> teaching the faith?

learning experiences, a mix of online and face-to-face interactions with
a teacher and classmates. What are the implications of this blended and
online learning revolution when it comes to teaching the faith? Is it possible to teach the faith online or in blended-learning classrooms? If so,
what are the benefits and limitations of such a practice? Following are a
series of tips for thinking through such questions.

Put the Revolution in Historical Perspective

Many people think of blended and distance learning as innovations of
the digital age, but they have a much longer history. In fact, Christians
have used blended and distance learning for millennia. Take an example from the Early Christian Church. Many books in the New Testament
were letters written to people in another location. Sometimes the letter
came before a personal visit and teaching. Sometimes they came after a
personal visit. However, the letters themselves can be seen as a form of
distance learning, leveraging the dominant communication technology
of the day. As such, when Christians today think about using blended

and online learning for teaching the faith, they are joining a truly ancient practice in Christianity.

THINK ABOUT AFFORDANCE AND LIMITATIONS, NOT JUST GOOD AND BAD

Sometimes people are tempted to make broad judgments about blended and online learning. It can be much more helpful to think about what blended learning does well, what online learning does well, and what each type does less effectively. In other words, there are affordances and limitations to face-to-face learning environments, and there are affordances and limitations to online learning environments. The key is not to choose one or the other, but rather to consider how we can best use both to accomplish our goals in teaching the faith.

Consider, for example, how some research indicates the benefits of an asynchronous, online discussion (a discussion where students can type and share their answers with a group, but at different times of day, reading and replying to others at yet another time). Researchers find that students who might not speak up in class are sometimes more inclined to share their ideas in an online discussion. It allows them to read other responses, reflect in the privacy of their own home, and then construct a careful and thoughtful reply. Such a practice levels the playing field for discussions while also encouraging people to engage in more carefully considered responses, which can be helpful as we encourage students to meditate on the Scriptures and to consider the implications for their lives. At the same time, many of these online discussions lack the spontaneity or personal touch of sharing the same physical space with a teacher and small number of others. This is one example of hundreds of different benefits and limitations to online versus face-to-face instruction. By getting more informed about the others, you can learn to leverage a blend of both online and face-to-face instruction in powerful ways.

REMEMBER THAT NOT ALL CLASSES ARE THE SAME

When people start to talk about their opinions of blended and online learning, they sometimes make a novice mistake. They assume that all online classes are the same. The reality is that online learning can vary from one class or teacher to another as much as face-to-face classes differ. Many factors come into play: the size of the class, the teacher, the background of the students, the content and resources, the learning strategies employed, the assessment practices included, to name a few. As such, do not be too quick to rule out blended or online learning because of one bad experience or example. Learn about the many options and types, giving yourself a larger toolbox to use as you teach the faith.

Not All Teaching Is the Same

Suppose that I asked if you can drive. How would you respond? Most adults would reply in the affirmative, but what if I then pulled up a tractor trailer and asked you to drive it? Or what about a race car in the Indy 500? Being able to drive in one context doesn't mean you can easily drive in another. The same is true when it comes to teaching with blended and online learning. Yes, there are many teaching skills that transfer from one to another, but in another way, you are learning to drive in a new context. As such, respect the differences. Have the humility and curiosity to read and learn about effective and less-effective strategies for teaching in blended and online environments. There are a wealth of resources on the topic that we can use to deepen our knowledge and skill to teach in these different contexts.

Start with the Learning Goals and the Needs of Students

Who are you trying to reach and teach? What are the learning goals that you have in mind? By starting with these two questions, you will be able to more effectively decide when to employ blended and online learning. For example, perhaps your school wants to find new ways to support and connect with homeschool families, and these families do not have schedules that align with the school day. Then blended or online learning activities might be a solution. Or what if you are trying to teach confirmation across five rural parishes and you can't be at every place weekly? Perhaps there is a way to design a blended learning experience to address this problem. Maybe you want to find a way to help students spend more time reflecting, thinking about what they are learning, or sharing their ideas with one another between classes. Again, a blended or online learning strategy might help you achieve that goal. Blended and online learning might, in some instances, be a way to meet the needs of people whom you are serving or teach others who were otherwise unreached.

Think like a Designer

Designing effective blended and online learning experiences is not a matter of showing up for class and presenting a bunch of content. Of course, that is rarely effective in face-to-face teaching either. Instead, creating effective blended and online learning requires planning and designing. What do you want your students to learn? How will you know when they have learned it? How will you monitor their progress? How will you help them learn it? How will you help them remain engaged and active in the learning? How will you nurture a positive learning community? These are the questions that you want to ask and answer as you think about designing blended and online learning experiences for teaching the faith.

You Do Not Need to Be a Lone-Ranger Teacher

The good news is that there are tens of thousands of people online who have rich expertise in these practices, and most are happy to share their insights. Reach out to them and lean on them as you explore the benefits and limitations of teaching the faith through blended and online learning. There are at least three different fully online Lutheran high schools functioning today, and the higher education institutions in the Lutheran Church all have one or more people with expertise in these areas. Take advantage of their experience to refine your skill.

Blended and Online Learning Can Help Us Help One Another

Consider a rural Christian school with limited teachers and resources. Through blended and online learning, they can now connect with other Christian schools and ministries around the world to enhance the curriculum and learning experience for students. Classes can connect with missionaries on the mission field. Teachers can pull in experts in various areas of study. We are no longer bound to the people and resources in our immediate physical location, and this provides promising possibilities for designing rich and engaging teaching-the-faith lessons. It can be as simple as a key pal (the digital version of a pen pal) program or a quick videoconference with a person or group in another location. It can also be as complex as designing full online resources and coursework that can be used and shared among schools around the world. Many Christian educators, leaders, and schools are just beginning to tap into the power of being the Body of Christ in a connected world.

BLENDED AND ONLINE LEARNING CAN HELP US MEET THE NEEDS OF INDIVIDUAL STUDENTS

One strength of blended and online learning is that they both give us new ways of thinking about teaching and learning that sometimes help us meet individual needs of students. What if you have students in your class with widely different backgrounds when it comes to the Christian faith? You can use blended and online learning options to accommodate those differences instead of trying to use a single strategy that works for some and not for others. You can provide lessons that adjust the amount of time spent on something, the pace at which different students learn, and even the learning pathways they take to learn something new. If we believe that each person is a unique child of God, full of potential, then how can we use blended and online learning to honor God's unique handiwork of each person?

> If we believe that each person is a unique child of God, full of potential, then how can we use blended and online learning to honor God's unique handiwork of each person?

CONCLUSION

Physical community is an important part of the Christian Church and Christian education. The author of Hebrews reminds us not to neglect meeting together (10:25). God sent His Son in the flesh to this world and designed us as physical beings; making personal connections in a shared physical space is a powerful way to nurture Christian community and relationships. At the same time, embracing these gifts does not mean that we must reject or neglect the promise and possibilities of blended and online learning. Both can help us to teach the faith in our increasingly digital and connected world.

25

THE ROLE OF MUSIC IN TEACHING THE FAITH

Kenneth Kosche

Words and music independently affect heart and mind significantly. Combining language with music may at times seem to exceed the sum of the two parts, so powerful is the symbiosis. Madison Avenue has successfully exploited the technique for decades.[1] The worlds of sports, politics, and pop culture know and celebrate this power.[2] Propagandists of every era wrote words and tunes to influence public behavior, not especially altruistically. St. Paul also knew the power of word and music combined, but he expressed a far different perspective.

> *Let the word of Christ dwell in you richly, teaching and admonishing one another in all wisdom, singing psalms and hymns and spiritual songs, with thankfulness in your hearts to God. (Colossians 3:16)*

In a single sentence, St. Paul encapsulates the theme of this essay, linking the rich indwelling of the Word of Christ with the thankful response of singing. There is no doubt he believed such singing reinforced the indwelling of the Word of Christ. St. Paul is not engaged in sales or propaganda; nor does he advocate for a particular genre of music.[3] For

---

1   For a fascinating read, see Steve Karmen, *Through the Jingle Jungle: The Art and Business of Making Music for Commercials* (Lakewood, NJ: Billboard Books, 1989), 262. Try a little experiment: sing these jingles and fill in the blanks. "You deserve a break today at _____." "We are _____. Bum, ba dum, bum bum bum bum." "_____ is on your side." Getting rid of earworms like these may prove challenging. That is part of the marketing plan.

2   For instance, regarding pop culture, refer to the song "I Write the Songs" by the former Beach Boy Bruce Johnston, made popular by Frank Sinatra, Barry Manilow, and others. For a less sentimental expression, consider the genre of rap music and lyrics and its possible influence on thought and behavior.

3   We try too hard to separate "psalms, hymns, and spiritual songs." Paul's statement encompasses all of the kinds of sacred music familiar to the people of the time. Throughout his epistles, he quotes portions of hymns known to his readers. Cf. Romans 11:33–35; Ephesians 2:19–22; 5:14; Philippians 2:6–11; 1 Timothy 1:17; 6:15–16; Titus 3:4–7, among others.

the child of God, singing the faith is simultaneously a natural and powerfully effective activity. True in St. Paul's day, it is still true for us in the twenty-first century. Since this essay seeks to present a Lutheran perspective on the role of music in teaching the faith, let us do so by asking two uniquely Lutheran questions, namely, "What does this mean?" and "How are these things done?" In other words, what is meant by "the Word of Christ," which music and lyrics are best suited to faith formation, and how might we shape our pedagogy?

> For the child of God, singing the faith is simultaneously a natural and powerfully effective activity.

St. Paul also tells us, "So faith comes from hearing, and hearing through the word of Christ" (Romans 10:17). We sing of faith in its simplest form:

> Jesus loves me! This I know,
>
> For the Bible tells me so.
>
>> Little ones to Him belong;
>>
>> They are weak, but He is strong.
>
> Yes, Jesus loves me!
>
> Yes, Jesus loves me!
>
> Yes, Jesus loves me!
>
> The Bible tells me so.
>
> Jesus loves me! He who died
>
> Heaven's gates to open wide.
>
>> He has washed away my sin,
>>
>> Lets His little child come in. (*LSB* 588)

Countless little children have sung, memorized, and loved this simple song of faith. Perhaps you have as well. It tells us that the Word of Christ is *about* Him and *comes from* Him—"for the *Bible* tells me so."

Of course, children need eventually to be drawn into deeper biblical truths, which should be done through teaching the Word of Christ and singing about it.[4] Simple songs must be supplemented by other expressions of the faith as children grow in intellect and experience. A

---

4   Christ Himself tells us, ". . . teaching them to observe *all* that I have commanded you" (Matthew 28:20, emphasis added).

mistaken assumption holds that since children cannot understand more complicated matters, we should not challenge them with more complicated words and songs. Of course, common sense indicates the truth of this statement to a point, but it is also proper to challenge children to help them grow. An experienced teacher related that one of the favorite songs sung by her first and second graders years ago was "Christ Is Arisen" (*LSB* 459). Some adults shrink at the prospect of singing the tune in public worship (they ought not), but these children learned the tune and words and sang them with joy. When a substitute teacher asked her class for their favorite songs, they volunteered this one, causing quite a surprise for the substitute!

> **Songs learned in youth revisit a person throughout life.**

Songs learned in youth revisit a person throughout life. Concepts that were not clearly formed as a child may develop over time and bring richness to an adult's faith experience at an appropriate time. Some early challenges are worthwhile and may also prove the means for classroom discussion and explanation. This is true also for the Christian congregation and for pastors who shy away from hymns they consider "difficult" or unfamiliar.[5] Given the challenge, children and adults might actually learn to *like* the once unfamiliar songs!

The other side of the coin is true as well. My teaching career began in a unified public school system in which I taught music to the whole range of first graders through high schoolers. The first graders were excited to sing "Frère Jacques." It was a fun tune with odd words. The second graders liked it because they were singing in French *and* they could sing it as a round. But by third grade, they had outgrown it and were quite tired of it. The lesson learned was the need to stretch, grow, and learn new songs with more advanced ideas. The analogy to teaching the faith through music should be obvious. Singing about Noah and his "arky" is fun, but it teaches only so much and lasts only so long.

Where does one find music to sing that is well-suited to the development of faith? I say "sing" because purely instrumental or keyboard music, unless it reminds one of Christian texts, does nothing for faith formation. There is much music that sounds noble and can stir the emotions, such as Bach organ music. However, faith comes from "the Word of Christ." For purely aesthetic reasons, please do teach your children

---

5   A dear ninety-two-year-old congregant laughingly once chided me, "No more than one 'new' hymn on a Sunday morning!"—a valid point. However, singing no "new" hymns means the congregation's musical faith expression remains static.

Bach, but for faith formation, you must sing words. There are many fine collections of Christian songs for children. Sunday School and Vacation Bible School programs often provide songs written around a particular theme that can be taught and discussed. These have limited long-term benefits largely because the children never sing the songs again once the program has been presented. Concordia Publishing House has excellent materials for the general classroom and for children's choirs. Organizations like Choristers Guild[6] have developed a graded series of songs for children. However, a word of caution must be noted: whenever using literature from non-Lutheran organizations, check the lyrics for sound theology. Many a catchy tune has sold unsound theology. If you cannot embrace the words, do not promote the tune.

Consider teaching children hymns and portions of the liturgy. Unlike transient programs, worship regularly contains hymns and music from various liturgies. Liturgy is based upon or directly quotes Scripture. Learning hymns and liturgy as a child allows the child to become an active worshiper from an early age. If the classroom teacher, the parish musician, and the pastor can coordinate and do some advanced planning, this will not be a hit-or-miss proposition. Sadly, a close pastor friend of mine recently related that the teachers in his parish school refused to teach the *Venite* from Matins.[7] Their reason? "Why should we teach children something *they will never use*?"—this statement coming from teachers in a church that regularly worships using various settings of the Divine Service and the Office of Matins with a called Lutheran parish musician. Lord willing, their reaction is an anomaly, but I have observed an increasing number of Lutheran chapels and worship based on YouTube rather than being musically led personally by classroom teachers. Perhaps the dazzle of highly elaborate accompaniments combined with engaging visuals has beguiled teachers away from regularly singing with their children in a clear, pleasant, unpretentious voice, with or without keyboard accompaniment.

Somehow in our media-immersed society, we unfortunately accept the notion that unless there is a soundtrack with full orchestra, or at minimum a keyboard part blaring, singers cannot learn. On the contrary, modeling lyrics and melodies unadorned by accompaniment proves to be a far more effective teaching tool. The teacher can model specific pitches, words or phrases, and the *affect* of the song admirably without all the

6 See www.choristersguild.org.
7 The *Venite* is a setting of Psalm 95. See *LSB*, pp. 220–21.

distractions media can present. The teacher can also assess the accuracy of the singers immediately and make corrections as needed. The piano can be a crutch. Singing unaccompanied actually builds singers' confidence over time rather than teaching dependency on a keyboard or electronic device. Singers, especially young singers, can sense if the teacher lacks confidence, and they will mirror it in their own singing. If you are such a person, rather than avoid singing, sing all the more so that you can become self-assured in doing so with your students.

Consider the value in selecting a specific and finite repertoire and learning it thoroughly. In the age of Google, we unwittingly believe we can always search and find information, thus suggesting memorizing is an old-fashioned, outdated idea. Read a portion of the Collect for the Word, in which we pray:

> Grant that we may so hear them [the Scriptures], read, mark, learn, and inwardly digest them. (LSB, p. 308)

Something truly learned (memorized) can stay in the mind forever. "Knowing" means *knowing*; "knowing about" or "where to find it" signifies *less than knowing*. That which is securely known may be taken to heart. If a hymn or song is lengthy, consider memorizing only the beginning stanza, or if the song has a chorus, memorize the chorus or the refrain.

Finally, select lyrics that cover the whole range of human experience and interaction with the Almighty. Select music with a wide range of emotional affect. "Happy clappy" music represents only a tiny portion of a child's emotional and faith experience. Use words and music that have intense emotional impact as well as the more "cheerful" manifestations. For this reason, a valuable part of a child's repertoire ought to include settings of the Psalms either verbatim or in paraphrase. No other part of Scripture covers such a wide expression of the faith and human emotion. Here is an example. Together, sing Psalm 27:1: "The LORD is my light and my salvation; whom shall I fear? The LORD is the stronghold of my life; of whom shall I be afraid?" Then explain the text with questions: "Have you ever been afraid, perhaps afraid of the dark? What does it mean for the Lord to be your 'light' and your 'salvation?' How does He help you to not be fearful?" and so forth. In this way, faith is nurtured and the Word of Christ dwells richly in a child—and develops later as an adult. This is how a child takes it to heart.

Christian music serves an amazingly vital role in teaching and nurturing the faith, as the hymn "When in Our Music God Is Glorified" states so well:

> How often, making music, we have found
>
> A new dimension in the world of sound
>
> As worship moved us to a more profound
>
> > Alleluia!

> Let ev'ry instrument be tuned for praise!
>
> Let all rejoice who have a voice to raise!
>
> And may God give us faith to sing always:
>
> > Alleluia! (*LSB* 796:2, 5)[8]

---

8 Hymn text by Fred Pratt Green, copyright © 1972 Hope Publishing, Carol Stream, IL. Used by permission. All rights reserved.

26

GRADES, ASSESSMENT, AND FAITH FORMATION

Bernard Bull

Scan the Gospels for Jesus' approach to grading and assessment and you will notice something extraordinary. Jesus did not give a single popquiz or use tests aligned to national or state standards. He did not use multiple-choice or essay tests. He did not, at least not to the best of our knowledge, use a set of carefully planned formative and summative assessments to measure students' progress or document how they performed at the end of the "class." In fact, He did not even use letter grades. Yet, people learned from Him. At the same time, it would be a mistake to suggest that Jesus did not use assessments. Given these facts, what does it mean for those of us in Christian education? This essay is intended to serve as a tool for reflecting on the role of grading and assessment in teaching the faith. As such, I offer the following eight suggestions.

KEEP FIRST THINGS FIRST

The purpose of teaching the faith is just that, to teach the faith. We invite students into the study of God's Word. We teach Christian doctrine. We heed the words of Jesus in Matthew 28 by making disciples, teaching them to obey that which Jesus commanded. Whatever we choose to do with grades and assessment must be in service to this primary goal. As a result, instead of just assuming or embracing common schooling practice, we want to consider how these other approaches will help or hinder our goal of teaching the faith.

Pay Attention to the Difference between Formative and Summative Assessment

There are two common categories of assessment. Formative assessment is the type that is really about giving the teacher and student feedback on progress toward one or more learning goals. Summative assessment is the snapshot at the end, telling us what one did or did not learn. Formative assessment is like the checkup at the doctor's office, whereas summative assessment is like an autopsy. The checkup at the doctor's office allows the doctor to check on your health. The doctor conducts an exam and may perform tests that give the doctor and patient feedback on the patient's overall health. Based on that feedback, the doctor might suggest certain changes: eat differently, exercise more, get more rest. The more specific the suggestions, the more helpful. This is not a onetime event, but something done frequently enough that the patient has a chance to make changes and become healthier. The autopsy, on the other hand, does the patient no good. The information might help doctors learn how to better care for future patients, but it does nothing for the one being examined. That is sort of like the grades at the end of a class. While the student can learn something from the grade, it is in many ways too late. As such, when we are teaching the faith, formative assessments are among the most important forms of assessment for us. Our ultimate goal is to nurture students, not to grade, rank, rate, and sort them.

> Our ultimate goal is to nurture students, not to grade, rank, rate, and sort them.

When teaching the faith, we are not just trying to cover the material; we want students to learn. Formative checks for understanding (which do not necessarily need to be attached to grades at all) can be a helpful way to see when students are frustrated, confused, or misunderstanding a key teaching. We do not want students walking away from a lesson, unit, or class still confused or unclear about Christian doctrine, for example. That is why teachers of the faith are wise to engage in frequent, informal formative assessments.

Be Clear about What Grades and Assessments Do and Do Not Tell Us

If you opt to use traditional grades and assessments as part of teaching the faith, it is important to be clear (for ourselves, our students, and parents) what these grades tell us. If a student gets a C on a theology test,

Not being clear about the role and message of grades and scores may result in a Law and Gospel disaster.

what does that say about his faith? Does it mean that his faith is less or worse than the faith of a student who earned an A? If a student gets low scores on quizzes and tests, does it mean that the student is a bad Christian? Does God judge us according to our grades, tests scores, and quiz scores? These questions may seem silly to us, but not being clear about the role and message of grades and scores may result in a Law and Gospel disaster. The fact is that God's love for us in Christ does not change according to our performance in any class. Getting a lower grade or score may, however, indicate that a student did not understand an important concept or topic. That is the more important concern.

Consider the Purpose of Grading and Assessment

At its best, assessment in teaching the faith plays two important roles. First, it helps the teacher know how the student is doing. What does she understand? What confuses her? What gaps in knowledge exist? This is important information for a teacher, calling the teacher to adjust lessons accordingly, follow up with the student individually to clarify or address gaps, or provide additional encouragement and suggestions. Second, it provides feedback to the learners (and sometimes parents and others) about what they understand and what they do not. Feedback on progress toward a goal can be motivating and helpful. Just remember to keep the focus on the learning and not the assessments. The assessments exist to help people learn, help them see their progress, and help teachers adjust their teaching accordingly.

Consider the Role of Five Types of Assessment and Feedback

There are hundreds of ways to assess student learning, but they all fit into five main categories. Keeping these five in mind can be a helpful way to build a robust plan for feedback in the classroom, one that gives you and your students lots of information on how they are doing while also dealing with the reality that you, as a teacher, have only a limited number of hours in the day.

Instructor feedback. This is the type of feedback that we usually think about. It can be as simple as the teacher providing verbal or written direction to a learner. Of course, it can also be more complex. The teacher might use checklists, rubrics, or even audio- or video-recorded feedback as a student progresses on a project.

Peer feedback. Learners can help learners, using the same types of feedback listed for the instructor. Of course, some learners may not yet have much knowledge or ability in the subject; then it may be helpful to teach learners how to give good feedback, perhaps even using a rubric or checklist.

Self-feedback. The goal is for learners to be able to check their own progress and make the necessary adjustments. Again, some guides or structure may be helpful in certain cases, but as student confidence and competence increase, less direction is needed.

Computer-generated feedback. This could be something as simple as a self-paced tutorial (perhaps an uploaded presentation with a question on one slide and answers on the next). It could also be some sort of practice quiz that gives learners a sense of whether they understand basic concepts or vocabulary. Remember that this is formative, so it need not have a formal grade or mark associated with it. The important part is that it helps the individual learners (and the teacher) get feedback on how their learning progresses.

Mentor and outside adviser feedback. In this instance, I use *mentor* to mean people outside of the classroom. It could be an expert in the field, or it might be a family member or colleague who is willing to review work and give some helpful tips. This also has a way of adding some authenticity to the learning experience.

STRIVE FOR A CULTURE OF LEARNING OVER A CULTURE OF EARNING

Yes, letter grades motivate many students. The goal of earning an A or avoiding an F is often enough to help students study and prepare for that next exam. However, such a goal is not enough to help students develop a growing and persistent interest in what they are learning, one that will empower them to continue learning beyond the tests, or even to use or remember what they learned. While letter grades motivate, they also demotivate.

Letters grades don't have to be carrot-and-stick motivators. There are many educators who cultivate an environment that minimizes the role of grades as motivators while still using them. Ultimately, a teacher of the faith who depends upon letter grades as the sole or primary motivator risks missing out on the experience of cultivating a rich learning community of purpose and possibility. It is one thing to learn alongside a group that wants to get a good grade. It is a completely different experience to explore the wonders of God's Word with a group of people who develop a drive to learn for other reasons. There are many and better ways to help students stay engaged. Of course, many great teachers still use grades, but they do not use them as the primary motivator. That is a recipe for a culture of drudgery and compliance, something that can get in the way of our goal in teaching the faith.

MAKE SURE ASSESSMENTS ARE CONNECTED TO GOALS

Assessments are intended to check on student progress toward one or more goals in the lesson, unit, or class. If there are no clear goals, then we diminish the value of assessments. As such, we want to make sure we can clearly state what we want students to learn from each lesson, and then create ways to check on student progress toward meeting those goals. That relationship between goals and assessments is a powerful combination.

CONSIDER THE POSSIBILITIES

As we think about how to design classes and learning experiences for teaching the faith, it is helpful to recognize that there are no direct prescriptions in Scripture nor are we bound to use only traditional schooling practices. Tests, multiple-choice quizzes, essay exams, and letter grades are common realities in many schools; but it can be helpful to consider other ways to learn about how and what students are learning. In many modern education systems, grades and tests are a way of life, but we have immense freedom and flexibility. Allow yourself that freedom and flexibility as you consider how best to use assessments that truly help you nurture the faith of your students.

27

GOD IN THE SHINY OBJECTS

Leveraging Technology in Faith Formation
Matthew Bergholt

"Train up a child in the way he should go; even when he
is old he will not depart from it." (Proverbs 22:6)

One of the more talked about, if not controversial, topics in education today is the role of technology. In today's society, technology is embedded into almost every part of the world in which we live, and education is no exception. From a very early age, children are surrounded by smartphones, tablets, computers, and the immeasurable depth of media that such items present. Our students are unable to escape (nor may they want to) the stream of technology and information of which they are a part from before they roll out of bed in the morning until they finally drift off to sleep at night. Their time in the classroom is no exception. For the six or more hours of instructional time, students are faced with interactive whiteboards, mobile devices of every shape and size, and innumerable sources of educational media. Even if they are not surrounded by technology, it is a present thought throughout their day. "What am I going to play online when I get home?" "I wonder if I have any text messages so far today." "Did I remember to put my phone on vibrate before I put it in my locker?" All are possible thoughts running through the mind of a student on a constant basis. Society as a whole may need to take a step back to see how pervasive technology has become in our lives, especially for the youngest members of society.

Regardless where one falls on the continuum of the integration and role of technology in education, the single fact remains that technology is here to stay within society. It will not simply fade into the background as a fad or trend. The reality is that technology is and will be an integral part of the students in classrooms around the country for the rest of their lives.

So what are we to do with that reality? More important, what are we to do with this reality within Lutheran education? How do we embrace and encourage the idea of faith formation in the lives of students distracted and influenced by the ever-present buzz of technology? Or more simply put, how is the Word of God taught through, with, and among the "shiny objects"?

> How is the Word of God taught through, with, and among the "shiny objects"?

First and foremost, we cannot afford to run away from technology in the classroom. Gone is the time when educators could avoid technology in their personal life, let alone in their professional life. Students are quick to pick up on the educator who does not embrace, or at least acknowledge, the role of technology in the lives of students. Once students have this impression, it becomes much more difficult to build a relationship between the teacher and students. This relationship is perhaps the most critical component of faith formation in a student's life, regardless of technology. Without it, there is no foundation set in place for continued learning, growth, and development.

Second, educators need to embrace the idea of professional development and research in regard to educational technology. Ignorance is no longer an option. While it is okay to not keep up with all of the changes in the world of technology (a downright impossible task!), educators do need to set aside time in order to learn about what is new and emerging. This will benefit their classroom instruction as well as their interaction with students. Two easy ways to accomplish this are to find a regularly updated educational technology blog or website and visit it on a consistent basis; or take an online professional development course to enhance and hone skills related to technology you and your students already use in the classroom. Perhaps the easiest way would be to attend an educational technology conference and learn alongside fellow educators who find themselves in the same situation in the classroom as you. Whatever your decision, a specific dedication to professional growth regarding educational technology is essential to leveraging emerging technologies in the classroom.

Keeping these first two key points in mind, how can Lutheran educators leverage emerging technologies specifically to increase and strengthen their students' faith? How do we train up a student to be an upstanding child of God? How do we instill in them their role in society and the Church? Are we sending our students out into the world prepared for the society that they will enter? In reality, this is actually the easy part! The same conversations and discussions about Christian living and individual faith need to take place as they have in the past: discussions regarding the role of the Ten Commandments in a student's life today and in the future, discussions speaking to morality, and the role of a Christian in the world of the twenty-first century. The topics are endless. However, now these discussions may take place in a different medium, such as an online chat or virtual conversation. Students are now able to see and experience events around the globe as they happen in new and interactive ways. They have access to an unlimited amount of information, commentaries, and reactions to their faith as well as the faith of others. Additionally, new technologies bring new topics for discussion to the forefront of how it affects their faith. Online content creation and sharing can lead to a discussion about intellectual property and the Eighth Commandment. The rise of various instant-messaging apps and social-media platforms not only opens up conversations about digital citizenship and the lasting effect of an online presence, but it also allows for their use in the demonstration of student understanding and internalization of learning. There are so many new ways to approach these conversations and discussions regarding the role of technology in the life of a Christian, while at the same time leveraging them to facilitate and drive the interaction.

So, how does one effectively continue these discussions when a new technology emerges? There are four major stages necessary when looking at a new technology and how it can be used to strengthen the faith of a student instead of becoming just another shiny object.

The first stage is evaluation. Set aside time to take an in-depth look at what the technology is, what its integration within the classroom would look like, and whether it will drive conversation related to faith development. After evaluation, the next step is alignment. Looking at how the technology will fit within the existing structure or curriculum ensures a cohesive voice in alignment with existing resources. If, through evaluation and alignment, an emerging technology is found to be beneficial as a tool or to the conversation on faith development, then it is time to implement the emerging technology. This is where the individual educator or the school as a whole is actually able to put the technology into practice as a tool or embed it into the curriculum and begin seeing results among the students. The final and most often overlooked stage in effective implementation of emerging technology is the review process. Once a technology has been implemented as a tool or curricular piece, a reflective process needs to take place to gauge its effectiveness. Although many schools do this step informally, in reality it needs to be a formal process, as the reflective process is almost as important as the emerging technology itself. While these four stages are not hard-and-fast rules that must be followed word for word, it is beneficial to keep such a structure in mind when evaluating the role of an emerging technology in the faith development of a student.

In the coming years, new technologies will all make their way into mainstream society and, as such, into the educational setting. However, regardless of what appears in the realm of educational technology in the next years or even in the next week, the relationships, discussions, and conversations within Lutheran schools will still be driven by the same foundation that has existed for almost five hundred years. Christ as the cornerstone of faith development is the one thing that will not change, regardless of the shiny objects that seek to pull students away from that truth. Technology is and will remain a consistent presence in education for the indefinite future. Thus, it is up to the Lutheran educators to leverage the technologies of the world around them today in order to strengthen the faith development of students now and for the rest of their lives.

28

A Confirmation Primer: What, Why, and How

Mark Blanke

When you hear the word *confirmation*, what image pops into your head? Is it white-robed youth standing next to their pastor in the chancel of the church, smiling, red carnations on their robes, holding their confirmation certificates in hand? Is it a group of junior high students sitting on both sides of a long table in the church basement on a Wednesday afternoon?

We in the Lutheran Church are shaped by our own confirmation experience along with the traditions and expectations that have been placed on confirmation in our church for the past hundred-plus years. Any serious review of confirmation must try to separate the anecdotal evidence that informs our confirmation models from the biblical, confessional, and historical directives for confirmation practice. But before we can construct the what, why, and how, we need to unpack some of what we commonly understand as "confirmation."

> Any serious review of confirmation must try to separate the anecdotal evidence that informs our confirmation models from the biblical, confessional, and historical directives for confirmation practice.

This is where things get interesting. There isn't a biblical directive for confirmation as practiced today. Neither do our Lutheran Confessions contain explicit guidelines that would influence how we practice confirmation. As for a historical directive, the things that have been said about confirmation and the variance of practices that we have seen make it difficult to find any solid footing for a "preferred practice." Some will find this lack of directives to be uncomfortable, and some will discover

> There are questions that must be asked and answered if we are to make effective use of this wonderful learning opportunity that we call "confirmation."

a newfound freedom in that news. However, there are questions that must be asked and answered if we are to make effective use of this wonderful learning opportunity that we call "confirmation."

What is confirmation? In Early Church history, confirmation was just the dismissal after one was baptized. In the 1400s, the Catholic Church declared it a sacrament. Luther cautioned against an overemphasis on confirmation for fear that it may detract from Baptism. He said, "I would permit confirmation as long as it is understood that God knows nothing of it, and has said nothing about it, and that what the bishops claim for it is untrue."[1] In the 1960s, the LCMS participated in a study of confirmation. From this study, the following definition was developed and approved by the Synod: "Confirmation is a pastoral and educational ministry of the church which helps the baptized child through Word and Sacrament to identify more deeply with the Christian community and participate more fully in its mission."[2] The Small Catechism defines confirmation as "a public rite of the church preceded by a period of instruction designed to help baptized Christians identify with the life and mission of the Christian community."

While these definitions vary, they seem to focus on two desired outcomes—participants will be more fully connected to their church and more able and willing to participate in its mission. Is that the outcome that you are seeing from your confirmation efforts? LCMS pastors reported that only 46 percent of members were still active in the church just four years after completing their confirmation experience.[3] With those type of results, we have reason to be skeptical that we are achieving these stated outcomes for confirmation.

Perhaps these definitions do not highlight the outcomes really owned by the Church. Anecdotal evidence and evidence from research completed by Dr. Marvin Bergman in 2010[4] indicates that many deliver a confirmation program that constitutes a type of doctrinal primer for our youth.

---

1   LW 45:24.

2   "The Report of the Joint Commission on the Theology and Practice of Conformation to the Honorable Presidents of the American Lutheran Church, Lutheran Church in America, and The Lutheran Church—Missouri Synod" (1970), 39.

3   Institute for Religious Education, "The State of Christian Education in The Lutheran Church—Missouri Synod" (2006). Unpublished.

4   Marvin Bergman, *What's Happening in LCMS Confirmation?: A Summary of Findings Based on Nine Populations*, accessed February 25, 2016, http://www.cune.edu/resources/docs/Research/youth-confirmation-report-July-2010.pdf.

If the hoped-for outcome is a clearer understanding of our doctrine, how are we doing?

In his research, Milo Brekke sought to determine how children who attended Lutheran schools were different than those who didn't. Brekke found that there were some negative outcomes for those students who only attended during their junior high years (seventh through ninth grades). Brekke posited that the negative outcomes correlated with the students' inability to handle abstract concepts and went on to say,

> The research . . . also raises important questions about the relevance of the methods being used in confirmation instruction and parochial education in general at that point in the developmental process of the youth. The research . . . supports the contention that inability to handle high level abstractions is characteristic of the majority of young people of average ability at grades 7–8. For most of them such ability is not fully developed. At least they are unable to cope well with the highly abstract, logically structured, and doctrinal instruction typical of a religious education and confirmation instruction given at that age. The research indicated that an expected outcome of such instruction is a kind of learning that fixes immature, concrete, and rigid conceptualization that is highly resistant to later influences and developments necessary for the maturing of an articulate adult faith.[5]

Bergman's research provides data supportive of Brekke's concerns. For example, 97 percent of confirmation leaders said that the topic of Holy Communion was given "major" attention in their program. When asked how frequently the topic of Holy Communion was discussed in classes, 97 percent of recent confirmands stated that the topic was "discussed often" or "discussed sometimes." Only 6 percent of confirmation leaders stated that "prepare to receive Holy Communion" was not an important goal in their confirmation program. In fact, 96 percent of new confirmands believed that the goal to "prepare to receive Holy Communion" was either fully or mostly achieved through their confirmation experience. Yet, when asked to complete the statement, "In Holy Communion, one receives . . ." only 36 percent of confirmands responded by saying "Christ's body and blood and bread and wine." Despite the strong emphasis on this topic by confirmation leaders, approximately

---

5   Milo Brekke, *How Different Are People Who Attended Lutheran Schools?* (St. Louis: Concordia, 1974), 116.

two-thirds of confirmands could not identify the Lutheran response.[6] Could it be that students at the seventh- and eighth-grade level were just developmentally incapable of understanding this highly abstract concept? This is just one example of a challenge that we may face if we seek to focus primarily on confirmation as a doctrinal primer.

Without a biblical or confessional directive mandating confirmation instruction, and with anecdotal and statistical evidence that our current methods are not achieving our stated or unstated goals, we need to look anew at the what, why, and how of confirmation.

WHAT?

When district executives and university and seminary professors were asked, "What is the level of clarity of the purpose and goals of confirmation among pastors?" 15 percent of respondents said "High," 34 percent said "Moderate," and 51 percent said "Low."[7] Clarifying the "what" is not an easy task.

A formative question when asking what confirmation is, is to first ask, "Who confirms?" Any growth of faith in the heart of a believer is always the work of the Spirit, but there is also a participatory nature of the confirmation experience. When pastors were asked, "In your perspective, who does the confirming in the Rite of Confirmation?" 37 percent said "the pastor," 16 percent said "the congregation," 34 percent said "the youth," and 14 percent said "other."[8]

Clarifying who is confirming will help to define the "what." If the learner is confirming his or her desire to participate more fully in the mission of the Church, then that should clarify the goal or purpose of the learning experience. If the pastor is confirming that the learner has demonstrated a grasp of the key teachings of the Church, then that should also help define the "what." Since confirmation fits firmly into the adiaphora category of Church practices, then any answer to the question of "Who confirms?" is valid (as long as the Spirit's role in developing and sustaining faith is clearly affirmed and it isn't perceived as adding anything to Baptism); but how we answer that question will drive our understanding of what it is.

---

6   Bergman, *What's Happening in LCMS Confirmation?*
7   Bergman, *What's Happening in LCMS Confirmation?*
8   Bergman, *What's Happening in LCMS Confirmation?*

WHY?

We practice confirmation because it provides a valuable time to connect with our youth on matters uniquely related to the Church. Ninety percent of parents of confirmands agree with the statement that "for most Lutherans, confirmation is the most important Christian education event in their lives," as do 81 percent of pastors.[9] While one may argue regarding the virtue of such opinions, the data provides us with an understanding about the perception of value that key stakeholders have for the confirmation experience. Parents and pastors are likely to support and encourage this learning experience, and that might be enough of a "why" in these days of decreasing dedication to Church practices and influence.

HOW?

If you accept the definition of confirmation as helping the confirmand to identify with and participate in the life and mission of the Church, the way we practice it might look a lot different than what we see today in many churches and Lutheran schools.

If ongoing participation is a goal, we should do everything we can to make the rite look as little like a graduation as possible. (Some have suggested having the rite when students *start* their confirmation experience.) If we want confirmands to identify with their church, we better do more to help them understand the mission and ministry of their church . . . and equip them for participation. If we think having a good grasp of our doctrine is crucial to identifying with that mission, we need to teach the more abstract concepts when they have the mental capabilities to handle those concepts.

The 1970 report recommended that we implement a "longer and later" confirmation experience, starting at fifth grade and ending around tenth grade. It also recommended separating first communion from the completion of confirmation. We know that families have the greatest influence on the faith development of children, so if faith development is seen as a priority, one would be negligent not to include family participation.

Best practices related to confirmation start by first defining your preferred outcomes and designing an experience that has the best potential to achieve those outcomes. Start by deconstructing what you thought

---

9   Bergman, *What's Happening in LCMS Confirmation?*

confirmation had to be and reconstruct it with the freedom of knowing that there isn't a single way that it has to be done. Use innovation coupled with effective educational methodologies to shine the hidden gem that is confirmation in the Lutheran Church.

29

INTERGENERATIONAL APPROACHES TO TEACHING THE FAITH

Jill Hasstedt

Paul wrote to Timothy, "I am reminded of your sincere faith, a faith that dwelt first in your grandmother Lois and your mother Eunice and now, I am sure, dwells in you as well" (2 Timothy 1:5). The home was the heart of Timothy's faith formation, but Paul became his spiritual father. The gathering of believers was also a "household of faith." This frequently iterated Pauline concept is perhaps most fully developed in Galatians: "So then, as we have opportunity, let us do good to everyone, and especially to those who are of the household of faith" (6:10). The Church is pictured as a collection of adopted sons and daughters of the Father with an elder brother, Paul, teaching his spiritually younger brothers and sisters as little children and all being heirs of the Kingdom "in Christ" (Galatians 4:1–20).[1]

The North American culture is changing. Nearly one in five United States residents will be age 65 or older by 2030. At the same time, the youngest generation, "Generation Z," will make up a quarter of the population sometime in the 2020s,[2] and these younger generations are moving back in with their parents. "Multigenerational families bunking together is hardly news in certain cultures. In 2009, 9.4 percent of Asian households, 9.5 percent of African American ones and 10.3 percent of Latino homes were multigenerational (compared with 3.7 percent of non-Hispanic white households). But strong indications show that

---

1   Leland Ryken, James C. Wilhoit, Tremper Longman III, eds. "Galatians" in *Dictionary of Biblical Imagery* (Downers Grove, IL: InterVarsity Press, 1998).
2   Grayson K. Vincent and Victoria A. Velkoff, "The Next Four Decades: The Older Population in the United States: 2010 to 2050," US Census Bureau (May 2010), accessed February 25, 2016, http://www.census.gov/prod/2010pubs/p25-1138.pdf.

> We are returning to a more intergenerational and historically "normal" model of household life but in a far more multicultural landscape.

multigenerational living is on the rise."[3] We are returning to a more intergenerational and historically "normal" model of household life but in a far more multicultural landscape. In the midst of this great change, God's people have an important role to play in offering light and hope.

At any given time, most Christian congregations have a ministry that includes five or six generations. While older models of pedagogy typically separated generations, a revival of sorts is taking place as recognition of emerging cultural patterns affects educational models. Paul's concept of the "household of faith" is ripe for recapture.

Likely Objections

Can a four-year-old, a fourteen-year-old, a forty-four-year-old, and an eighty-four-year-old learn anything together? If you simplify things for the four-year-old, will anyone else learn anything? These objections are real and should be acknowledged, but they misunderstand the overall purpose of intergenerational learning strategies. This style of instruction is not meant for every situation. There will always be a need for age-specific ministry and programming. However, extreme age stratification and separation is not healthy for the Church or society.

The Purpose of Intergenerational Learning Strategies

Charlotte's Web is a well-known children's story with an adult message about the importance of love, sacrifice, and interconnectedness. In the story, an "intergenerational relationship" exists between a childlike pig named Wilbur, a little girl named Fern, and a wise and mature barn spider named Charlotte. When Wilbur boasts that he could spin a web if he tried, it is Fern who ponders that even though spider webs are strong, the individual threads can still get torn and broken by the insects they capture. Charlotte must be watchful, mending and tending the strands of her web to reconnect them and reweave the web when it becomes full of holes.[4]

---

3   Sally Abrahms, "3 Generations Under One Roof," *AARP Bulletin* (April 2013), accessed February 25, 2016, http://www.aarp.org/home-family/friends-family/info-04-2013/three-generations-household-american-family.html.
4   E. B. White, *Charlotte's Web* (New York: HarperCollins, 1980), 55.

Intentionally building bridges between generations reduces the "isolation and extreme independence that are like insects in the web that cause it to tear in places." This web is "like the safety net that lies below circus performers ready to catch them if they fall. It is of little use if it is full of holes. Small holes might still provide some measure of safety but small holes in a safety net allow the smallest bodies to fall through first."[5] Intergenerational education helps to reweave the web that allows generations to connect deeply, to pass on their faith and their values, and to more ably live out their Christian vocations in their homes, workplaces, communities, and the world.

Intergenerational educational approaches should be used when the purpose of the event or process is to

- build social relationships and understanding across generations;
- improve relational skills and communication across generations;
- facilitate faith sharing and faith building beyond mere accumulation of knowledge (to know God rather than to just know about God[6]);
- model lifelong learning;
- provide pathways for older and younger people to become more accessible to one another;
- decrease the isolation of the old and the insulation of the young;
- provide opportunities for mutual coaching and mentoring;
- pray for one another;
- "stir up one another to love and good works" (Hebrews 10:24); and
- reduce extreme age stratification and isolation.

PRINCIPLES FOR INTERGENERATIONAL EDUCATION

While there is a science to intergenerational teaching and learning, there is also an art to it that requires intuition, creativity, and innovation. Some principles may help:

1. **Keep in mind that process is more important than product.** Bringing generations together for a positive relational

---

5 Jill Hasstedt, "Reweaving the Web for Families" (master's thesis, University of Illinois, Springfield, 1994), 4.

6 Holly C. Allen, "Nurturing Children's Spirituality in Intergenerational Settings," *Lutheran Educational Journal* 139, no. 2 (2004): 114.

experience is more important than the activity you are using to do so or the finished product you are trying to create. One church worked together to build a playground. A small group of men grabbed the power tools and set to work to get the job done, but when reminded of the importance of process, they became tutors showing those with less experience how to use tools and practice safety. Five-year-olds hammered. Preteens and teens cut wood with a table saw as older workers helped guide boards and coached novices. Preschoolers helped deliver water to workers. It took longer, but it worked better.

2. **Have a clearly defined purpose.** Whatever your purpose, be sure to think it through and state it clearly. See the above list for ideas and examples.

3. **Seed understanding.** There is a big difference between the expectations the oldest generations had of life as they started out and those of the youngest.[7] The Korean and Vietnam War generations saw changes wrought by the Civil Rights and women's movements of the mid-1900s, and they largely still benefited from the American Dream and a burgeoning middle class. The emerging Generation Zs or Plurals[8] are starting the twenty-first century with the continuance of a four-decade decline in two-parent families, a wide cultural acceptance of gay marriage, and a diminishing belief in the American Dream at a time when the middle class is shrinking. Knowing generational research and teaching some of it as we develop intergenerational programming is essential to seeding understanding. (And no one does generational research better then William Strauss and Neil Howe.)

4. **Teach relational skills.** Don't assume people know how to interact. Teaching the "five finger rule" helps if one person or group dominates conversation. If someone speaks, he is instructed to raise his thumb in his lap. Four other people must speak (raise the other four fin-

> Don't assume people know how to interact.

---

7   William Strauss and Neil Howe, *Generations: The History of America's Future, 1584 to 2069* (New York: William Morrow and Company, 1991).

8   Magid Generational Strategies, "The First Generation of the Twenty-First Century: An Introduction to the Pluralist Generation," accessed February 25, 2016, http://www.magid.com/sites/default/files/pdf/MagidPluralistGenerationWhitepaper.pdf.

gers to count) before that person may speak again. Help people learn or remember good listening skills or how to work at understanding.

5. **Start somewhere.** If you see a pattern of extreme age stratification and want to ameliorate it, pick one program or event that already exists and ask, "What can be done to make this become more intergenerational-friendly?"

6. **Identify key influencers.**[9] Gather several generations and pull them together for a conversation about ideas, challenges, problems (holes) they see, and possibilities before you begin. Then fill any "holes" they identify before someone falls through them.

7. **Do something together.** "Doing" builds bridges of cooperation and communication in nonthreatening ways. A devotion using Romans 8:28 on how God works to make good come from difficult circumstances can reference the old phrase "When life gives you lemons, make lemonade," and groups can work together to make lemonade from scratch while discussing key questions for faith sharing.

8. **Plan good questions.** Good questions invite great sharing. For the lemonade-making activity above, try these: How does God work? If everything doesn't turn out all right, does God still love us? What is God's ultimate plan for us? Where have you seen God make things work together for good in your life?

9. **Understand differing ability levels**. An older adult might not be able to kneel on cement to do a chalk drawing, and a younger child might not have scissor skills for cutting felt, but they could work together to accomplish both.

10. **Be prepared to modify time or content.** If the group goes off on a tangent but communication and process are working well, let it happen. Be flexible.

11. **Involve learners as leaders.** The young and old should be teaching and learning from one another. Design ways for each generation to shine.

9 Brad Griffin, "Intergenerational Ministry beyond the Rhetoric," Sticky Faith Leader, accessed February 25, 2016, http://www.stickyfaith.org/articles/intergenerational -ministry-beyond-the-rhetoric.

12. **Use scaffolding.** In education, scaffolding is the support given during the learning process. As competence is achieved, the support structures are removed and more responsibility is given to the student. Plan in such a way as to have the participants be as responsible as possible for what happens and as successful as possible.

13. **Divide and conquer.** If an activity is too complicated to be done in one session, parcel it out to two or more. A church making nativity characters out of 2 × 4 blocks and felt for Advent could make Mary and Joseph and Jesus one year, angels the next, and the Wise Men a third year. Over three years, participants would make a whole set. All kinds of households could be encouraged to post "selfies" of their sets being used at home.

14. **Evaluate.** Involve participants (and key influencers) in evaluation. Learn from what worked and what didn't, and listen for other approaches they might suggest.

Intergenerational learning strategies that build strong relationships between generations help to create a strong safety net of relationships that protects the youngest and reduces isolation of the old while enriching the lives of all. Bonds are formed. Wisdom is shared. Faith challenges are tackled. Most important, these relationships bind people to the Church and to one another in Jesus' name so that the passing of faith from generation to generation can happen in the most organic way possible.

Context
and Culture

In 1 Corinthians 9:22–23, the apostle Paul tells us, "I have become all things to all people, that by all means I might save some. I do it all for the sake of the gospel, that I may share with them in its blessings." In 1 Peter 3:15, Peter reminds us, "Always [be] prepared to make a defense to anyone who asks you for a reason for the hope that is in you; yet do it with gentleness and respect." These and many other passages remind us about the importance of remaining faithful to the unchanging truths of God's Word, but also responding to the times in which we live, attending to the distinct contexts and cultures where we live and serve. These truths are also an important part of Lutheran education. As such, the final section of essays in this text are devoted to culture and context, considering what it means and looks like to engage in the Lutheran teaching ministry in the contemporary world.

As a way of remembering that Lutheran education is much larger than our local context, Jonathan Laabs, a long-standing champion for a global perspective on Lutheran education, writes the introductory essay for this final section. In it, he reminds all of us in Lutheran education that we are part of a worldwide ministry that spans centuries and nurtures the faith in a broad cross section of people from diverse cultures and contexts. Right after that, John Mehl gives us a missionary perspective on Lutheran education; he reminds us about the importance of listening and learning, building relationships, approaching our work with humility, and embracing the opportunity to proclaim the Gospel. After all, our education is not only one that prepares people for life in this world but also one that equips people for eternity.

For many serving in Lutheran education, it has become increasingly clear that our world has changed. People who once found themselves in contexts that were largely welcoming of a distinctly Christian understanding of the world now find themselves in a post-Christian setting. Jill Hasstedt helps us reflect on what it means to teach the faith in a post-Christian context, and Grant Carey writes about teaching the faith to many who hold a worldview and belief system that clashes with a confessional Lutheran understanding of faith and life. How do you teach the faith to a generation of many who believe, for example, that ultimately God just wants us all to be good, nice, and fair to one another? Marty Kohlwey addresses this worldview and other attacks on our faith, naming the challenges that come our way as well as providing questions to use as a way to approach these challenges in faith and trust in our Lord.

In addition, I offer an essay that examines the way in which the digital world has affected the beliefs and values of people around the world. What does it mean and look like to engage in Lutheran education in an increasingly digital and post-Christian world? Harvey Schmit adds an important voice about how Lutheran schools can make sense of external standards and expectations on academics while remaining faithful to that which is distinct about what we teach.

Yet another contextual consideration for those in Lutheran education is the diversity of teaching and learning models. As such, Cheryl Swope explores homeschooling, providing us with a primer and overview of the homeschool movement, one of the faster growing types of K–12 schooling. Don and Joyce Kortze extend the conversation about homeschooling by introducing us to how the Lutheran school community might embrace and partner with homeschool families.

Having examined various approaches to the cultures and the contexts in which we engage in Lutheran education, we finish this text with a final essay from Kim Marxhausen. She provides a wonderful conclusion to our collection by helping us think about nurturing a distinctly Christian learning community. In an increasingly post-Christian context, Kim provides a guide for maintaining a truly distinctive Christian community, one that honors and supports the primary calling of parents to nurture the faith of their children.

May this final section of essays further fuel the fire of your reflection about and preparation for the teaching ministry. As Martin Luther wrote in reference to the universities of his day, "I greatly fear that schools for higher learning are wide gates to hell if they do not diligently teach the Holy Scriptures and impress them on the young folk."[10] Yet, those of us serving in Lutheran education have the great honor and responsibility of making sure that Luther's fears about schools do not come to reality, that we continue to provide havens where the Gospel reigns supreme, and where the words of Deuteronomy 6:4–9 are lived out daily.

> Hear, O Israel: The LORD our God, the LORD is one. You shall love the LORD your God with all your heart and with all your soul and with all your might. And these words that I command you today shall be on your heart. You shall teach them diligently to your children, and shall talk of them when you sit in your house, and when you walk by the way, and when you lie down, and when

---

10 Martin Luther, *What Luther Says* (St. Louis: Concordia, 1959), § 1327.

*you rise. You shall bind them as a sign on your hand, and they
shall be as frontlets between your eyes. You shall write them on
the doorposts of your house and on your gates.*

30

LUTHERAN EDUCATION: A GLOBAL PERSPECTIVE

Jonathan C. Laabs

It was Martin Luther who first set the tone for global Lutheran education almost five hundred years ago: "When schools flourish, things go well and the church is secure"[1] and "I greatly fear that schools for higher learning are wide gates to hell if they do not diligently teach the Holy Scriptures and impress them on the young folk."[2] Luther's passion for education and the theology behind his words propelled Christian education in a new direction and inspired church leaders to develop new strategies for outreach.

Even the most visionary of reformers and education leaders could not have anticipated the significant growth and expansion of Lutheran education in all parts of the world. As Christians are called to carry out the Great Commission ("Go therefore and make disciples of all nations, baptizing them in the name of the Father and of the Son and of the Holy Spirit" [Matthew 28:19]), it is only natural that teaching has been a basis for spreading the Word of God through the centuries. Factors such as travel opportunities, publication innovations (remember the Gutenberg Press?), and the vast array of technological innovations have made possible what could never be dreamed in previous centuries. But at the center of global Lutheran education is still the mission heart.

> But at the center of global Lutheran education is still the mission heart.

Following the Reformation in Europe, the growth of the Church took new forms as communities of believers spread into many parts of the

---

1   LW 54:452.
2   Martin Luther, *What Luther Says* (St. Louis: Concordia, 1959), § 1327.

world. Such travel was motivated both by the simple desire to carry God's Word to other lands and by the need to escape religious conflict (and sometimes persecution) occurring as a result of changes in the church and in society. Missionaries took along with them their traditions, their languages, and their cultures. As they settled in new lands, their influence on the indigenous people was significant. One thing they all had in common was the desire to spread the Word of God to places and people who had not yet heard and to "make disciples of all nations." Pastors led, and congregations were formed. In their earliest efforts, and on the basis of the teaching of Martin Luther, this instruction was also initiated in the home and developed through formal education in schools.

EDUCATIONAL MISSION FOUNDATIONS

Many stories have been told about the early days of mission work from Europe to other countries. Some major examples of such movements were the sending of missionaries through some twenty-three German mission societies in the early and middle part of the nineteenth century. After many years of struggle and search for identity in these Lutherans' own homeland, numerous missionary efforts resulted in new locations of congregations and schools on several continents. During the early 1800s, German settlers found their way to locations such as South Africa, Australia, southern Brazil, Latin America, Palestine, India, and North America. In each place, priority was placed on establishing schools for the children of the missionaries, but they also offered an education for the children of the people they were serving. Such a model established the beginning of today's outreach and mission orientation.

In many of the countries where early missionary activity took place and congregations grew, formal church organizations formed, and denominations were often the result of this coordinated effort. Such church bodies usually kept close ties to their founding church affiliates and other bodies who shared their doctrinal beliefs, resulting in many forms of fellowship; there were also divisions caused by disagreements among those bodies. But Christian education remained a priority at the local level.

As the church systems grew, so did the school population. In many cases—such as in Australia, the United States, Canada, Hong Kong, and Brazil, where the quantity of Lutheran schools blossomed over the years—systems were established to provide ongoing support for the educators, boards, and congregations engaged in operating the programs. School offices were formed at the national levels in many of the denominations and often at a district or regional level as well. Professional organizations and other supporting agencies were also formed in response to the demand for growth. In recent years, new initiatives for the development of such professional organizations have been seen in Asia, Africa, and Central America.

In places such as China, Papua New Guinea, Indonesia, and many parts of Africa, formal missionary work was the result of new outreach originating in the very countries that benefited from the original German and other European mission efforts of previous decades. Beginning in the early 1900s and growing significantly through the twentieth century, mission sites were established by denominations, mission organizations, and even individual congregations in countries throughout Africa, Central and South America, and Asia. Many of these later mission starts also resulted in the establishment of their own church bodies, and the relationship among the denominations grew. Schools were almost always associated with the growth of the Lutheran Church as it has developed in the last century. Christian education has remained at the center of outreach.

Most schools connected in some way with the Lutheran Church around the world serve primarily those students who are residents of their own country. However, the past five decades have seen an increase in the development of international schools, which reach beyond the national students and serve expatriates who live in their midst. Three international schools in Hong Kong, Shanghai, and Hanoi are currently operated by The Lutheran Church—Missouri Synod. Highland Lutheran International School in Papua New Guinea and Buena Vista Concordia International School in China are other examples of international schools located along the Pacific Rim. It is likely that such growth will continue. Parents who find themselves in foreign countries want the same type of quality education for their children as if they were at home. The added value of a Christian context for their students is attractive. For the Church, the presence of Christian schools in predominantly non-Christian communities provides a rich opportunity for outreach and meaningful ministry, often in places where no other approach is allowed.

CHALLENGES AND QUESTIONS

Lutheran education has experienced its share of problems and changes over the centuries since Martin Luther challenged the conventional church. Schools have been the victims of theological and structural obstacles within the church itself: education has sometimes been diminished as a ministry priority, leadership has changed, and denominational differences have restricted growth.

However, most of the challenges experienced by Lutheran schools through the years have come from outside. Demographic decline in areas that once were Lutheran strongholds, economic problems that increasingly have global implications, and societal pressures from many angles are all responsible for changes to the kind of Lutheran education that our forefathers developed and nurtured. In some cases, this has caused school closings; in a disturbing number of new cases, these factors have been responsible for an erosion in what the Lutheran school can and should bring to its community.

> How can the Church provide the most relevant education opportunities for children of all ages, both those who are affiliated with the Church and those whom the Church can clearly reach in new ways?

Important questions about the future of Lutheran education have been raised in recent years, such as how to best fund Lutheran schools, how to ensure qualified and committed educators (in response to a significant reduction in the output of trained Lutheran college graduates), and what constitutes the best school for the community it serves. It is clear that people's needs are changing, and their expectations of schools are higher than ever.

How can the Church provide the most relevant education opportunities for children of all ages, both those who are affiliated with the Church and those whom the Church can clearly reach in new ways? In a changing post-Christian world, how can the basic mission of the Church—commanded of us in Matthew 28—be best focused on the people and communities in which it is clearly embedded?

OPPORTUNITIES AND JOYS

If Martin Luther were around today, he would probably have stated most of the things he said and wrote in exactly the same way. He would likely have been intrigued, however, with the myriad new opportunities that God has given the Church to take His saving Word into all the world.

The years since Luther's ministry in the sixteenth century have opened doors that he could not have imagined, but would have enjoyed seeing in action. With the current opportunities that God has provided in this world and a vision for new things to come, the Church and education communities might consider the following directions for the future of global Lutheran education:

- Continue to develop and coordinate the training programs and service opportunities at Lutheran higher education institutions.
- Activate new organizations, conferences, and professional development opportunities in countries around the world that have Lutheran schools and other Christian education programs. Build upon the global Lutheran education initiatives already undertaken by Lutheran Education Association (LEA), Lutheran Education Australia, and Asia Lutheran Education Association.
- Establish alliances of agencies and church organizations across denominational lines that focus on Christian education in the context of the Lutheran Church.
- Provide exposure to global Lutheran education experiences for university students, field educators, and retired educators through servant events and short-term and long-term opportunities.
- Facilitate the identification of and support for professional educators to serve in Lutheran education settings at the national and international levels.
- Publicize and support the work of mission organizations that specifically emphasize education as the basis for their ministry (e.g., Garuna Foundation and LeadaChild).
- Identify the countries that currently have schools as part of their Lutheran ministry outreach and include their educators in LEA's Global Lutheran Educators Network.
- Bring together (both physically and virtually) leaders and educators from all parts of the world who have in common the vision for Lutheran education in their settings.

NEW DIRECTION FOR MISSION AND MINISTRY

Many church leaders, local congregations, missionaries, and leaders worldwide have observed that education may increasingly be the best opportunity for outreach, foundation for evangelism, and means

> Education may increasingly be the best opportunity for outreach, foundation for evangelism, and means of reaching the lost that Christians have for mission work today.

of reaching the lost that Christians have for mission work today. In some cases, it is the *only* way of having a formal presence in a country. God has blessed the work of countless missionaries and all those who have supported them through the last five centuries. The charge of Martin Luther to stay rooted in Holy Scripture so that "when schools flourish, things go well and the church is secure" has remained at the heart of Lutheran education growth and development through the decades. Schools, educators, leaders, and supporting agencies have made it possible for people of all ages to hear the Word of God, practice it in their daily lives, and share it with others in many places throughout the world.

Today's innovations and global interdependence have made it possible for each of us to become part of a worldwide Lutheran education mission in ways never before available. Getting involved personally in experiences, travel, and events is more possible than ever. Countless resources are available on the Internet, as well as many opportunities to be connected to the global Lutheran education network. More important, each person who understands the value of education as a foundational part of every person's life and catches the vision for how the Church can use this God-given ministry can pray each day for all those who serve in so many countries and for the continuing growth of Lutheran education around the world.

31

A MISSIONARY MIND-SET

Our God Is a Sending God

John Mehl

Our English word *mission* comes from the Latin noun *missio*, which can be translated as "a sending." In the Bible, we see how God sends Himself and others, sometimes to proclaim judgment but more often in attempts to rebuild broken relationships with His children. Some of the most beautiful words in the Bible come immediately after the fall when Adam and Eve are hiding. God comes looking for them in the garden and asks, "Where are you?" (Genesis 3:9). He wants His children back. In the Old Testament, we read how when His children wandered away, He sent judges and prophets to recall them. In the New Testament, we see the disciples sent to call the lost and suffering and proclaim the kingdom of God. The message is always the same: "Where are you? Your God wants a right relationship with you."

The ultimate sending, of course, is when Jesus is sent to suffer the punishment we deserve. Paul reminds us that "for our sake He made Him to be sin who knew no sin, so that in Him we might become the righteousness of God" (2 Corinthians 5:21). When Jesus asked, "My God, My God, why have You forsaken Me?" (Matthew 27:46), Luther wrote that Christ's "deep spiritual suffering . . . far surpassed all bodily suffering. . . . For to be forsaken of God is much worse than is death."[1] When we think of mission proclamation in schools, we need to be clear that Jesus isn't just martyred for a good cause like a TV hero. He suffered the consequences of the broken relationship caused by our sin.

---

1 Francis Pieper, *Christian Dogmatics* (St. Louis: Concordia, 1951), 2:311.

183

On the very first Easter Sunday, Jesus appeared to His disciples and said, "As the Father has sent Me, even so I am sending you" (John 20:21). This sending is for all Christians—for all members of the priesthood of believers. In one of Luther's sermons on this text, he said,

> This is said and written for us, as if to say: . . . "For whatever remains of your life, live as those sent by Christ." It is the office of everyone to instruct his neighbor, etc. And this power is given not to the clergy alone (though [here it is] spoken to the apostles) but to all believers. When you have performed this highest work, seek to become Christ's apostle, to serve all people, so that they may come unto God as you have.[2]

It can be exciting to know that Lutheran teachers, as part of God's mission, have beautiful mission fields of students, parents, and extended family. At the same time, this can be uncomfortable, because in God's sending, we don't get a map. God told Abraham and Sarah, "Go from your country and your kindred and your father's house to the land that I will show you" (Genesis 12:1). In other words, leave everything that is familiar and go to some unknown place. As we think about being sent by God, we would like to know the plan and see the backward design of this plan. We want instructions that clearly state that if we do A, then B will be the result. We want output to be proportional to input. And most important, we would like a program that gives us some control.

> The only place to which God calls us is the cross, and from there He sends us out to a place we can't know—to the world where we have ample opportunity in our vocations to be His instruments who share His love through word and deed.

The only place to which God calls us is the cross, and from there He sends us out to a place we can't know—to the world where we have ample opportunity in our vocations to be His instruments who share His love through word and deed.

WE ARE SENT INTO RELATIONSHIPS

The places God often sends us are difficult. In order for God to have a relationship with people who are separated from Him, we will likely need to mix with unsavory folks. For some reason, it seems okay for Jesus to spend time with sinners and prostitutes, but the ungodly are the very people that our parents suggested we avoid. Teachers, however, have a very natural relationship with students—even unbelieving students.

---

2   LW 69:336–37.

This is certainly part of our Lutheran understanding of vocation, but it also plays a part in how we witness. God will use our teaching relationships to be "ambassadors for Christ, God making His appeal through us" (2 Corinthians 5:20).

> God will use our teaching relationships to be "ambassadors for Christ, God making His appeal through us" (2 Corinthians 5:20).

Just as Jesus came in the flesh "and dwelt among us" (John 1:14) in the incarnation, we, too, are sent to have personal relationships. In those relationships, we risk being hurt, but it is worth the risk as we are privileged to be sent to do the King's work, to proclaim salvation in Christ in face-to-face situations. These are not simply one-way text or email encounters; rather, we are sent to engage the lives of those filled with brokenness and sin. We need to be able to believe that the Spirit can change the heart of anyone—even the most hopeless, disobedient, disrespectful, and ornery child.

THE SPIRIT CREATES FAITH

It is vital for us to remember that it is not we who change hearts, but the Holy Spirit who was sent to work faith. Paul reminds us, "We have this treasure in jars of clay, to show that the surpassing power belongs to God and not to us" (2 Corinthians 4:7). In Luther's explanation of the Third Article in the Small Catechism, he writes, "I believe that I cannot by my own reason or strength believe in Jesus Christ, my Lord, or come to Him; but the Holy Spirit has called me by the Gospel, enlightened me with His gifts, sanctified and kept me in the true faith." It is never our job to create the relationship with God—it is His job.

It is our privilege, however, to proclaim His Word. The Holy Spirit works through the Word to create faith. God's promise is that His Word is all we need. Paul says, "So faith comes from hearing, and hearing through the word of Christ" (Romans 10:17). In Isaiah 55:11, God tells us that His Word is efficacious: "So shall My word be that goes out from My mouth; it shall not return to Me empty, but it shall accomplish that which I purpose, and shall succeed in the thing for which I sent it."

We must remember that the mission is God's. He is the one who sends. He is the one who works faith and builds relationships through the Word. It should be easy then, right? Don't we just speak God's Word and stand back and watch things happen? Rarely is it so simple.

HIGH-IMPACT ENGAGEMENT

> The relationships that have the highest impact, even with children, are personal relationships that include one-on-one interaction.

The relationships that have the highest impact, even with children, are personal relationships that include one-on-one interaction. These relationships require a lot of time and patience that is focused on listening. Listening is necessary to know what our students have heard. We need to understand what they feel and value. We need to know where they place their trust and that what they believe is truly real. We need to discover how they see themselves in relationship to God. Knowing these things helps us to proclaim God's Word in a way that allows the Spirit to work on hearts.

The old mission conundrum is this: if I speak the Gospel and it is not heard, have I been faithful in my task to proclaim Christ? It is easy to understand how a foreign language can be a barrier to proclamation. Luther is an excellent example of one who saw that the use of Latin in church was keeping the German people from clearly hearing God's Word. It is certainly not our job to make God's Word pertinent, because it is relevant to every culture in all time, but even if we are all speaking the same language, our very words can raise barriers so the listener doesn't hear the Gospel.

We now deal with this same conundrum in our teaching. The words of our Western Christian culture can be confusing, even to children raised in the United States. Think of how we use the word *church*. Is church a building or an assembly of people? What does it mean to "go to church"? What is a "heathen"? What does it mean to "be saved"? For example, students from Asian backgrounds, which often emphasize a collective nature of community, may not understand individual confession or even the "I believe" in the Apostles' Creed. But they can point out that Jesus taught us to say "Our Father." We need to be proclaiming Christ in a way that the barriers are lowered and the Spirit has the opportunity to work on hearts. To do this, we take the time to listen to what our students hear. We need to be respectful in conversation, even with young students.

THE LAW AND THE GOSPEL

Sharing both Law and Gospel, as appropriate, makes it possible for the Spirit to work on hearts. Both the Law and the Gospel need to be proclaimed. People cannot hear the Gospel if the Spirit doesn't convince them that sin has broken their relationship with God. Our job, then, is not to "Christianize" students by coercing them into loveless and hypocritical "good works." The Law reveals sin but does not solve it. While good order in the classroom is important, the Law is not a classroom management tool. ("Jesus won't love you if you don't sit down.") The Law does convict sinners—even children—but it does not change the heart and cannot modify behavior.

Only the Gospel has the power to transform hearts and create a right relationship with our Lord. The Gospel needs to be proclaimed in a personal way, so use the personal pronoun *you*. A broad statement about love has almost no impact in a marriage proposal compared to a simple "I love you." A general statement about Jesus dying for the sins of the world is true, but it lacks the power of these words: "Jimmy, Jesus loves you. Jesus paid the punishment for your sins because He wants a relationship with you."

You Will Be My Witnesses

As Jesus ascended into heaven, He told those assembled, "You will be My witnesses in Jerusalem and in all Judea and Samaria, and to the end of the earth" (Acts 1:8). He doesn't say we "should be" witnesses, but "you will be." It is who we are, part of our baptismal identity (Romans 6). Our God doesn't demand results or success. The mission is His, and everything happens on His timeline. Paul reminds us, "I planted, Apollos watered, but God gave the growth" (1 Corinthians 3:6). As people sent by Jesus into the world, we proclaim Christ as our Savior. "Where are you?" we ask. "Your Lord wants a right relationship with you now and forever."

32

TEACHING THE FAITH IN A POST-CHRISTIAN CONTEXT

Jill Hasstedt

A post-Christian context can be defined as one in which Christianity has lost its place as a cultural footing where it was once the dominant "civil religion" that formed a nation's values, public rituals, and symbols. Over time, the Christian civil religion, if it ever existed, absorbed world-views, cultural beliefs, and values and incorporated them in a cultural mulligan stew. It may well be argued that the civil religion of any nation never was truly Christian, but it is even less so today. How might one effectively teach the true Christian faith within a culture whose civil religion has strayed far from Christian core beliefs or become hostile to them? This is, in essence, both a first-century and a twenty-first-century question.

> How might one effectively teach the true Christian faith within a culture whose civil religion has strayed far from Christian core beliefs or become hostile to them?

Christians are not alone in feeling disoriented and displaced in the postmodern era. The rise of postmodernism in the still rising dust storm of the information revolution at the onset of the digital age is affecting every institution of society that was once considered a source of authority in culture: churches, schools, government, family, police, military, and so on. This upheaval is not unlike that caused by the game-changing invention of the printing press by Gutenberg in the 1400s. The rapid spread and democratization of knowledge seeded the Reformation in the sixteenth century.[1]

---

1 Evan Andrews, "11 Innovations that Changed History," History Lists, posted December 18, 2012, accessed February 26, 2016, http://www.history.com/news/history-lists/11-innovations-that-changed-history.

Martin Luther and other reformers famously challenged and contributed to the dismantling or restructuring of many authority structures of their time. Certainly the Roman Catholic Church felt the impact. However, the pace of change in the Reformation could be considered snaillike compared to that being faced since the dawn of the Internet.

The rapid deconstruction of institutional authority is an indicator of postmodernism in the digital age.[2] It is the not-so-invisible elephant in the room. The new cultural rationale might go something like this:

1. "Knowledge is power."[3]

2. Institutions are no longer the source of knowledge; the Internet is.

3. Therefore, institutions no longer have the power.[4]

The role of the teacher as a disseminator of knowledge or information becomes suspect if that role is supplanted by technology. The role of institutions becomes suspect if they are no longer the keepers of the knowledge of a culture. If all ideas are equivalent in the "cultural supermarket of ideas,"[5] then why not just create one's own worldview or religion or values by shopping from the shelves of available options?

The individual then becomes the source of power, because any individual can access all the knowledge he or she needs somewhere on the Internet. There is great appeal, especially for the young, in being able to sidestep the "control" of authority. Instead of going to authorities, individuals are willing to trust the opinions of nonexperts they don't even know as long as they are accessing that source on their own. If the new locus of power and control lies with those who know how to access the information most successfully (or to hide it), the potential for misuse of power is great. If knowledge is power, it is wise to learn that power corrupts and can be manipulated.

> If knowledge is power, it is wise to learn that power corrupts and can be manipulated.

How do these challenges shape effective, integrity-based pedagogy in such a new and developing landscape? In this dismantling of central

---

2   Manuel Castells, "Communication, Power and Counter-power in the Network Society," *International Journal of Communication* 1 (2007), accessed February 26, 2016, http://www.ijoc.org/index.php/ijoc/article/viewFile/46/35.

3   Attributed to Francis Bacon, 1597.

4   Barry Burke, "Post-modernism, Post-modernity and Education," infed.org, accessed February 26, 2016, http://www.infed.org/mobi/post-modernism-and-post-modernity.

5   Phil Cohen, *Rethinking the Youth Question: Education, Labour, and Cultural Studies* (London: Macmillan, 1997), 390.1, as quoted by Burke in "Post-modernism, Post-modernity and Education."

power, institutions may see decline. Churches, especially the old established ones, will see decline. However, the potential of the multiplied impact of individual Christians faithfully living out their vocations with a Christlike servant heart has never been greater. The Church is, after all, the sum total of all believers living now and who have already entered into heaven. Jesus' command to "teach all nations" continues to grow the Body of Christ.

STRATEGIES FOR EFFECTIVE PEDAGOGY IN A POSTMODERN ERA

1. **Be transparent, not manipulative.** A persuasive teacher can move students in a direction with intellect or charisma, but so can a cult leader. In the long run, helping students of the faith to spot less honorable forms of communication will protect them. The Word of God does not need persuasive tricks to work. The Gospel has the power of truth and the work of the Holy Spirit behind it. God promises that His Word will not return empty but will accomplish His purpose (Isaiah 55:11). Trust that.

2. **Be attentive to welcoming differences.** Teach students that welcoming diversity is different than embracing it. Understanding cultural practices and beliefs in context is different than believing one must blindly accept them in order to value the people who hold them.

3. **De-westernize Christianity.** Jesus was not western. The gift of grace and forgiveness, the atoning sacrifice and victorious resurrection are not western. The Gospel has taken root in every culture, bringing with it a radical philosophy of love and divine truth that defies the relativistic and very western idea that every person decides individually what is true for them. Jesus said, "I am the way, and the truth, and the life" (John 14:6).

4. **You can't deal with what's not "on the table," so put it there!** The Christian teacher will bring these concepts to the table:

   a. **Help students identify the inefficacies of relativism.** Radical relativism has made deep inroads into civil religion, proclaiming there is no absolute truth, only individual truth. Teach students to challenge the idea of individual truth and morality, "so that we may no longer be children, tossed to and fro by the waves and carried about by every wind of doctrine, by human cunning, by craftiness in deceitful schemes" (Ephesians 4:14).

b. **Help students identify dangers of syncretism**, the combining and merging of ideas from other cultures and belief systems. Does the truth ever change? Paul coached Timothy in the Pastoral Epistles, often warning him to fight false teaching (see, for example, 1 Timothy 4). Challenging the encroachment of syncretic beliefs is perhaps the single largest issue Christian teachers will face in teaching the children of millennial families. "Leading the charge in the move to customize one's package of beliefs are people under the age of 25, among whom more than four out of five (82%) said they develop their own combination of beliefs rather than adopt a set proposed by a church."[6]

c. **Be open to questions** and willing to coach students in dealing with tough ones, listening with humility.

d. **Think exhortation, not prescription.** Urge and equip students to develop the tools for evaluation and discernment.

5. **While still teaching what "authority" is** and how Christians are to submit to it as part of the "mystery of godliness" (1 Timothy 3:16), **change the premise of teaching** so that instead of being about an authority giving knowledge to a less-learned student, it is about how to question authority and evaluate what is trustworthy (Acts 17:11).

6. **Understand that the individual is more important than the institution**. Bring it down to "one." Faith is not institutional, it is individual. First bring it down to the gift of the One to one (Ephesians 2:8–9), then bring it back to the one Body (Romans 12).

---

6 Barna Group, Ltd., "Christianity Is No Longer Americans' Default Faith," barna.org, posted January 28, 2009, accessed February 26, 2016, http://www.barna.org/barna-update/faith-spirituality/15-christianity-is-no-longer-americans-default-faith.

7. **Intentionally use a forked (multipronged) approach.**[7]

   a. Build biblical literacy to the highest level possible.

   b. Work to create a strong relational community.

   c. Teach truth and how to evaluate the measures of truth.

8. **Promote stewardship of faith.** Stewardship is taking care of what has been entrusted to us, and there is no greater gift entrusted to us than that of faith. We show care for this gift by active participation in worship, studying God's Word, receiving the Sacraments, having an active prayer life, and serving others.[8]

9. **Think process, not results.** Results are important, but in a postmodern era, the process of getting there—the journey—may be more so. Collaborative, patient, relational approaches that trust the truth of God's Word and the work of the Holy Spirit to do their work over time will be more effective than emphasizing content.

10. **Remember that trust matters.** Help students to anchor the faith in their minds with the highest values of Christianity. As a teacher, express those values, live them out personally and actively, and involve students in living them out in ways that make a difference locally, nationally, or globally.[9] In this era, nothing stays secret for long, and trust is earned not by being perfect, but by being transparent, open, honest, and genuine.

Ultimately, the greatest tool a teacher has is love.

You may have heard the saying "People don't care how much you know until they know how much you care." The powerful pedagogue in a post-Christian context cannot simply be a good scholar who is able to learn well. The strongest weapon against radical relativism is radical love.

---

7   John Burke, *Mud and the Masterpiece: Seeing Yourself and Others Through the Eyes of Jesus* (Grand Rapids, MI: Baker Books, 2013).

8   Karpenko Institute for Nurturing and Developing Leadership Excellence, "KINDLE Christ-like Servant Leader Outcomes," accessed February 26, 2016, http://www .kindleservantleaders.org/wordpress/wp-content/uploads/2012/04/SPO-Version -25.1.1-FINAL-05-100120122.pdf.

9   Nathalie Nahai, "The Secret Psychology of Persuasive Copy," accessed February 26, 2016, http://www.slideshare.net/nathalienahai.

Peter said it:

> *Above all, keep loving one another earnestly, since love covers a multitude of sins. Show hospitality to one another without grumbling. As each has received a gift, use it to serve one another, as good stewards of God's varied grace: whoever speaks, as one who speaks oracles of God; whoever serves, as one who serves by the strength that God supplies—in order that in everything God may be glorified through Jesus Christ. To Him belong glory and dominion forever and ever. Amen. (1 Peter 4:8–11)*

And so did Paul:

> *If I speak in the tongues of men and of angels, but have not love, I am a noisy gong or a clanging cymbal. (1 Corinthians 13:1)*

But Jesus said it first:

> *A new commandment I give to you, that you love one another: just as I have loved you, you also are to love one another. By this all people will know that you are My disciples, if you have love for one another. (John 13:34–35)*

33

HELPING STUDENTS GROW SPIRITUALLY IN AN AGE OF MORALISTIC THERAPEUTIC DEISM

New Christian vs. Old Christian Challenges and Approaches

Grant Carey

Students today live in a challenging world that is significantly differ-ent from the one you and I experienced. They are busier, more connected, and over-informed through social media. Because of this and a change in how the world views Christianity, helping students develop a lasting faith has become more challenging. This essay will address the unique challenges teachers of the faith have in nurturing students in a lifelong relationship with Jesus.

THE PREDOMINATE FAITH OF THIS GENERATION

Researchers have found that a majority of teenagers in the United States have a faith that is contrary to mainstream Christianity, and they have labeled this "worldview" as Moralistic Therapeutic Deism (MTD). In her book *Almost Christian*, Kenda Creasy Dean gives five guiding beliefs of MTD:

1. A god exists who created and orders the world and watches over life on earth.

2. God wants people to be good, nice, and fair to each other, as taught in the Bible and by most world religions.

3. The central goal of life is to be happy and feel good about oneself.

4. God is not involved in my life except when I need God to resolve a problem.

5. Good people go to heaven when they die.[1]

With our current generation, faith is seen as a good thing for moral upbringing, but unnecessary for an integrated and holistic life. Religion, which was once a central part of family life, now has less influence when it comes to most adolescents' obligations, schedules, routines, and habits. Because of this, the faith of teenagers has become compartmentalized, and religion is seen as just another activity to go along with band, soccer, and school. Most young people would never say they subscribe to this faith, but MTD accurately describes the overarching belief of today's students and can be summarized by breaking down the three descriptive title words: *moralistic*, *therapeutic*, and *deism*.

> Most young people would never say they subscribe to this faith, but MTD accurately describes the overarching belief of today's students.

Moralistic is primarily about doing well in the world and being a good person. While there is nothing wrong with being a good person, moralism tends to develop into a form of works-righteousness in which a person believes he or she has to produce good works in order to be saved and earn the favor of God. It is an "if/then" faith: *if* I do something good, *then* something good will happen to me. This moralistic faith takes Jesus' sacrifice and grace out of the picture and replaces it with a distorted view of karma, a concept found in Hinduism and Buddhism. One of the central thoughts that come out of the moralistic faith is that God wants everyone to get along. While this is most certainly true and good, Christianity is not a faith of just "being nice" or "helping people." Dean shares the danger of this view by saying, "The church's accommodating impulse does not stem from God's call to us to share our lives with the stranger or to share God's love with others. Instead it grows out of our need as a church to be liked and approved."[2]

The ***therapeutic*** part of MTD equates to a feel-good faith. Some of the key creeds of teenagers with a therapeutic-focused faith are "When I need something, God is there," or "God wants me to be happy," or

---

1 Kenda Creasy Dean, *Almost Christian: What the Faith of Our Teenagers Is Telling the American Church* (New York: Oxford, 2010), 14. By permission of Oxford University Press, USA.

2 Dean, *Almost Christian*, 34.

"Knowing God is there makes me feel good." None of these phrases are inherently wrong, but they lack a true knowledge and grasp of God and His work in and through us. MTD is not a religion of repentance from sin, living as a servant of a holy God, steadfastly saying one's prayers, or building character through suffering; rather, it is about feeling good, happy, secure, and at peace while being able to resolve problems. Jesus told His disciples that they would have trouble in this world, that people would hate them because of Him, and that they should deny themselves and take up their cross and follow Him. None of Jesus' admonitions to His disciples sounds like the happy, feel-good, therapeutic faith of MTD.

Lastly, **deism** is the part of MTD that speaks to God's character, or lack thereof. The core tenet is that there is one who exists, created the world, and defines our general moral order; but he is not particularly personally involved in one's affairs, especially affairs in which one would prefer not to have god involved. Most of the time, the god of this faith keeps a safe distance and does not get too involved in the lives of the adherents, unless they need him for something in their life. Deism is more a self-serving faith rather than a faith of holiness and transformation. In fact, according to Dean, MTD is "all about us. God's primary role in Moralistic Therapeutic Deism is to stand back and approvingly watch us evolve."[3]

The outlook that comes from MTD is an empty and searching faith that fails when times get tough. Is it any wonder that teenagers are leaving the Church, and their faith, when they view God in this manner? This may leave you wondering, what can we do to help students better know the truths of God and the amazing Good News of Jesus Christ?

USING OUR LUTHERAN FAITH AND THEOLOGY TO COMBAT MTD

As educators and spiritual mentors, we can easily grow frustrated or downtrodden by the culture that seems to speak contrary to our students' Christian faith. But this is one of the reasons God has called us to be teachers of the faith. God called the prophets to speak truth and comfort to the Israelites, even when it was hard. God empowered the disciples to go and share a better way of life through Christ, even though it cost many their lives. God spoke through Martin Luther when the papacy seemed to lose sight of grace. Change starts small and grows as others

---

3   Dean, *Almost Christian*, 39.

are transformed. Here are just a few ways we, as educators of the Christian faith, can better help our students experience a lasting faith that is rooted in the Word of God.

Overcoming Moralism

Use Law and Gospel. I once had a middle-school-age girl come to me and ask if abortion was wrong. Fear came over me as I searched for the right answer, but suddenly I remembered to ask the question, "Why do you want to know?" I once learned that asking this one question helps determine the direction we should take in answering tough questions such as this one. If she had responded that she had recently had an abortion, it would be fitting to talk about grace and new beginnings. However, if she was thinking about having one, then it would be fitting to talk about God's Law and desire for life as found in the Fifth Commandment. One of the things I love most about our Lutheran faith is the emphasis on Law and Gospel. We are able to talk about God's standard for our lives, but we are also able to talk constantly about His incredible grace for us when we fail to live up to those standards. When students understand that we are all in need of a Savior and that we can never fulfill God's perfect standard, it helps them to understand that moralism doesn't work in our world. We will never be good enough or nice enough without the love and forgiveness of Jesus in our lives.

"Why do you want to know?" I once learned that asking this one question helps determine the direction we should take in answering tough questions.

Use Christian ethics. Allowing students to talk and wrestle with tough issues better prepares them for the world they will enter when they are one day on their own. An excellent way to do this is by using case studies and examples with your students when they are in a controlled and grace-filled environment, so that when they are one day confronted with real-life examples, they are able to respond with a healthy and informed worldview.

Teaching a True Therapeutic Faith

Use the theology of the cross. When we help students realize that life is hard but we have a God who is faithful, even to the point of death for us on a cross, we help them understand that they can find true comfort in their faith. This can be seen time after time in Scripture as God provides daily for the Israelites in the desert, as He rescues the disciples from the storm when they were on the lake, and ultimately, as Jesus took up a cross and suffered and died for all of humanity. A true therapeutic faith is not one that makes us happy by taking away all the pain and suffering in the world, but rather one that helps us weather the storms of life.

Use Confession (and Absolution!). As we teach students to confess and ask for absolution for the things they have done and left undone, we help them see that their sin is real, and it hurts themselves and others. But we also help them know that God heals that hurt through His sacrifice, which is therapeutic and incredibly freeing.

Showing That Jesus Is Better Than Deism

Use prayer. One of the tenets of MTD is that one goes to God in prayer only when one needs Him or has a request of Him. However, when we teach students to pray in the good and the tough times, they are able to see God's faithfulness in all areas of their life. Keeping track of prayer requests (and answers to the prayers) in your classroom or youth group is a great way to help students see that God is present in all circumstances. This type of praying without ceasing (1 Thessalonians 5:17) helps them recognize God's omnipresence in their life and that He truly cares for them.

Use apologetics and world religions. Students need a solid foundation for their faith, and one of the best ways to provide that is by teaching why we believe what we do. When they are able to see that Jesus was actually a real person in history, that He really did die and rise from the dead, and that there is evidence that supports it all, they are able to understand that their faith is credible and worth holding on to. Playing "devil's advocate" with them helps them think through responses and reasons why they believe what they do. In addition, by exposing them to the various world religions and worldviews, we help prepare our students for what they will one day encounter by giving them the tools and knowledge for what is truth in a world with so many differences.

Lutheran education has always been about providing a solid foundation to students. However, the approach we take in teaching our students about their faith must be intentional as we strive to help them live in a world that embraces a faith of Moralistic Therapeutic Deism. The good news is that by proclaiming Jesus and His amazing grace, we are already effective spiritual teachers.

34

TEACHING THE FAITH IN A CONTEXT OF STANDARDS, COMPLIANCE, AND REGULATIONS

Harvey Schmit

A group of principals are talking at the monthly breakfast meeting.

Dave mentions, "Did you see the article yesterday from the state board of education? We're getting a revised set of curriculum standards."

Henry jumps in, "Great, just what we need, another mandate from afar. Was this one written by some ivory tower professor, or some know-it-all legislator? Doesn't matter, I'm sure neither of them have been in a real classroom in twenty years."

Pete offers, "Doesn't matter to us. We just use what's in the textbook. Certainly the people who write them know more about curriculum and standards than I do!"

The fourth principal, Pat, just sits back and smiles, waiting for the initial reactions to pass before offering the solution she has found to the focus on standards in the present educational environment.

Dave argues that education as a profession brings with it more regulation than any other field. "Not only are there local standards, as seen in our local public school district, but there are also statewide expectations, encouragement from the district and Synod, accrediting agencies both regionally and nationally, and the feelings and beliefs of the general populace. It's the parents who are the most challenging. They would never debate the specific medical advice they receive, or the legal explanation from a lawyer, but they will readily offer an opinion regarding the appropriate way for my school, and particularly their child's teacher, to educate."

With so many cooks in the kitchen, educators cannot help but react, particularly in regard to standards. Such responses can be considered in four broad categories: ignore, implore, explore, and create.

IGNORE (PETE)

Pete claims that his approach, ignore, is the simplest one. He is correct; it requires the least effort in the short run, but it has the greatest potential for problems in the long run.

Pete continues the discussion. "My school simply follows the textbooks that have been selected, without regard to standards. If standards are raised as a concern, we point to the authors of the texts. They are trusted experts in their fields who should incorporate standards well. Further, the publisher promises to weave the standards throughout the grades. This way, we address both the standards and the overall curricular plan for the school. It's two birds with one stone, and I don't have to do anything!"

Pete's argument may seem reasonable at first blush, but the pitfalls are many and deeply dug. Even if the textbooks truly meet the ideal described, they are still being applied by individual teachers. Creative teachers regularly pick and choose, modify, and expand their instructional content, and it is wonderful that they do so. However, this often results in classroom experiences that do not perfectly mirror the intent of the text's author. The wandering away from the standard begins. In this scenario, the administrator's responsibility is that of policeman, carefully monitoring the teacher's lockstep application of the text.

Creative teachers who move beyond those boundaries need to be brought into compliance, and certainly there is no allowance for student-centered variation. How many people aspired to be teachers so that their creativity might be limited? How many administrators chose that position to be able to police this kind of instruction? How many parents wish to have their child in a classroom in which the individual needs of the child are ignored? The alternative to this is to allow everyone to be creative and go their own way. This feels right at the time of application, but completely destroys the opportunity for a comprehensive course of study in which earlier learning serves as a foundation for that which comes later.

> This feels right at the time of application, but completely destroys the opportunity for a comprehensive course of study in which earlier learning serves as a foundation for that which comes later.

If that does happen, it would only be by chance. Is there support for a system that succeeds by chance?

IMPLORE (HENRY)

At the next level, implore, the principal has a different role. When the new standards emerge, they are not ignored.

Henry explains, "Our faculty also start with the text series, but we match it to the new standard. My task is to implore the teachers, the local experts, to each review their textbooks and connect that material with the standards for their subject and grade level. We've been doing one subject each year; so this year we would have been half done, until the new standards came out! Guess we'll have to return to the one-week blitz this summer. Monday, it's math standards and done. Tuesday, we're on to language arts. It's a long week, but I make sure a parent brings in lunch each day, and we usually have a staff social at the end. When I first became a principal, I did it all myself, tediously pounding away a text and a grade level at a time. Believe me, it's a lot easier to implore the faculty to help. They're more invested, and I actually get a summer break."

While the faculty, administrator, or both feel an initial burst of pride at a difficult task completed, this does not last for long. The end product is usually a three-ring binder or an electronic version of one. Several next steps are possible, none of them desirable. If the task is a one-person job done by the administrator, the faculty views the product as the principal's idea of what the faculty ought to do. Should the faculty ignore the product, the administrator's imploring continues into the future, possibly including a monitoring process.

If it is a group activity, again several possibilities await. Should the method of choice be the "one subject a year" variety, it is quite likely that a new set of standards will emerge before the entire process is completed. In such cases, the group is highly tempted to toss the whole process and move to the "ignore" approach. Should the process be blitzed, or even completed over time, the binder or electronic file that results is seldom a truly living document. Rather, the binder is placed on a shelf where it gathers dust, or it disappears into the hard drive of despair until a new computer is purchased.

In either case, the product is usually a plan that is not realistically affecting everyday practice. When the plan is noticed, the result is probably guilt, as the administrator and faculty see it as one more reminder of the many things that should be done but is prohibited by limited time and competing needs. Not only has pride been replaced by guilt, but the final result is no better than the ignore approach. What frustration, after great application of time and effort, to realize that the end result could have been attained as effectively by doing nothing!

Explore (Dave)

The explore option, although not the ideal, provides opportunity for both engagement and application.

Dave explains, "We do something similar, but we start with the standard or curriculum list, and then review the textbooks and other class activities. The teachers enjoy the challenge of matching their instruction to the expectations. Each teacher hopes that each standard is already done in his or her classroom. If a standard is not in the textbook, perhaps it could be considered at the next book review. In the meantime, I challenge each teacher to creatively fill the gap with other resources. They enjoy bringing creative skills to bear. Some of them even have the students generate ideas. My teachers are engaged because they truly plead their own case successfully or expand their practice. Either way, actual application of the standards is likely to occur. My role is resource and cheerleader rather than taskmaster. When it works well, the faculty is more focused and free to creatively move education forward to the benefit of each learner. Wow, I must be a great administrator!"

What could be better? As good as this may sound, there are still a number of potential trouble spots in this approach. One is that the administrator must be very skillful in presenting the task so that faculty can perceive it as an intriguing challenge. The task is still a lot of work, as most things worth doing are. The potential is great that this challenge is perceived as an onerous task rather than an intriguing opportunity. Further, not all teachers will accept concepts in the standards as preferable to their own. Standards may place the fourth grade teacher's favorite activity in a different grade. Temptation will be great to connect such pet activities to that teacher's grade level, even if an authentic connection is not truly there. The administrator is in the unhappy position of pointing out such inauthentic connections. The teacher is then likely to respond in a defensive manner, and the slippery downward slope to disaster has begun. The next steps are to either move back to unengaged compliance (see "Implore" above) or to a posture that ignores the process completely. Should all of these be avoided, another danger awaits, as the emergence of a new or revised set of standards means the process must be reinitiated with all of the same challenges.

CREATE (PAT)

Pat, who has been quietly listening, offers her thoughts. "The three of you are really working hard at this, each in your own way. What helped me is to move beyond the standards to the larger goal. What did I want our school to model? One goal was the opportunity for teacher creativity. We all seek student-centered learning. All of you have mentioned faculty engagement. A professional presence by the school to the larger community is also paramount. We all work on this, but it seems that every time a new set of standards is generated, we're back to square one. The solution cannot be a one-time solution, but rather one that is durable. We need something known, such as the textbooks, but also something that we own—not because we bought it, but because we believe in it.

"Each of our respective schools, and faculties, has a set of values. While probably not written down, there is a common understanding of purpose, vision, and mission. My faculty and I took several days (including mealtimes) to identify those goals and write them down. Now, instead of an outside group dictating to us, we have our own set of values and beliefs, clearly stated and connected to actual activities."

> "Now, instead of an outside group dictating to us, we have our own set of values and beliefs, clearly stated and connected to actual activities."

Henry interrupted, "Isn't that just writing your own standards? How does that meet the new common core or any external standards?"

Pat continued, "The key concept here is that most standards are common to most schools. It's why our teachers balk at formal processes with standards; they believe they already know what they're doing and why. So, what possible motivation is there to invest in a process that formalizes or documents adherence to an outside agency? The goal statements, or framework, that the faculty generates is known to them and owned by them. It reflects local needs and practices. It is known to stakeholders, and it reflects their beliefs and continuing attraction to the school. This framework is durable, not requiring frequent review and recasting. The discipline we needed to apply was to be sure every activity, existing or proposed, had an authentic tie to the framework. Thus such review happens every time a new activity is proposed."

Dave spoke up, "We could do that, and in many ways probably have already, but how does that solve your compliance with new standards?"

"That's the beauty of it," Pat continued. "We relate those external and evolving items to the local school through our own framework. Most of the standards are already occurring. However, now the entire program does not need to be revised; we simply revise the connection between the standards and the existing framework."

She continued, "This allows for only three possibilities. One, the framework matches the standards perfectly, process complete! Two, the framework includes more than the standards do. Wonderful, the school goes beyond the standards, process complete! Three, the framework does not include something in the standards. Now we don't have to apply each standard, only those that are identified as beyond the framework. Discussion focuses on those few disconnects. The result is either expansion of the framework, which makes the school better, or an appeal to the source group for the standard, which may make the standards better."

It was quiet for a minute. Then Henry said, "Well, that's something to think about. Our time for today is gone, but I'm intrigued. Let's take this up again next month."

35

CONFRONT THE CHALLENGES TO YOUR FAITH

Marty Kohlwey

As I think over the years of my life and the lives of those I have been blessed to share life with, I am brought to deep emotion reflecting on the turbulent challenges we struggle through as adolescents and young adults (Psalm 90; 2 Corinthians 1).

In my college class this morning, as many as one-third of my students shared that they have struggled with depression or other mental disorders. Others in class have families suffering with divorce, drugs, cancer, abuse, and/or death. These events attack us with questions about the goodness of God and sometimes even His reality.

Other challenges to our faith are many and constant. Daily, whether we realize it or not, we are confronted with conflicting beliefs. Sports, social media, news, and entertainment present a very different value system than what God desires for us. These often push us to base our identity and meaning on abilities, appearance, wealth, and material things.

We are only moments away from the highest highs and the lowest lows. How do we navigate through this life and the world in which we live? Where can we find strength and clarity to maintain a fulfilled identity, true meaning, and everlasting hope?

> Where can we find strength and clarity to maintain a fulfilled identity, true meaning, and everlasting hope?

In reflecting on these questions, I thought of a few more questions that are crucial to handling the previous ones. From deeply questioning my faith, I personally have found there is no better answer that gives me a coherent understanding of life and the world than what you will find below.

Who Are You?

> Ironically, when we accept ourselves as broken and come face-to-face with our mess of a life, we find out who we really are: lost but found, broken but healed.

On what do you base your identity? What makes you who you are? Is it your job? your hobby or sport? your grades? your status in your peer group? your relationship with your girlfriend or boyfriend, husband or wife? How you answer this question (and the next two) will determine whether you survive the challenges to your faith. They speak to what we really believe.

I think I know who I am. . . . I don't know about you, but I am . . . a mess. I feel like a failure. I can't make this life work. I am thankful that, the first time I realized this, Jesus was there to show me it was okay to be a loser (Luke 9:24; 19:10). He showed me I am a child of God (1 John 3:1), chosen by Him, holy and dearly loved (Colossians 3:12; 1 Peter 2:9). Ironically, when we accept ourselves as broken and come face-to-face with our mess of a life, we find out who we really are: lost but found, broken but healed.

Ralph Underwager, in a book called *I Hurt Inside* (Augsburg, 1973), reveals that whenever we feel we need to compare ourselves to others or feel a need to be better than what we are (or different than what we are), we are under the Law. Satan bombards us with this by the minute. We compare our body, our clothes, our car, and our home. We compete for relationships, jobs, and just about anything in life. Comparison and competition breed despair over unmet expectations and goals, so we beat ourselves up for not measuring up. Somehow this covert operation of the Law needs to lead us to the amazing news that we are in need of someone bigger and better than us—someone who meets the standards of perfection and of God. This leads us to the only God who provides us with a very personal friendship with the One who made us, saved us, and lives with us. A healthy understanding of our identity in Christ on a daily basis is vital.

Why Am I Here?

What is my purpose? Does my life have meaning? Do I matter to this world? We, at certain times of life, scream these questions in our mind and sometimes out loud. Most people don't really know. This question goes beyond our career and our place in our family, physical talents, and academic abilities. I have abilities and talents, but I am not always sure

I am using them the way I should. Doubts and questions arise. I still ask myself what I am going to do when I grow up, and I am fifty-three!

At our very core, we are made to be lovers. Not in a sexual sense, even though that is true also. We were made to love and to be loved. We long to share our deepest self with someone who understands us. We were made to join the beautiful love relationship between the Father, His Son, and the Holy Spirit!

> We were made to love and to be loved. We long to share our deepest self with someone who understands us.

We are made to worship. We all worship something. All day long we worship sports and celebrities. We consume ourselves with the latest news of what is going on with the people we idolize. In 1 Peter 2, we are told that our worship is tied into our identity. This is no surprise. We identify with a team and then can't wait to talk about the big win they had the other night.

No matter what we can or can't do, love and worship are our purpose. Enjoy His love and help others to see what a big deal He is! Pretty simple. Let people know of the person who saved your lost life, just like you talk to others about the great shot your favorite player made to win the game.

IS THERE ANY HOPE?

Is there hope for the future, your future? This is my last question but certainly not the least important. We have to have hope. Without it, we give up. We become desperate. Hopeless. Have you ever felt hopelessness? If you haven't, imagine thinking that you have nothing to live for—maybe more important, nothing to die for. Imagine having nothing to care about, no one to care for you. Atheists can come to this conclusion easily if they are honest with themselves. Unfortunately, this is where our society is pointing us. No creator, no meaning, and no hope. This undercurrent, created by the rejection of God, leads to despondency. It is the undercurrent in many of us without a clear understanding of faith in Jesus (Hebrews 11:1–3).

Many have turned to atheism because they felt God let them down by allowing a crisis to happen in their life. They can't believe in a God who would let such a bad thing happen. The question is what are your options? If there isn't a God, then what better answers are given? If there is no God, then there is no meaning beyond this life and no hope beyond the grave.

Or is there a God we can't understand because He is bigger than us? As a father, there have been many times when my children have had no way to understand my decisions. Some of my decisions were best for my children even though they did not understand. Some were best for others and as a result caused my children pain. We are in a similar situation with God. We cannot see the whole picture right now (1 Corinthians 13:12).

The flip side of hopelessness is joy in a never-ending hope. When we are in love with our special someone, hope abounds. The future is exciting. Adventure is around every corner. This is our life in Christ. Even in tumultuous times, we can be confident that He will work things out for our good (Romans 8:28) and that life has meaning.

Read these knowing they apply to you!

- He knows me by name. It is engraved in His hand with the nails of the cross.
- I am worth the life of the Son of God. He died so I could have an amazing and adventure-filled relationship with Him.
- I am dearly loved. I am a beloved son or daughter.
- I belong to Him. He chose me to be His.
- I am forgiven. Being an eternal God not hindered by time, He knows my past, present, and future. This means He has forgiven *all* my sin. I am accepted by Him just the way I am—no matter how many times I have let Him down, pushed Him out of my mind, promised not to do that particular sin and did it anyway. As Brennan Manning says in his book *The Relentless Tenderness of Jesus*, "He expects more failure from you than you expect from yourself."[1] My sin, my failure, and the mess I have made of my life are all covered by grace.
- I have been made new, a new creation. I am now being transformed by the Holy Spirit.
- He has made me different than anyone else with gifts and talents unique to me. I can share what He has done for me.

I have chosen to fill my day with these reminders, guarding my heart and my mind (Proverbs 4:23). My attitude is profoundly affected by what my mind is taking in all day long. The verses below indicate that our mind,

---

1   Brennan Manning, *The Relentless Tenderness of Jesus* (Grand Rapids, MI: Fleming H. Revell, 2004), 163.

attitude, and heart are encouraged by the Spirit and at peace when we rest in His certain hope and in who we are and why we are here. During tough times, depressed moods, prideful moments, or harsh criticism, I must go back to these three foundational cornerstones of my worldview. I can do this by being in His Word, by listening to His music and praising Him (Colossians 3:15–17), and through sound teaching and the people of God (Acts 2:42–47). I think about these things, and He reminds me I am loved, my life has purpose, and He will never leave me nor forsake me (Ephesians 4:22–24; Colossians 3:1–3; Philippians 4:4–9; 1 Peter 2:9).

Please take time to write down your thoughts now and answer the three questions I posed above. Take time for each question; pause and reflect on what it would be like not to have a relationship with God, and then finish with how this changes with Jesus in your life, considering the thoughts shared above. Once you have come to grips with the stark contrast in the answers to these questions from both the Christian worldview and a postmodern or pluralistic point of view, consider how you might share this with your students.

Here are some ideas for introducing this to your students and also teaching to this everyday:

- Contrast three popular song lyrics from the Billboard Top 20 and Christian Top 20. What worldview is behind the lyrics? How does this affect us? Contemplate Colossians 3:16.

- Consider a popular entertainer and his or her worldview. Shia LaBeouf gave an interview years ago that revealed his need to have these three questions answered. "Sometimes I feel I'm living a meaningless life, and I get frightened." "I have no idea where this insecurity comes from, but it's a God-sized hole. If I knew, I'd fill it, and I'd be on my way."[2]

- Discuss what makes people who they are. Bring the discussion back to those things that are not based on what you do. Review 1 Peter 2:9.

- How can life have meaning if you are limited in your abilities? Can God still use you? Consider Colossians 3:17.

- Have your students create "life maps." John Trent's book *Life Mapping* (WaterBrook Press, 1998) can serve as a guide, but the basic idea is to walk through memories and milestones of your

---

2   Dotson Rader, "The Mixed-Up Life of Shia LaBeouf" *Parade*, June 14, 2009, accessed February 26, 2016, http://www.parade.com/130832/dotsonrader/shia-labeouf-mixed-up-life.

life. Students can do this by writing them down in a list chrono-logically or by drawing pictures for each event. This is a great way to show students how God can use the good and bad to make you who you are today. Be prepared for difficult memories and reali-zations that may need counseling referrals.

- Have your students interview family or friends, asking the ques-tion "What is your purpose in life?"

- Help students find their passion. What are they good at doing? What do their families and friends think they are gifted with? What do they love to do, especially for others?

- Do a servant event for your school or church, or for an organiza-tion in your town. Debrief by asking questions that bring them back to "Who are you?" "Why are you here?" and "Is there hope?"

36

EDUCATIONAL MINISTRY IN A DIGITAL WORLD

Challenges, Opportunities, and Considerations

Bernard Bull

The Christian Church has a long history of using technology in the service of ministry, and today is no different. The most notable early example is the technology of writing, eventually followed by the mass-produced book. In Exodus, we read that God commanded Moses to create written accounts. (See Exodus 17:14 and 34:1, 27–28 for examples.) Much of the New Testament consists of letters, or epistles. One could argue that these represented an early form of distance or blended learning, with teaching shared across time and space using the technologies of writing and letters. This continued through the Reformation, when the printing press started a revolution that early Christian educators embraced, creating catechisms and primers used in some of our earliest Protestant schools. Thanks to such technology, for the first time in history, individuals were eventually able to take readings home with them.

Fast-forward to today, to the digital age. Computer technology, the Internet, and communication technologies are the dominant technologies of the age. As with our predecessors across millennia, Christian educators have the challenge and opportunity to consider the benefits and limitations of using current technology to teach the faith. How do Christians go about evaluating and prayerfully considering ways to use technology in service to teaching the faith? While the technology is constantly changing, I offer the following five thoughts as starting points. These points do not include tips on specific tools or technology, but they do offer a sort of Christian philosophy for evaluating and using technology in ministry.

TECHNOLOGY IS INTERCONNECTED WITH CULTURE

"Technology" is applied scientific knowledge. Or from another perspective, it is the use of scientific (or some just say systematic) knowledge in applied or practical ways. This definition includes much of the modern world: the appliances in our kitchen; our means of transportation as well as the system of roadways and traffic laws; the medicine in our cabinets; the entertainment devices in our living rooms and basements; the tools we use for communication; the systems we use for measuring the size of a room, grading students, planning the school schedule, organizing lessons and curricula, collecting tuition, paying teachers from year to year, managing classrooms, refining our golf swing, and planning a family trip. Now consider the definition of culture, which usually includes something like "the beliefs, values, practices, and arts of a group of people." Technology is interconnected with culture. It reflects our beliefs, values, and traditions. It also sometimes shapes or shifts those beliefs, values, and traditions. There is a constant interaction between the two. As such, our reflection about the use of technology in ministry is part of a large conversation about Christianity and culture.

TECHNOLOGY IS NOT NEUTRAL

Given the definitions just shared, notice that technology is not just some neutral tool that one can choose to use for any purpose without unexpected side effects and implications. Replace the practice of washing dishes by hand with a dishwasher, and that changes life in a household. It might change certain traditions, communication patterns in the home, the electric or water bill, or what sort of dishes you buy and use (they have to be dishwasher safe now, right?). Or consider the technology of the automobile. That is definitely not a neutral tool. Just look at how the world changed due to the ability of people to travel long distances in a fraction of the time. People can live in one town and work in another. The concept of commuting was brought into existence by the automobile. We even have an entire genre of movie called "road movies," illustrating the deep sense of values and beliefs that people attach to having their own car, traveling cross-country, and hitting the road.

Technology shifts, tweaks, amplifies, or completely changes important aspects of one or more parts of a culture, including a school or classroom culture. Consider, for example, how the value of being connected to others at all times (and even beliefs about what it means to be safe) emerged with mobile phones. None of these are neutral devices or systems. For this reason, Neil Postman argued that a given technology is always a Faustian bargain.[1] There are benefits and limitations. Notice that I am not saying right and wrong. While that may be the case, it is more difficult to discern in some of these areas. Is it morally right or wrong to commute two hours to work each day? People have different opinions on that matter, and they can make compelling cases for a given situation. While there is certainly biblical wisdom to help one grapple with such decisions, I am cautious of legalistic claims and assertions.

There Are Spiritual and Theological Implications to Technology

If technology does indeed influence the beliefs, values, traditions, and practices of people, then that means there is a spiritual dimension to considering the nature of life in a technological world. It could be said that it is important to explore a theology of technology in society. Religious doctrines, beliefs, moral issues, and value systems have something to say about our lives in a technological world. The Amish understand this. Many mistakenly think that the Amish are anti-technology. If that were true, they would not use plows, buggies, saddles, shoes, or tools. Some argue that it is more accurate to see the Amish as pro-community rather than anti-technology. They seek to consider the impact a given technology (whether it be an object or a system) has upon their core values and beliefs. If there is valid concern that a given technology will jeopardize their beliefs and values, then they may well decide to exclude or limit it in their community life. While I am not arguing that we should imitate the Amish, there is a general lesson worth noting. They take the time to consider the implications of a technology. How does it amplify or muffle the beliefs, values, and mission of our classrooms and schools?

---

1   Neil Postman, "Five Things We Need to Know About Technological Change." Talk delivered in Denver, Colorado, March 28, 1998; http://web.cs.ucdavis.edu/~rogaway/classes/188/materials/postman.pdf.

THE ANSWER IS OFTEN NOT REJECTION

The Lutheran tradition has a rich historical connection to technological innovation, one that often includes embracing the use of emerging technologies. The printing press is the one that comes to mind right away. However, if we go back earlier in Christianity, we see that God used the technologies of a given day and time. Simply scan any book of the Bible in search of technologies, and you will likely be amazed to see how many are present. At the same time, these technologies all had benefits and limitations. They were not neutral. In other words, God's work can and will be accomplished amid the ever-changing, complex technological world. While there are dangers and blessings, benefits and limitations, we are called to live in this world. Even as we live in the world, God uses us in our vocations to love our neighbors, and new vocations will emerge as a result of technological innovation. Consider the concept of digital culture and digital citizenship. It is becoming increasingly necessary to engage in the digital world in order to be an active participant in society. Similarly, a growing number of people connect and live out parts of their lives in the digital world. As such, there is opportunity for Christians to live out vocations in love to these neighbors in the digital world, even with current and emerging technologies.

DISCERNMENT IS VALUABLE

While we are called to live in this increasingly technological world, there is immense benefit to prayerful consideration and study of the Scriptures with the contemporary world in mind. We seek out how the Ten Commandments inform life in a digital context. We revisit the promises of God and His declaration of our life in Christ as we see media representations of goodness, truth, beauty, and life and claims about what it means to be successful. God's Word is unchanging, and it can provide us with stability in this ever-changing world. A Christian education in the digital age finds ways to help students cultivate such discernment. Martin Luther's Large Catechism is a wonderful example of this as he not only teaches about the meaning of the Ten Commandments but also does it using specific examples and illustrations, even cases and scenarios from daily life. As such, we use that model to reflect upon God's Law and Gospel in the contemporary world, even life in social media and the blogosphere. Part of our mission as Christian educators is to challenge people to persistently consider the significance of the Christian world-view in light of modern life, thought, trends, and events.

CONCLUSION

These are five foundations for thinking about the role of technology in faith formation and religious education. As we explore these together, we can move on to thinking about different ways that we might use specific technologies. There are endless possibilities, and each will have benefits and limitations. The answer is not to reject or embrace it all. Rather, it is to keep our beliefs and values central (speaking and thinking about them often) and then to prayerfully, with the Scriptures open, live out those beliefs and values in this digital world, helping our learners to grow in the grace and knowledge of our Lord and Savior Jesus Christ.

As we explore the broad theme of educational ministry in the digital world, I'll conclude by drawing your attention to three different approaches or perspectives. The first involves illustrations from the digital world. A fundamental lesson about teaching is that the better you get to know your audience, the more easily you can help the learners connect with what you are teaching. With that in mind, one approach to digital ministry is simply getting to know what is going on in the digital world. We then use information about digital culture to create illustrations and examples that will help our learners. We might not actually use digital tools or get involved in the digital world, but we may create a lesson about how being connected to God is like having an unlimited cell-phone plan. We might then explain how connectivity with God is so much better. This sort of teaching, using examples from the lives of the listeners, is what Jesus did. When we read the parables, we read examples from the daily life of the people. Through those, Jesus taught important truths.

A second approach to ministry in the digital world is what I sometimes refer to as "preparing for battle." This perspective goes a step further than the first. Not only do we get to know the digital world, but we also make a concerted effort to help others critique this world in view of God's Word. And we go even further

> How can I prepare people for uncompromising faith and life in the digital world?

than that. We make it our mission to prepare and equip people with everything they will need to stand firm in their faith amid the challenges and opportunities of the digital age. This focus asks one main question. How can I prepare people for uncompromising faith and life in the digital world? This will require careful study of God's Word along with a deep-dive investigation into digital culture.

A third approach is outreach in the digital world. This perspective goes even further. It uses illustrations like in the first approach and tries to equip people like the second approach, but it also seeks to set up camp in the digital world. It is an effort to actually use the digital tools, spaces, and places for educational ministry. This is where people are setting up a presence in social media, starting a Christian podcast, creating a Christian blog, or participating in other online networks and communities. With this approach, people are actually engaging in ministry within the digital world. They set up a residence in the digital world and move from being an observer to a participant. Some might even compare this to what Jesus did. He did not simply hang out in the safe and ordinary places. He spent time in Samaritan country. He interacted with a woman of questionable reputation at a public well. He spent time with tax collectors. In other words, He met people in the spaces and places of their daily lives. Of course, He also sought to help them find a different way.

All three of these perspectives warrant attention. There is really no need to rate the value of the three. There is a time and season for each. Some may not be interested in or ready for the third approach. However, those same people may find it hard to deny that the second approach is important, that we need to prepare people of all ages for the challenges they will face in the digital world (predators, cyberbullying, pornography, building relationships, etc.). Ultimately, these three approaches are helpful distinctions as teachers of the faith consider the role of technology in their educational ministries. When might there be benefit in pulling examples and illustrations to communicate the unchanging truths of God's Word? When and how can we prepare people for faith and life in a technological world? When might there also be opportunity to reach new people through educational ministry that takes place in online spaces and communities? Answers to these questions will vary depending upon one's ministry context, but asking them remains valuable in almost all modern settings.

37

UNDERSTANDING THE GROWING HOMESCHOOL MOVEMENT

Cheryl Swope

There's no place like home. For an estimated 2.2 million children in the United States, this expression carries far more than mere sentiment.[1] Despite the abundant availability of public, private, charter, and parochial schools, "home" supplants "classroom" as the primary locus of learning for a conspicuously enlarging number of families.[2]

Why do so many families educate their children at home? Furthermore, why do so many *more* families decide to homeschool every year? At regional homeschooling conventions across the country, hosting as many as ten thousand homeschoolers and their children, onlookers can expect to find young mothers and fathers, some holding hands, walking the vast aisles of curriculum choices, as they discuss their plans, hopes, and dreams for their children. What motivates parents to teach their own children, often in the Christian faith, and often with sacrificial—even biblical—dedication? Perhaps more important, what are the hidden implications of answers to such questions for the Church and her schools?

In order to examine any movement, we ought first to examine its recent historical context. If only for a narrow window of time, home education today enjoys greater acceptance, better teaching resources, and broader legal freedoms in the United States than at any time in the past

---

1   Brian D. Ray, "Research Facts on Homeschooling," National Home Education Research Institute, accessed February 26, 2016, http://www.nheri.org/research/research-facts-on -homeschooling.html.

2   In the spring of 2010, an estimated 1.7 to 2.4 million children (in grades K–12) were home educated in the United States, with an estimated growth rate of 2 percent to 8 percent annually over the past few years. Homeschooling has also been growing around the world in nations such as Australia, Canada, France, Hungary, Japan, Kenya, Russia, Mexico, South Korea, Thailand, and the United Kingdom (Ray, "Research Facts on Homeschooling").

> If only for a narrow window of time, home education today enjoys greater acceptance, better teaching resources, and broader legal freedoms in the United States than at any time in the past four decades.

four decades. However, as recently as the 1980s, parents now dubbed "homeschool pioneers" received ridicule, alienation, and even imprisonment for their decision to educate their children at home. Yet they determined to homeschool anyway. Why?

By the 1960s, '70s, and '80s, the steady infiltration of progressivism, pragmatism, and utilitarianism in US education over prior decades resulted in widespread shifts in pedagogical purpose, content, and methods. Seemingly simple questions, such as "Why educate?" "Who is the child?" and "What is the role of the teacher?" began to receive varying and contradictory answers. Great formative literature and the classical languages all but disappeared from public schools during this time. Even Aesop's Fables, treasured by Martin Luther and taught for millennia to develop moral character, fell out of favor. Teaching methods successful from before the time of Christ—memorization, recitation, and Socratic questioning—were exchanged for socializing, "progressive," experimental education.[3] The decline in education is, perhaps, most evident in the current culture it produced.

Some brave and industrious teachers resisted experimental education within their own classrooms. Others founded new schools designed to reclaim the pedagogical purpose, content, and methods discarded by their colleagues. Perhaps most notably, Marva Collins (1936–2015) founded the Westside Preparatory Academy in 1975. Her school received national media attention for her "innovative" and highly effective teaching techniques such as memorization, recitation, and the Socratic Method. Her students lived in inner-city Chicago, yet Marva Collins read to them from the great works of Western civilization—including those by Cicero, Shakespeare, and Dickens.[4]

---

3 For timeless readings on education, including selections from Melanchthon and Luther, see Richard Gamble, ed., *The Great Tradition: Classic Readings on What It Means to Be an Educated Human Being* (Wilmington, DE: ISI Books, 2007). For more reading on the influence of progressivism in academia and in schools, see various writings penned from within the public school context by John Taylor Gatto. See also Victor Davis Hanson and John Heath, *Who Killed Homer? The Demise of Classical Education and the Recovery of Greek Wisdom* (New York: Encounter Books, 2001). For the alternative to progressive influences, see Gene Edward Veith Jr. and Andrew Kern, *Classical Education: The Movement Sweeping America* (Concord, NC: CiRCE Institute, 2015).

4 See Clifford Campion, *The Marva Collins Story*, directed by Peter Levin (1981; Burbank, CA: Warner Home Video, 2008), DVD.

Even with such models, the majority of public, private, and parochial schools continued to embrace an increasingly common experimental education founded on a persistent blend of progressive, pragmatic, and utilitarian ideologies. By the 1980s, schools, and the students educated by them, received unfavorable national attention for abysmal academic performance. Relativism masked as values clarification continued to spread in schools, and moral decline became undeniable. Parents and children found educational options dwindling rapidly.

Educational leaders such as E. D. Hirsch Jr. began to illuminate the pedagogical precursors to the dilemma parents faced. In *The Schools We Need and Why We Don't Have Them* (Anchor Books, 1996), Hirsch examined the ineffective methods and incomplete curricula adopted in premeditated ways by progressive educational theorists and their willing, or sometimes unsuspecting, disciples. Through the new theories, or perhaps to mask them, educational jargon had exploded. State-trained experts supplanted parents, if only in the educators' own minds, as the authority over children. Just as insidiously, progressive-minded educators within the Church deemed themselves experts in matters of teaching the faith. This resulted in new methods, new curricula, and a glaring fragmentation between clergy, educator, and home. All of this became detrimental to the family, as such fragmentation undermined sound catechesis and, ultimately, even our profound educational history as Lutherans.[5]

In 1529, Martin Luther created the German Catechism, later known as the Large Catechism, "for pastors and teachers to use in their own study and preparation."[6] The companion Small Catechism was created for use in the church, school, and home, with instructions as "the head of the family should teach it in a simple way to his household."[7] Luther elaborated with these words: "With the young people stick to one fixed, permanent form and manner, . . . so that they, too, can repeat it in the same way after you and commit it to memory."[8]

Martin Luther emphasized catechesis in schools, and he instructed pastors, "After you have taught them this short catechism, then take up

---

5   For a full treatment of the Lutheran educational heritage, see Thomas Korcok, *Lutheran Education: From Wittenberg to the Future* (St. Louis: Concordia, 2011).
6   James A. Nestingen, *Martin Luther: His Life and Teachings* (Eugene, OR: Wipf and Stock Publishers, 2004), 47.
7   See the introductions to each of the Six Chief Parts in the Small Catechism.
8   Luther's Preface to the Small Catechism.

the Large Catechism and give them also a richer and fuller knowledge."[9] Faith instruction was to be united in purpose, methods, and content in church, school, and home. Before and during the Reformation, the liberal arts tradition strengthened and broadened to educate boys and girls, princes and peasants. Visionary pastors, teachers, and schoolmasters created a wholly unified pedagogical and theological heritage for all Christians.[10] This our Lutheran educational heritage.

As confessional Lutherans, we are familiar with denouncing relativism in political, social, and moral arenas; however, we also need to shun pedagogical relativism for the sake of both the academic and spiritual instruction of our children. Common sense prevailed in church schools for a time, but as new church educators became inculcated with "new and improved" educational notions, and as the accompanying progressive jargon tantalized even otherwise reasonable people, we began to lose our way.

> [God] assures you that He will reveal Himself as having sent His Son into the world out of paternal love, as is written John 3:16, "that whoever believes in Him should not perish but have eternal life." Then you hear that God . . . gave His Son for you, let Him die for you, and raised Him again from the dead. He directs you to the Son and has Him proclaimed to you. And if this is correctly taught, then we come to Him. That is meant by the expression "to be drawn."[11]

This proclamation of the Gospel is our unified Christian calling, no matter the setting. An unwavering education supports this task, so that we might equip children drawn by the Holy Spirit to freely share the Gospel of Jesus Christ with others.

The Church and her schools must understand that the typical Christian homeschooler seeks only to do *better* than that which many schools are not doing well. The most common reasons given for homeschooling include the following:

- Accomplish more academically than is being accomplished in schools

---

9 Luther's Preface to the Small Catechism.
10 See Rev. John Hill, "Luther on Education," in Steven A. Hein, Cheryl Swope, Paul J Cain, and Tom Strickland, eds., *A Handbook for Classical Lutheran Education* (CCLE Press, 2013), especially pp. 130–46.
11 LW 23:86–87.

- Use pedagogical approaches other than those found in institutional schools
- Enhance family relationships (between children and parents, and among siblings)
- Customize the curriculum and learning environment for each child (as with special needs)
- Provide a safer environment for children and youth
- Teach and impart a particular set of values, beliefs, and worldview to children and youth[12]

Homeschooling families seeking to reclaim theological truths, restore moral purpose, instill respect for natural law, and share the Christian faith with their own children in the context of a clear, historic pedagogy can be embraced and even championed by the Church.

Some Lutheran parents combine home education with appreciated access to strong Lutheran Day Schools. Some families supplement home education with the new options for Lutheran online classes. Still others join or create homeschooling communities for cooperative education within a Lutheran congregation. Lutheran Day Schools serve these families well when they invite them to participate in daily chapel, special field trips, concerts, sports activities, clubs, and musical groups. As emphasized in the new LCMS book *Eternal Treasures: Teaching Your Child at Home,* when we remember our common cause of historic, effective, Lutheran education, unity abounds.[13]

Within a nation in which broad culture wars seem unlikely ever to be won by anyone who upholds absolute truth, Christian parents can at least be encouraged by the Church to live out their own vocations as father and mother with their own children. "As for me and my house"[14] becomes a motto for Lutheran homeschoolers—not as a profession of obedience as if trusting in their own good works, but rather as a confession of the home-based mission to rest in God's promises in Christ alone for salvation and to share these promises with their own children, even as they teach their children "in the discipline and instruction of the Lord" (Ephesians 6:4).

---

12 Ray, "Research Facts on Homeschooling."

13 Cheryl Swope and Rachel Whiting, *Eternal Treasures: Teaching Your Child at Home,* with a foreword by Matthew C. Harrison (St. Louis, MO: The Lutheran Church—Missouri Synod, 2015). See especially chapter 6, "Our Unity: Working Together in Home, Church, and School," 191–212.

14 Joshua 24:15.

For parents who provide a strong Christian education at home, just as for parents who enroll their children in a strong, historically faithful Lutheran Day School, benefits multiply for this life and the life to come. Strong family bonds become forged through memorable and even beautiful time spent together, whether sharing lessons, literature, hymns, or the Holy Scriptures. Strong academic performance emerges, as do surprisingly confident interpersonal skills. With steadfast instruction, children become engaged in intellectual discussions about world history; geography; classic writings, classical and biblical languages, along with deeply objective and yet eternally personal catechetical truths.

Freed from overly sentimental child-centered methods and unencumbered by socially progressive curricular content, homeschooled children, just as children who attend a strong Christian school, can become the grateful recipients of an education that appreciates the individual while strengthening the family and transcending time. With such an education, the student receives personal and familial benefits. Furthermore, homeschooled students typically score fifteen to thirty percentile points above their government-school peers on standardized achievement tests, regardless of whether their parents were ever certified teachers, regardless of household income, and regardless of whether their parents even received a high-school diploma.[15] Likewise, homeschooled students typically perform above average on measures of social, emotional, and psychological development, including measures of peer interaction, leadership skills, family cohesion, and participation in community service.[16]

Congregations, Sunday Schools, Day Schools, and educational experts would do well to support, if not perhaps learn from, these dedicated parents, just as homeschoolers can learn much from excellent schools. With over two million children taught at home, and with that number growing every year, homeschooling is currently more "mainstream" than at any time in our country's recent history. So long as children remain well

15 Ray, "Research Facts on Homeschooling."
16 Ray, "Research Facts on Homeschooling."

served by home education in faith instruction, academics, and the formative nature of nurturing the child on truth, beauty, and goodness—all the while depending on Christ alone for mercy, life, and salvation—many of our families will continue to proclaim in grateful unison, *"There's no place like home."*

38

WELCOMING AND INCORPORATING THE HOMESCHOOL FAMILY INTO THE LUTHERAN SCHOOL COMMUNITY

Don and Joyce Kortze

> However, taking time to understand the uniqueness of the homeschooling family will frequently result in a beneficial educational and ministry experience for all involved.

The integration of the homeschool family into the ministry of a Lutheran school is a challenging, even daunting, prospect that many in reality seek to avoid. There are numerous preconceptions to address, challenges to deliberate, and long-standing traditions to reconsider. This frequently puts a Lutheran school community on the defensive and results in a lost opportunity for ministry. However, taking time to understand the uniqueness of the homeschooling family will frequently result in a beneficial educational and ministry experience for all involved.

Each experience integrating the homeschool family into the Lutheran school community will be as unique as the family involved. There are certain characteristics that are common among homeschoolers; however, the desire to train their children in a home environment speaks to the willingness of these families to be distinctive. As Lutheran schools consider the opportunity to partner with homeschool families, it may be helpful to discuss common characteristics found among these families. A greater knowledge and understanding of the homeschooling process by the faculty and administration will be advantageous to the integration of both the part-time homeschooling student and those integrated full time into the traditional classroom. For the sake of this discussion, the concept of integration of a homeschool family into a Lutheran school assumes that these students are participating on a part-time basis. Homeschool families who choose to discontinue education at home and enroll their students in a Lutheran school full time would typically face a similar experience as a family that moves in from out of the area.

Homeschool families are quite passionate about the spiritual growth of their children. They are frequently very deliberate about the incorporation of the teaching of the faith not only into multiple components of the educational experience, but also into every facet of life. For this reason, they will be deeply interested in the religious context of the Lutheran school with which they are considering to partner. The concern over doctrinal issues, however, may be of less consequence than the extent to which they see the social and disciplinary framework of the Lutheran school displayed through traditional Christian values.

Academic excellence is also a central concern for homeschool families. This should not be construed to infer that Lutheran schools are inferior in their academic expectations. However, if we consider that the level of rigor is relative to the ability of the student, it is clear that a classroom environment will typically not be able to provide the unique expectations that are available in the one-on-one environment that is standard in a homeschool setting.

There are common needs among homeschooling families that may cause them to seek out partnership with a Lutheran school. Frequently, families are pursuing expertise and additional resources concerning challenging curricular subjects. This is more typical at a secondary level, where homeschool families will seek out specialists in upper-level mathematics, science, or foreign language. Many Lutheran elementary schools are also offering attractive specialized subject areas such as music, art, and drama, which may interest a growing family as well. Students who can be successfully integrated into these settings can experience the best of both educational worlds.

> Many Lutheran elementary schools are also offering attractive specialized subject areas such as music, art, and drama, which may interest a growing family as well.

Extracurricular opportunities attract many homeschooling parents who desire opportunities for their children to develop athletically and participate in interscholastic competition. This arena of integration can be particularly challenging for school administration; it is possibly the most challenging aspect of assimilating a homeschool student into the traditional school setting. Issues of team selection must be discussed when considering the addition of part-time students. Clear understandings of how to address issues of playing time, academic eligibility (particularly for classes completed at home), scheduling considerations, and more will need to be shared among all parties involved. Significant discussions to address important details would likely involve coaches, parents, and school administration.

> The willingness of the school culture to reach out to others who are distinctive will be the greatest determining factor in the success of this experience.

Although recognizing the common characteristics of homeschool families and anticipating their needs are important components of the integration process, the successful incorporation of these families into the Lutheran school will ultimately rest with the school itself. The willingness of the school culture to reach out to others who are distinctive will be the greatest determining factor in the success of this experience. That culture, and its degree of acceptance, is greatly shaped by those in leadership positions. A desire to reach out and welcome homeschool families must begin with those who will lead the process, prepare the environment, and address the concerns. In a traditional Lutheran setting, this would certainly involve the principal and school board. In some cases, depending on the structure of the school, this would also involve the pastor. The principal, in particular, will play a vital role in addressing this potential to the faculty. This can be a challenging consideration.

A culture of acceptance is the goal. This culture can be nurtured by helping the faculty and staff better understand this educational movement, rather than reject or judge it based on preconceived notions about its value, quality, or motives. Teachers can easily become defensive when considering such integration, as many feel that these parents deem the home experience superior to that provided by the Lutheran school and thus the Lutheran teacher. Yet, creating a positive bridge from the homeschool to the traditional school is vital for the sake of the students involved, and it can be a progressive springboard toward greater learning if handled intentionally and informatively. The tension between the educators of these two worlds is real. Just as traditional teachers may feel threatened by homeschool parents, homeschool parents often feel devalued by traditional teachers. However, if the adults lose focus, the ones who really lose out are the students.

226

To help bring a greater understanding of the homeschool student to the Lutheran school community and lower the defenses of all involved, consider offering an informational session on homeschooling as part of fall faculty meetings. We all have a visual of what a traditional school setting looks like; yet many who discredit home education do so without knowledge of how it works. It may be helpful to have a seasoned homeschool parent share his or her experience, paint a picture of the values of homeschooling, and explain how a homeschool setting differs from the traditional classroom. Speaking as educators who have spent time in both of these settings, we can say with confidence that a traditional classroom teacher would benefit from this, as it would help to better understand the homeschool student.

Homeschool families operate from a perspective of uniqueness. Families make the commitment to homeschool for a variety of reasons. However, they all stem from the understanding that there are unique aspects of the experience provided in a home setting that are not replicable in any traditional school environment. This often revolves around faith issues and academic rigor, as previously mentioned. However, there are many other intangibles that are central to the home environment that become important core considerations to the homeschooling family.

The opportunity for a family to spend the bulk of their day together—learning, growing, and experiencing life as a family unit—creates a uniquely deep bond that cannot be replicated with a similar investment of time and shared experience. The family dynamic created through the spiritual, emotional, and academic growth in which parents and siblings participate results in relationships that are fashioned to an inimitable depth. Children are trained not just in academics but in all facets of life. Character building and teaching respect and honor among every member of the family are all aspects of the learning environment. Understanding these varied aspects of the homeschool experience will help dispel the defensive and sometimes antagonistic tendency that can exist. For in reality, it must be considered that if the culture of the Lutheran school is not amenable to this understanding of homeschooling and its purposes, it may be best not to subject families to the school environment.

As we think about nurturing the faith in the students of our Lutheran school communities, it is important to understand that faith issues are a shared priority with the homeschooling family. Parents who choose to take the primary role in nurturing their children's faith are to be

As we think about nurturing the faith in the students of our Lutheran school communities, it is important to understand that faith issues are a shared priority with the homeschooling family.

applauded. Homeschooling parents take educating, nurturing, and caring for their children very seriously. Most have chosen this path not because the school setting is not good enough but because they feel a calling to their families. Parents who are passionate about this aspect of their children's lives will often be more than willing to continue in that role as their children enter a traditional school setting. They will frequently be very willing volunteers for parent associations and athletic organizations. They should be invited as full partners in the responsibilities of supporting the ministry of the school, its fund-raisers, and its social events. Using these parents as resources regarding faith integration would be another avenue to bridge the gap, enrich the traditional school, and help homeschool parents feel like they are on the same team with the school their children are now attending.

It is also important that the other Lutheran school families are accepting of these new members of the school community. The faculty and administration will need to speak to them with one voice concerning the desire to partner with homeschoolers in providing the blessings of Lutheran education to the community. They will also need to be informed about how various matters, particularly related to extracurricular activities, could affect their student.

Whether we are administrators or teachers in a traditional Lutheran school setting or Christian parents seeking to develop deep spiritual roots, family values, and academic excellence, it seems that our mission is very much the same. Our goal is to raise kids who love and serve the Lord; our goal is to create an educational community that is based on excellence; our goal is to mold and mentor children into young adults who have the necessary tools to move forward through life and make a difference in their world. When we focus on the similarities of our mission, we will realize the importance and responsibility we have to bring these two educational worlds together. The students themselves will be the ones who benefit when they are involved in a wide variety of experiences in a welcoming environment.

39

FOSTERING A CHRISTIAN LEARNING COMMUNITY AT SCHOOL AND HOME

Kim Marxhausen

In developmental psychology, a recurring theme identifies characteristics of a healthy home environment, an effective classroom management program, and successful schools, especially those working with high-risk students.

In the late sixties, research by Diana Baumrind[1] recognized three parenting styles, identified as permissive, authoritarian, and authoritative. Permissive parents are highly responsive to the needs of their children but low in expectations. Conversely, authoritarian parents are strict regarding expectations but do not show much responsiveness. Authoritative parents blend the two characteristics. The results of this research indicate that authoritative parenting is the most effective in producing happy, healthy children.

These characteristics also apply to discipline styles in the classroom. Authoritative teachers are those who create a classroom environment that supports autonomy. Deci and Ryan[2] describe such a classroom as one that provides needed structure while encouraging individual choice. Students learn from the consequences of their choices while teachers set expectations and attend to individual needs. An underlying principle of an autonomy-supporting classroom is the insistence that all students receive unconditional respect and care. This means that students are not left believing they must earn care as if it were a reward for good behavior.

---

1   Diana Baumrind, "Current Patterns of Parental Authority," *Developmental Psychology*, 4, no. 1, pt. 2 (1971).
2   Edward Deci and Richard Ryan, *Intrinsic Motivation and Self-Determination in Human Behavior* (New York: Plenum, 1985).

This means that students are not left believing they must earn care as if it were a reward for good behavior.

Students in an autonomy-supporting classroom know they belong, even when they make mistakes.

The term *warm-demander pedagogy* is one associated with culturally responsive teaching[3] and is observed in many successful programs working with high-risk students. A warm-demander pedagogy shows in a school that emphasizes both authority figures applying strict expectations for students and the nurture and care each student requires for success in learning and behavior. When the school sets high expectations with consistent consequences, it teaches children to develop self-regulation and gives a strong message that each student is capable of doing great things. This sense of discipline is successfully realized when it is accompanied by warmth and attention, allowing all students to feel a sense of belonging.

What similar thread weaves its way through all three of these ideas? Each one attempts to create a loving home, an effectual classroom environment, or a successful school by balancing expectations with responsiveness. It seems that each of these theorists has stumbled upon, and is trying to imitate, a basic doctrine Lutheran educators know well: the balance between Law and Gospel.

Our model for Law and Gospel comes from God's example as seen in Scripture. The Law tells us what is expected of us. It keeps order, shows us our sin, and promotes a God-pleasing life. The Law is preached to us when we are secure sinners. The Gospel, on the other hand, is our salvation without condition. It is God's expression of unconditional love—a love that is neither earned nor finite. The Gospel is realized in forgiveness and mercy and is preached to us when we are alarmed sinners.[4]

It is easy to identify Law in schools. Every community needs rules. Furthermore, for rules to be effective, every rule needs consequences. Lutheran schools are certainly no exception as they are full of sinners in need of Law. In addition to rules and consequences, we see Law in posters on the wall encouraging helpful behaviors, and we hear Law on the playground when teachers remind students to be safe. We find Law in conferences with parents when child behavior is discussed and plans are made to help that child change his or her behavior.

---

3   Franita Ware, "Warm Demander Pedagogy: Culturally Responsive Teaching That Supports a Culture of Achievement for African American Students," *Urban Education* 41, no. 4 (2006): 427–56.
4   See C. F. W. Walther, *Law and Gospel: How to Read and Apply the Bible* (St. Louis: Concordia, 2010).

If we name rules and consequences as Law, it is easy to assume that reward and praise are expressions of Gospel. After all, reward and praise are pleasant to receive. However, Law is what is expected of us, and Gospel is what is given out of *no merit of our own*. In school, students suffer consequences when they do not meet expectations and garner praise when they do. Both are expressions of Law, because both address expectations. It is interesting to note that research has found praise can produce anxiety, as the recipient will wonder if praise will continue to be earned.[5] Additionally, educators are warned that excessive use of extrinsic motivation (such as rewards) has been documented to stifle creativity and the intrinsic motivation to perform.[6] Even in a positive form, the Law judges.

In addition to Law, individuals in a community need Gospel in everyday life. We need the gift of God's Word and Sacraments to nurture our faith. We need forgiveness and mercy to enable us to learn from mistakes. We need unconditional love to know we belong to God because He has made us His. At school or at home, it is not safe to assume that all members feel and understand the Gospel. We must directly express it in words, actions, and policy.

What happens in a Christian community when Law overbalances Gospel?

Parents who live under the Law and feel that pressure for their children might work to protect them from the blessings of repentance and forgiveness. Parents do this by excusing behavior in their children instead of seeking to deal with the reasons behind the behavior. These parents shun repentance because they lack the assurance of forgiveness. Parents must understand and practice the gifts involved in repentance and forgiveness for children to feel they are growing and learning as a part of the community.

Classrooms that rely heavily on Law will be focused on what the students need to do instead of considering what the teacher can provide to encourage successful behavior and learning. This situation makes it highly unlikely that student needs will be accommodated. Unfortunately, the lack of necessary accommodation is likely to lead to behavior problems. Teachers who rely only on punishment and rewards will find

---

5   Carol Dweck, *Self-theories: Their Role in Motivation, Personality, and Development* (Philadelphia: Taylor and Francis Group, 2000).
6   Alfie Kohn, *Punished by Rewards: The Trouble with Gold Stars, Incentive Plans, A's, Praise, and Other Bribes* (Boston: Houghton Mifflin, 1993).

some children for whom no incentive is strong enough to shape behavior. Teacher time must be spent identifying and addressing the need behind the behavior as well as the behavior itself.

Schools that emphasize the Law in both punishment and reward but neglect to make the message of the Gospel clear will inadvertently promote bully behaviors. Children who have difficulty following rules may congregate and take out their anger on other students. Those who are successful at meeting expectations may also congregate and convince themselves that they earn their success. Soon, those in the group feel justified in demeaning those outside the group. This behavior results in rejected children. Bully behavior is what naturally happens when sinners begin to believe they are saving themselves. It is a familiar story of sin, and we should not be surprised when we see it play out in our Lutheran schools.

Lutheran teachers have the blessing of the doctrine of Law and Gospel to guide instruction. It is also an important aspect of building school community. Members of a community need the Law to guide behavior and consequences to encourage change. Nonetheless, members of a Christian community need to know that change is not possible without sanctification. The secular world will tell a child, "I know you can do better." In a Christian community, we remind one another that anything we accomplish comes through the power and love of our God.

Keeping in mind the proper use of Law and Gospel, fostering a Christian learning community involves four basic elements: God's Word, rules, repentance, and acceptance.

God's Word

It is essential for schools to worship together and for students to study God's Word, in direct instruction as well as integration into all learning. It is also essential that faculty members, as a group and as individuals, practice daily Bible study. Living and working in the Word is vital to building faith and community. Members of a community must connect each aspect of personal and public life to the Scriptures. In Scripture, God reveals His will to His people.

Rules

A healthy Christian community needs rules and consequences so that the members know what is expected and feel comfortable and safe. Consequences need to be appropriate to the behavior and age of the recipient.

The discipline process must make a point of pairing grace with Law as a reminder that the Holy Spirit can create change. Along with this, a healthy community needs praise and encouragement for work well done. This important feedback both informs and motivates.

Repentance

Repentance and forgiveness are an everyday occurrence easy to take for granted. Because we are so practiced in this ritual, it is too easy to forget the wonder of this gift. Repentance and forgiveness give us a chance to admit our mistakes, which means we will also have a chance to learn from them. We do not have to deny the existence of our imperfection. Instead, we can bring it out into the open and feel the burden of shame lifted from our shoulders. This is how God sustains community. Repentance and forgiveness teach us empathy. In empathy, a community avoids misunderstandings and learns how to care for the needs of each member.

Acceptance

As humans, we are hardwired to seek acceptance. God created us to be in fellowship, to work together, and to care for one another. The need for acceptance is why a healthy Christian community is indispensable. Students who feel they belong are free from stress and able to learn. Teachers who feel acceptance are better able to accommodate the needs of their students and to work with parents and fellow faculty members. Acceptance is not tolerance for wrong behavior. Instead, acceptance is part of the unconditional love that says we are members of God's family—even when we sin.

A Lutheran school that preserves a healthy community will also model community building for parents. In this way, a school extends its understanding of teaching parents how to teach the faith to their children by helping them to create a home environment that is conducive to faith learning. When families study God's Word, create and enforce rules, give feedback, repent and forgive, teach empathy, and show unconditional love, they are living the faith given to them by God.

CONTRIBUTORS

Matthew T. Bergholt (BA, Concordia University Chicago) is the coordinator of Online Support and Services for the School Ministry Office of The Lutheran Church—Missouri Synod. He is currently pursuing an MA in Educational Design and Technology from Concordia University Wisconsin. His published essays have appeared in the School Ministry Mailings of the Lutheran School Portal.

David Black (MA, Butler University) is a teacher and the director of Lights Academy at Lutheran High School, Parker, Colorado. He also serves as an adjunct professor at Concordia University Wisconsin and regularly writes, speaks, and consults on issues of faith, education, and technology.

Mark S. Blanke (MS, California Lutheran University; MA, Concordia University, Nebraska; EdD, Northern Illinois University) serves as professor of education, DCE Program director, and director of Strategic Planning at Concordia University, Nebraska. He has written for *NADCE Quarterly*, *Issues in Christian Education*, *Lutheran Education*, and other publications.

Paul Buchheimer (MS and EdD, Nova Southeastern University, Fort Lauderdale, Florida) has taught for thirty-five years and has been a principal in Lutheran schools for thirteen years. He is currently the placement director for Concordia University Texas. He also teaches graduate courses for the university.

Bernard D. Bull (MA, Concordia University Chicago; MLS, University of Wisconsin—Milwaukee; EdD, Northern Illinois University) is assistant vice-president of academics and associate professor of education at Concordia University Wisconsin. He has over twenty years of experience in Lutheran education ranging from middle school to graduate school. He is a frequent consultant and speaker on topics related to educational innovation, the intersection of educational and digital culture, the future of education, and Lutheran education in the twenty-first century.

Grant E. Carey (MA, Fuller Theological Seminary; DMin, George Fox Evangelical Seminary) is professor of religious education at Concordia University Texas. He has written for *Sunday School Matters*, *NADCE*

234

Quarterly, youthESource, and Lutheran Hour Ministries. He is currently working on a book entitled *Holistic Formation in Youth Ministry*.

Randall Ferguson (MA, Bowling Green State University; MDiv, Concordia Seminary, St. Louis; PhD, University of Minnesota, Minneapolis) has been on the faculty and in administration in various capacities at Concordia University Wisconsin since 1991. His published works include two custom textbooks: *Let's Get Interpersonal* (McGraw-Hill Primis, 2000, 2002) and *Reaching, Exploring, Serving: The Freshman Seminar* (Concordia University Wisconsin, 2008, 2010). He has made several presentations at national conferences such as The First Year Experience and The Leadership Challenge.

Laurie A. Friedrich (MS, Concordia University, Nebraska; PhD, University of Nebraska—Lincoln) is instructor of education at the University of Nebraska—Lincoln, where her research interests include the role of new literacies in elementary literacy education and technology integration in literacy methods courses for preservice and inservice teachers. She and her colleague received the 2016 Innovative Use of Technology Best Practice Award from the American Association of Colleges for Teacher Education (AACTE) for five years of preparing preservice teachers, classroom teachers, and university instructors to integrate technology through Tech EDGE. She also facilitates technology integration with Lutheran teachers through TEC21. Dr. Friedrich presents extensively nationally and locally. She is published in *Teachers Interaction* and *Children's Social Development*.

Amanda B. Geidel (MA, University of Nebraska—Lincoln; EdD, Northcentral University, Prescott Valley, Arizona) is director of special education and assistant professor of education at Concordia University, Nebraska. She often presents at conferences and to school faculties on the topics of pre-referral intervention for struggling students and educational techniques for the successful inclusion of students with disabilities. In 2011, she wrote an article for *Teachers Interaction*, a Concordia Publishing House magazine, entitled "See How They Grow."

Jill A. Hasstedt (MA, University of Illinois, Springfield) is director of family ministry and web administration at Zion Lutheran Church, Belleville, Illinois, where she also oversees adult education. She has written for

Concordia Publishing House, youthESource, *The Lutheran Witness*, and Lutheran Hour Ministries. She serves currently as a Finishing Well Instructor for the Karpenko Institute for Nurturing and Developing Leadership Excellence (KINDLE). She has also led multigenerational events for more than thirty years in school, parish, and camp settings.

Patricia A. Hoffman (MA, Concordia University Chicago; PhD, University of Wisconsin—Madison) is professor emerita of early childhood at Concordia University Chicago. She recently retired after serving Lutheran early childhood and elementary schools as well as the Concordia University System for thirty-nine years. She is a national and international speaker whose writings appear in numerous publications. She is now busy consulting, traveling, and spending time with family.

Martin R. Kohlwey (MS, Concordia University, Nebraska) serves at Concordia University, Nebraska as coordinator of first-year experience, instructor, and coach. He served fourteen years at the high school level as spiritual life director, head of the religion department, Bible teacher, and head basketball coach.

Donald E. Kortze (MA, Concordia University, Nebraska) served nine years as classroom teacher and twenty-three years as principal at Rockford Lutheran High School, Rockford, Illinois; he now serves at Rockford Lutheran as academic dean.

Joyce M. Kortze (BS, Concordia University, Nebraska; Lay Ministry Certification, Concordia University Wisconsin) has worked outside the home as teacher and coach and served her family as full-time homeschooling mom for twenty-five years. She now serves as worship planner at Mount Olive Lutheran Church in Rockford, Illinois, and is pursuing publication of her Bible study, entitled *Joy for the Journey*, various worship materials, and a devotional journal entitled *Life Lessons in the Passion*.

Kenneth T. Kosche (MS, University of Illinois at Urbana-Champaign; DMA, University of Washington) is professor emeritus of music at Concordia University Wisconsin, where he taught for thirty-one years. An active parish musician for over fifty years, he is also a hymnwriter and composer with more than four hundred publications among seventeen publishers. He has served as a music clinician and guest organist and conductor and has contributed articles for journals of the Association of Lutheran Church Musicians and other publications.

Jonathan C. Laabs (MA, Concordia University Chicago; EdD, University of Michigan) currently serves as executive director of Lutheran Education Association (LEA) and is adjunct professor at Concordia University Chicago. His thirty-nine years in Lutheran education have included teaching; administration; speaking at the regional, national, and international levels; and serving on a variety of national boards and committees. Dr. Laabs has visited and consulted with Lutheran schools on six continents. He has been a regular contributor to LEA's *Shaping the Future* magazine and written articles for *Lutheran Education Journal* and other Lutheran education publications.

Kim Marxhausen (MA, Concordia University, Nebraska; PhD, University of Nebraska—Lincoln) works at Faith Lutheran Church in Lincoln, Nebraska, in family and child ministry and teaches for Nebraska Wesleyan University and the University of Nebraska—Lincoln. She serves as a keynote speaker for LCMS district conferences and writes for LCMS School Ministry as well as for periodicals such as *Shaping the Future* (Lutheran Education Association) and *Lutheran Education Journal* (Concordia University Chicago).

John L. Mehl (MDiv and DMin, Concordia Seminary, St. Louis) is the director of mission partnerships and church relations at Concordia University, Nebraska. Before coming to Concordia, he served as the pastor of a rural parish in Kansas and spent twenty years as an LCMS missionary based in Moscow, Frankfurt, and Hong Kong.

Russ Moulds (MS, Loyola University; PhD, University of Nebraska—Lincoln) is professor of psychology and education at Concordia University, Nebraska, where he also serves as director of the Two Kingdoms Network and editor for *Issues in Christian Education*. He writes regularly on Lutheran education and was both editor and a contributing author for *A Teacher of the Church* (Wipf and Stock, 2007).

John W. Oberdeck, (MDiv, Concordia Seminary, St. Louis; PhD, University of Missouri—Columbia) is professor of theology and director for lay ministry at Concordia University Wisconsin. He has served parishes in central and southern Illinois and taught for thirteen years in the practical department of Concordia Seminary, St. Louis. He's been teaching at Concordia University Wisconsin since 2002. He is the author of *Eutychus Youth: Applied Theology for Youth Ministry* (Concordia, 2010) and has had essays in *Concordia Journal*, *Teachers Interaction*, *Concordia Pulpit Resources*, *Issues in Lutheran Education*, and *Shaping the Future*.

Rebecca R. Peters (EdD, Talbot School of Theology at Biola University) is professor of education at Concordia University, Irvine, where she also teaches in Christ College in the Church Vocation classes. Her writing includes the book *Building Faith One Child at a Time* (Concordia, 1997; second edition forthcoming in the summer of 2016) and articles in periodicals such as *Issues in Christian Education*, *Christian Education Journal*, and the LEA publication *Shaping the Future*.

James Pingel (MA, Marquette University; MA, Concordia University Wisconsin; PhD, Cardinal Stritch University) is associate professor of education and history at Concordia University Wisconsin. His published essays have appeared in *Issues in Christian Education*, *The Caleb Comment*, *The Southern Historian*, and *Lutheran Digest*. He recently published *Confidence and Character: The Religious Life of George Washington* (Wipf and Stock, 2014). Pingel also served as SLeD (School Leadership Development) mentor (2010–2016); executive director of Mayer Lutheran High School, Mayer, Minnesota (2000–2004); and executive director of Sheboygan Lutheran High School, Sheboygan, Wisconsin (2004–2014). He was selected as the South Wisconsin District Administrator of the Year in 2012.

John T. Pless (MDiv, Trinity Lutheran Seminary, Columbus, Ohio; Colloquy, Concordia Theological Seminary, Fort Wayne) is assistant professor of pastoral ministry and missions at Concordia Theological Seminary in Fort Wayne, Indiana, where he also serves as director of field education. Since 2009, he has also served as a visiting lecturer at Lutheran Theological Seminary in Pretoria, South Africa. Professor Pless is the author of many works, including *Martin Luther: Preacher of the Cross* (Concordia, 2013), *Mercy at Life's End* (LCMS, 2013), *Handling the Word of Truth: Law and Gospel in the Church Today* (Concordia, 2015), and numerous chapters in other books published in both the United States and Germany. With Matthew Harrison, he is editor of *Women Pastors? The Ordination of Women in Biblical Lutheran Perspective* (Concordia, 2012). He is also book review editor for *Logia: A Journal of Lutheran Theology* and a member of the editorial council of *Lutheran Quarterly*.

Rodney L. Rathmann (MA, Concordia University Chicago; EdD, University of Missouri—St. Louis) is the former senior editor of school, midweek, and confirmation resources at Concordia Publishing House (CPH) and long-time associate adjunct professor in the College of Education at University of Missouri—St. Louis (UMSL). Published works include those created in conjunction with his association with CPH and UMSL. Among these are Bible studies and articles relating to parenting, class control, and brain-based learning for publications including *The Lutheran Witness* and *Teachers Interaction*; confirmation materials including *Charting the Course* and *My First Catechism*; and a teaching resource, *Integrating the Faith: A Guide for Curriculum in Lutheran Schools*.

Lorinda L. Sankey (MS, Southern Illinois University Edwardsville; PhD, St. Louis University) taught grades 2 through 8 for twenty years in Lutheran schools in Florida, Iowa, and Illinois. She has served as elementary education program coordinator and associate dean in the College of Education at Concordia University Chicago. She soon begins as associate dean, head of teacher education in the College of Education, Health, and Human Sciences at Concordia University, Nebraska.

Rebecca S. Schmidt (MA, Michigan State University; EdD, University of Arkansas, Little Rock; Colloquy, Concordia University Ann Arbor) is associate director of schools for the Office of National Mission of The Lutheran Church—Missouri Synod. Her area of expertise is focused in early childhood education and school leadership. Her experience includes serving as an early childhood educator, preschool director, and elementary principal in schools in Michigan, Arkansas, and Missouri.

Terry L. Schmidt (MEd, Concordia University Chicago; MA, Southern Illinois University Edwardsville) is director of schools for the Office of National Mission of The Lutheran Church—Missouri Synod. In this role, he assists schools and congregations to start schools (Genesis), improve schools (National Lutheran School Accreditation and Strengthening Schools and Congregations), and recruit and train new school leaders (School Leadership Development Project). Lutheran schools are located on the front line of the North American mission field, and Terry believes that the future success of The Lutheran Church—Missouri Synod is directly linked to the health and viability of Lutheran schools. Terry has served in Lutheran schools in Illinois and Wisconsin and began his teaching career in Papua New Guinea. He has received both the LEA Christus Magister Award as well as the Outreach Leader Award from the Lutheran Education Association. He also received the Ablaze Partner Award from LCMS World Missions in 2009.

Harvey M. Schmit (MA, Concordia University Chicago; EdD, University of Michigan) is currently campus dean in the School of Education at Concordia University Ann Arbor. Dr. Schmit spent several years of ministry in Lutheran elementary schools as teacher and principal and has also served on various boards and committees at the Synod, district, and regional levels.

Timothy J. Schumacher (MA, Pepperdine University) is assistant professor of educational technology at Concordia University, Irvine. He has had over twenty years of experience teaching in various Lutheran K–12 schools in the United States and Australia. He has made many presentations over the years to Lutheran educators in the United States, Australia, and Ghana on various topics in educational technology and Lutheran education. His writings have appeared in the Lutheran Education Association's periodical *Shaping the Future* and Lutheran Education Australia's periodical *SchooLink*. He was also a contributor to the *Concordia Curriculum Guide: Grade 8, Social Studies* (Concordia, 2006).

Cheryl Swope (MEd) is the coauthor of *Eternal Treasures: Teaching Your Child at Home,* with foreword by Matthew C. Harrison (LCMS, 2015) and *Curriculum Resource Guide for Classical Lutheran Education* (CCLE, 2015), author of *Simply Classical: A Beautiful Education for Any Child,* with foreword by Gene E. Veith (Memoria Press, 2013), and creator of the Simply Classical Curriculum for Special Needs for ages 2–21 (ClassicalSpecialNeeds.com, Memoria Press). Cheryl and her husband homeschooled their adopted twins with special needs (autism, learning disabilities, mental illness) from their infancy through high school graduation with a Christian classical education. Cheryl's published articles have appeared in *The Classical Teacher* (Memoria Press) and the *Classical Lutheran Education Journal* (CCLE Press). Cheryl serves as lifetime board member with the Consortium for Classical Lutheran Education.